The Art of American
Screen Acting,
1960 to Today

ALSO BY DAN CALLAHAN

*The Art of American Screen Acting,
1912–1960* (McFarland, 2018)

The Art of American Screen Acting, 1960 to Today

Dan Callahan

McFarland & Company, Inc., Publishers
Jefferson, North Carolina

LIBRARY OF CONGRESS CATALOGUING-IN-PUBLICATION DATA

Names: Callahan, Dan, 1977– author.
Title: The art of American screen acting, 1960 to today / Dan Callahan.
Description: Jefferson, North Carolina : McFarland & Company, Inc., Publishers, 2019. | Includes bibliographical references and index.
Identifiers: LCCN 2019001469 | ISBN 9781476676951 (softcover : acid free paper) ∞
Subjects: LCSH: Motion picture acting—History—20th century. | Motion picture actors and actresses—United States—History—20th century.
Classification: LCC PN1995.9.A26 C355 2019 | DDC 791.4302/8—dc23
LC record available at https://lccn.loc.gov/2019001469

BRITISH LIBRARY CATALOGUING DATA ARE AVAILABLE

**ISBN (print) 978-1-4766-7695-1
ISBN (ebook) 978-1-4766-3596-5**

© 2019 Dan Callahan. All rights reserved

No part of this book may be reproduced or transmitted in any form or by any means, electronic or mechanical, including photocopying or recording, or by any information storage and retrieval system, without permission in writing from the publisher.

Front cover: Al Pacino, 1972; background photograph © 2019 Shutterstock

Printed in the United States of America

*McFarland & Company, Inc., Publishers
Box 611, Jefferson, North Carolina 28640
www.mcfarlandpub.com*

For Nick Moore
The Best Friend and the Most Fun

Table of Contents

Introduction: Method and Meryl	1
Jack Nicholson: Dance with the Devil	5
Warren Beatty: Take Off Your Clothes	12
Al Pacino: Darkness on the Edge of Town	17
Dustin Hoffman: Midnight of the Method	26
Robert De Niro: Born to Lose	34
Harvey Keitel: Body Artist	42
Gene Hackman: Keep It Real	46
Albert Finney: Married People	49
Anthony Hopkins: High, Wide and Handsome	53
Daniel Day-Lewis: In Character	60
Jeff Bridges: Straight No Chaser	65
Nick Nolte: Crucified	68
Sean Penn: By Himself	74
River Phoenix: Only Once	78
Denzel Washington: The Duke in His Domain	84
Viggo Mortensen: Set Apart	87
Christian Bale: Transparency	89
Leonardo DiCaprio: Bad Influence	92
Michael Fassbender: Angel Eyes That Old Devil Sent	95
Ben Whishaw: Diamond in the Rough	99
Jane Fonda: The Search	104
Faye Dunaway: Touched to the Quick	111
Ellen Burstyn: The Shadow Self	118

Gena Rowlands: Love Streams	124
Maggie Smith: The Acid Queen	130
Julie Christie: Darling	136
Glenda Jackson: Tension Clenching	140
Diane Keaton: In the Moment	146
Sissy Spacek: Down Home	154
Debra Winger: Feathers in a Tornado	158
Sigourney Weaver: Above It All	164
Glenn Close: Command Performances	167
Kathleen Turner: Lust for Life	170
Alfre Woodard: Wait and See	175
Judy Davis: High Anxiety	179
Emma Thompson: A Star Danced	190
Jennifer Jason Leigh: Hard Knocks	194
Julianne Moore: Lying in Wait	198
Samantha Morton: Chaos/Control	201
Patricia Clarkson: On a Dare	204
Conclusion: Chaos Theory	208
Bibliography	211
Index	213

Introduction
Method and Meryl

Two figures loom over most of the actors in this book. The first is Lee Strasberg, a guru of Method acting who taught at the Actors Studio from the early 1950s to the early 1980s. The second is Laurence Olivier, whose technical influence was key for two of the major actors here, Anthony Hopkins and Maggie Smith, both of whom began their proper stage careers with him at the National Theatre. (There is an irony in the fact that these two diametrically opposed men started to give very similar "shameless old ham" performances on film in the late 1970s, for this illuminated both Olivier's security in his reputation and Strasberg's insecurity when not controlling others.)

Strasberg controversially led his students into the realms of sense memory and affective memory, where an actor is encouraged to use images and remembrances from their own lives for a role. Many of the performers in this book studied directly with Strasberg, most notably Al Pacino and Ellen Burstyn.

Strasberg's theories about acting could lead to disastrously limited and self-indulgent work. But they could also lead to the Italian restaurant scene in *The Godfather* (1972) where Pacino has to decide whether or not to murder two men, and to the "red dress" monologue from *Requiem for a Dream* (2000) where Burstyn lays bare the hopes and dreams and loneliness of her character Sara Goldfarb in a way that speaks for all older people. And so these two performances are stronger finally than anything Hopkins or Smith ever did, but Hopkins and Smith are more impressively rounded and versatile actors who in their prime could handle just about any classic theater role.

Sometimes the Strasberg way of working was just about making emotions more available to actors. "I find that my training with Lee Strasberg has made my emotional life very accessible to me, and I don't always have to call up a specific experience from the past," said Ellen Burstyn when I interviewed her in 2017. "When I started out, I did. But now, after years of accessing those dimensions of myself, I can pretty well go there without having to … it's years of training and working where I can just tap into it and it comes, you know."

Speaking to Charlie Rose about playing Sara Goldfarb in 2000, Burstyn said, "It's accessing your own pain creatively and transforming it ... in this case, it's her experience, but it's really the human experience. I think all people recognize when they're looking at someone's pain that they feel it in themselves." She told Rose that she was "elated" at the end of the day while shooting *Requiem for a Dream*. "It's cleansing," she said. "When you transform that energy, you get more energy from it. It's an exhilarating experience."

From the too-personal base of their work with Strasberg, both Pacino and Burstyn reached the universal and the collective. River Phoenix never studied with Strasberg, yet he seems to have destroyed himself by identifying too strongly with his role in *My Own Private Idaho* (1991), and this could be seen as an example of what can happen when an actor gets too deeply into a part. But of course Phoenix might have destroyed himself anyway, and his achievement in that movie is still there and still beguiling and still violent, and maybe an end point for the sexy and morbid influence of James Dean.

Robert De Niro studied with Stella Adler, a Method teacher who emphasized research and imagination rather than personal experience, and so De Niro's version of the Konstantin Stanislavski Method meant trying to live as a taxi driver or a boxer, and it also meant changing himself as much as he could for a part. Olivier would never have actually put on weight for a role as De Niro does in *Raging Bull* (1980), and he wouldn't have needed to stay in character at all times, as Daniel Day-Lewis often has.

Speaking about the noted differences between Adler and Strasberg as teachers, Burstyn told me, "It's all about the word 'if.' You know their argument about 'if'? Stella used 'as if.' Stella said you don't go directly to the experience, you don't say, 'Thus and so is happening.' You say, 'it's as if thus and so is happening.' Stella had a big thing about Lee. I studied with Stella for one scene study class. She had an objection to Lee ... there was something about Stella's experience with Lee that turned her off on him, and I think it was personal." Burstyn insisted to me that Strasberg was not doctrinaire about his version of the Stanislavski Method with her. She remembered him telling her, "You use whatever works, dahling."

In England, Olivier's example lingers. Olivier could have given Hopkins's performance in *The Remains of the Day* (1993) or Smith's performance in *The Lonely Passion of Judith Hearne* (1987), and he could have done the work that Meryl Streep did all through the 1980s and beyond. The influence of Streep is essential in the way she moved actors away from the Strasberg variant of the Method and in the way she emphasized Olivier-like externals and imagination, yet she herself utilized some Method hallmarks for some of her earlier film work. Streep stayed in character while she played in *Sophie's Choice* (1982) and *Ironweed* (1987), and that is because she wanted to disappear into those roles. Later on in her career, Streep was more like Bette Davis, able to snap in and out of character at will.

Of all the people in this book, one of the most crucial and unusual is Judy Davis, an actress that Streep herself admires. The Australian Davis nearly always plays in a heightened and old-fashioned style much like that of Bette Davis and Katharine Hepburn, and in this way she is freer than Streep, who always seems to be self-conscious about her own lack of naturalism, her inability to be spontaneous. Streep is not covered in this book only because she is too large a subject for an essay-length piece (and so in her own way is Streep's closest rival Jessica Lange, who represents the glory and mess of giving in to your most extravagant personal emotions).

What I hope to do here is analyze the strengths and drawbacks of the Strasberg Method as expressed in many of the performances under discussion, and to call attention to the more eclectic way of working for actors that is coming about in the 21st century. When I studied at the Stella Adler Conservatory in the late 1990s, we were told over and over again that Strasberg was a damaging and pernicious figure whose teaching led to chaos and ruin. This is true in the worst work that came out of the Actors Studio, as typified by a disastrous Studio production of Chekhov's *Three Sisters* in the 1960s, but his best actors took what he gave them as just a kind of permission and a spur.

An actor today can use anything that might help them, and most of them do not stick to one Method or one point of view. Everything is up for grabs now, and in this dissolution there is another kind of chaos, but out of this modern chaos might come someone like Ben Whishaw, who is unimaginable in any other time but our own. Categories are breaking down on all fronts. But before they did, the Method as taught by Strasberg and Adler was the united yet divided front for most American actors.

Streep rejected the teachers she had at Yale who wanted her to delve into her personal life for a role. It is Streep's rejection of this orthodoxy that is the secret dramatic happening that explains the change that occurs as this book goes on. And it is Streep saying "no" that explains our new freedom from any system that must be followed to the letter.

Jack Nicholson
Dance with the Devil

Maybe the major male movie star of the 1970s and beyond, Jack Nicholson paid his dues for ten years or so before he really caught on. He made his debut in a juvenile delinquent picture, *Cry Baby Killer* (1958), and he's a little green and skinny but already "Jack" for anyone who can see in *The Wild Ride* (1960), where he tells a cop, "Sarge, I don't break the law, I make my own." The script indicates that he is in love with his best male friend, but this isn't believable at all because Nicholson is so purely male in such a specifically blue collar, barroom manner. He projects a palpable sense of sexual insolence in the way he moves and the way he sits.

Unlike many of the male stars of this time, there's nothing androgynous about Nicholson. He is not a Method man but a star actor of an earlier type, a James Cagney mixed with a dash of Cary Grant and more than a dash of redneck. There's a kind of sexism about his screen persona, a need to bed women and then cast them aside, and this is partly what a lot of his best films are about: confronting and exposing this unseemly side of him.

Apart from his masochistic dental patient in Roger Corman's *The Little Shop of Horrors* (1960), it cannot be said that Nicholson gives too many signals of what he would become during his apprenticeship. He smoked marijuana most every day in this 1960s period, and this certainly impacted his slow, nearly glazed tempo. There were only glimmers of emotion in his eyes, set off by his devilish eyebrows.

Nicholson made four low-budget films with director Monte Hellman during the 1960s. In the war movie *Back Door to Hell* (1964), he deliberately holds back and uses a flat behavioral affect to work directly against some of his pious dialogue, and this seems like the urge of a hipster and a nonconformist, a rebel and a class clown. He is a gunman in *The Shooting* (1966), menacingly flashing his white teeth in the glare of the Utah sun, and he's so unsettling here because there are flashes of craziness in his eyes that signal he is capable of anything.

Nicholson toiled in Roger Corman movies and TV series, dabbled in screenwriting, did motorcycle movies, and then finally hit with *Easy Rider*

(1969). He is skinny in that movie and his voice is nasal, and he wears a baggy white suit and dark glasses. "To old D.H. Lawrence!" toasts his southern lawyer George Hanson as he takes a first drink of the day.

When the liquor goes down, Nicholson comes up with a very original way of expressing George's pleasure and pain: "Ahhh!" he shouts, and then he makes little noises that sound like "Neat! Neat! Neat!" as he works his elbow like a robot that has just been oiled. And the "Neat!" then changes to a "Phhft! Phhft!" sound that transitions into another much lower and more conventional "Ahh…" of satisfaction.

This is a large gesture made towards hedonism, towards pleasure, and these are major interests for Nicholson. He is a little James Cagney-ish here, but this is a Cagney who smokes a lot of pot. Nicholson is hyper-charged, yet his rhythms are more languid than the classic Hollywood actors. He simmers. He slows things down to enjoy them, and sometimes just to detach himself from what he does not want to accept about life.

George has the address to what he says is the best whorehouse in New Orleans, given to him, he claims, by the governor of Louisiana, and he would like to go down there with motorcycle rebels Wyatt (Peter Fonda) and Billy (Dennis Hopper). George smokes his first joint with them and tells them that aliens are already among us in a very reasonable voice, as if he is explaining something obvious to a little kid. Nicholson is not convincing as a man smoking marijuana for the first time, but maybe George is just putting them on and having his fun.

"You know," he says, "this used to be a helluva good country. I can't understand what's going wrong with it … it's real hard to be free when you're bought and sold in the marketplace." The iconic Nicholson emerges here, the group philosopher, the bad boy, the bull-shitter, the goofball and knucklehead, always going much further than you expect with his impulses until they seem slightly non-human, like Cagney's did. This is star quality, far larger than life, and always dangerously rebellious. Tell Nicholson to do something, or expect something from him, and you're likely to get an insult or a tantrum that you will never forget.

He gets killed off in *Easy Rider*, and then his career kicked into the highest gear. Over the next five years, Nicholson slipped into a run of films that made his reputation, each one topping the next, seven major movies from 1970 to 1975. The first of these was *Five Easy Pieces* (1970), where he is Robert Eroica Dupea, a man who fits in nowhere, a man who is always fleeing and rejecting.

Dupea is a fighter, a drinker, and a volatile wanderer smashing things the way Brando's Stanley Kowalski clears the table during Blanche DuBois's birthday dinner in *A Streetcar Named Desire* (1951). Dupea was brought up in a cultured family of musicians, and he has run away from that to work on an oilrig. His blue-collar life doesn't satisfy him, but his life back at home was stultifying. There seems to be nothing in between for him, and this gulf finally feels tragic.

Nicholson makes Dupea's self-destructive frustration exuberantly physical, letting it overtake him sometimes so that he is throwing himself all over the frame like a Tasmanian devil. His greatness here lies in his ability to go that far and to never forget the comic in the midst of profound alienation, his goofy verbal inspirations and love of sex buttressing the habitual contempt with which Bobby treats most of the people he encounters. When he confronts a barking dog in a car and starts to bark back at it, Nicholson hits on a kind of pissed-off energy that had seldom been seen on screen before, and the way he loses his temper with an officious waitress was felt as liberating, even if it is a largely pointless and even unfair gesture.

His none-too-bright girlfriend Rayette (Karen Black) says he is the "moodiest" man she has ever been with, and those moods are what made Nicholson matter in an angry, confused period in America. In the big scene where he talks to his silent, stroke-afflicted father (a disapproving patriarch), Nicholson is attacked by tears and fights against them, whereas most actors and actresses try to cry and give in all-too-easily. Nicholson's Dupea is a complex, three-dimensional, damaged and damaging soul, marked always by unease, wanderlust, and loss.

Nicholson directed an unruly movie, *Drive, He Said* (1971), about students who are rebelling against the establishment, and then he picked one outstanding and difficult part after another. Any actor interested only in popularity would never have taken roles like the repellant, misogynist Jonathan in the grim, closely observed *Carnal Knowledge* (1971) or the repressed radio host in *The King of Marvin Gardens* (1972), performances that gave no hint of likability or charm.

Nicholson is asked to sustain a six-minute take in extreme close-up with the self-consciously written monologue that opens *The King of Marvin Gardens*. When his far flashier brother (Bruce Dern) hugs him on the boardwalk at Atlantic City, Nicholson holds himself up and away from him, as if he has to signal his removal from life and people, yet he still radiates a kind of affection for his brother, too, even as he holds himself physically back. Only an actor working at the highest level of skill could get across both of these things at once so cleanly and simply.

His anger in *Carnal Knowledge* is not cleansing but childish and toxic, and it is meant to be so. When he cries, "I *am* the motherfucking shore patrol!" in a bar in *The Last Detail* (1973), it's enjoyably dominating in the moment, just as it's enjoyable for his sailor character "Bad Ass" Buddusky in the moment, but that very quiet, gentle, fatalistic movie knows that such displays are ultimately futile.

Jack Nicholson (left) signals both love and removal from brother Bruce Dern in *The King of Marvin Gardens*.

The Last Detail is about as un-commercial a picture as could be imagined, even with Nixon in the White House and a despairing national mood. It says that life is a set-up and that even its amusements don't last long. And so Nicholson's trademark goofiness, which often verges on cross-eyed cartoon, can make no real dent. These are films about masculine braggadocio and insecurity and powerlessness, and Nicholson serves them uncompromisingly, without flinching from the most painful areas of impotence and humiliation.

The early '70s Nicholson films all share one thing in common: first-rate scripts by writers like Carole Eastman, Jules Feiffer, Robert Towne, and Bo Goldman. The women in them are mainly anonymous prostitutes, sexpots, neurotics, or shrews, for that kind of representation was common in the 1970s too, alas. The exception to that is Faye Dunaway's faceted, victimized Evelyn Mulwray in *Chinatown* (1974), where Nicholson is the sly private investigator Jake Gittes, handily taking on Bogart territory with his own brand of hip, flip, knowing style, basically detached until his temperament explodes.

Gittes is a second-rate sort of guy, and maybe not the brightest. He really does look out solely for himself, unlike the Bogart characters who go noble in their own way, and once again Nicholson is a symbol of anger and impotence, spending much of the film with a bandage over his nose after a thug (played by director Roman Polanski) cuts it because Jake is being too nosy. Bogart would have gotten the conspiracy in *Chinatown* all tied up by the end, but Nicholson's Gittes is out of his depth, a loser who has to walk away.

The alienation in Nicholson's work reached a crest when he got Michelangelo Antonioni's *The Passenger* (1975) made and made himself open to it. Nicholson shuts down practically all vestiges of his star persona for this decidedly non-commercial venture, maybe Antonioni's finest film, where he plays a reporter who takes on another man's identity only to face further disquiet. Nicholson delivers the spare, rather high-flown dialogue with candor, rock-solid believability, and grace, no small feat. That same year, he crafted his ultimate outsider rebel, Randle P. McMurphy in *One Flew Over the Cuckoo's Nest* (1975), a masculine, low-down life force who gets extinguished in a mental hospital, a man who is rowdy, rabble-rousing, and too much fun for this world.

Nicholson's dangerous, improvisatory, sometimes cartoon-like vitality was at its larger-than-life yet believable height in *Cuckoo's Nest*, so that he is both a rare movie star and also someone you can imagine meeting at a bar in New Jersey. Towards the end of that movie, he plays maybe his finest single scene when McMurphy sits by an open window and seems to be overtaken by some kind of existential dread (all behind a blank, stoned face) and then combats it with little spurts of his bad-boy, rascally will to live. Nicholson was both lovable and a little scary here, so that bourgeois audiences could be tickled by his testing of propriety and rules but also somewhat reassured when his rude working class joie de vivre was taken down by the establishment.

Nicholson finally won an Oscar for *Cuckoo's Nest*, and in the next few years he rested, mainly, and did undemanding roles. The broad comedy *Goin' South* (1978), which he also directed, suggested that such frequent marijuana use had finally fried his brain, but he bounced back with his most extreme study in impotence and frustration: Jack Torrance in Stanley Kubrick's *The Shining* (1980), a man who wants to write but cannot, so that he turns into a rampaging demon.

This is a far broader performance than anything Nicholson had offered before, with his devilish eyebrows working overtime, and some of the mugging can get a little exhausting. His habitual contempt comes from insecurity and failure in *The Shining*, and so a monster emerges, a possessed man, and the actor playing him reached as far as he possibly could for non-human impulses.

Nicholson was a 1930s deadbeat in thrall to the sexual dynamism of Jessica Lange in *The Postman Always Rings Twice* (1981), where he offered a near-comic study in open-mouthed dumbness, hunger, and low cunning. And then, somewhat improbably, he was the playwright Eugene O'Neill in Warren Beatty's *Reds* (1981). His O'Neill is a brooder, and a man with intense feelings for Louise Bryant (Diane Keaton) that cannot be expressed. Both Lange and Keaton stimulated Nicholson out of his solitary detachment, and in *Reds* he uses that detachment to suggest the pride and hope of a man who keeps those things hidden from others. In the scenes of recrimination he has in that movie with Keaton, Nicholson reaches an impressively stark level of intensity.

He was at his very best—ordinary, hot-tempered, and fully present—in Tony Richardson's overlooked *The Border* (1982), where he played a corrupted border agent who tries to help a woman get her stolen baby back. That was followed by an exuberant star turn in *Terms of Endearment* (1983), which won him a second Oscar in the supporting category. As Garrett Breedlove, a hedonistic former astronaut, Nicholson toyed with his own public image and let his potbelly loose, which only added to his authority, to the feeling of love and even respect he occasioned.

He got two more Oscar nominations for best actor in the 1980s, for the strange comedy *Prizzi's Honor* (1985), where he was maybe the outright dumbest man he ever played, and for *Ironweed* (1987), where he tried to be a 1930s street bum but was too much the perceived off-screen "Jack" for that role, too sated by money and women. His horny devil in *The Witches of Eastwick* (1987) was close to an all-out cartoon, and this was capitalized on, to the maximum level of salary and influence, by his very hammy Joker in *Batman* (1989), a new kind of film in a new kind of Hollywood, and very far from his '70s prime.

Nicholson picked up another supporting nomination for a loud courtroom scene in *A Few Good Men* (1992), and then a second lead Oscar for the comedy-drama *As Good as It Gets* (1997), which spoke to his beloved status more than anything else. (His thoughts are so crudely legible on his face in that movie that they might as well have cartoon bubbles attached to them.) This was the time when he was omnipresent at award shows, sitting up front in his sunglasses, radiating power and love of sensation, stewing in all his own juices of reactive but blissfully removed humor and pleasure.

His creative swan song was *About Schmidt* (2002), which worked against Nicholson's image in very touching ways. When his put-upon, retiree character got up to make a speech at his daughter's wedding to a numbskull, the audience I saw the movie with tensed with delight at the prospect of an old-school Nicholson explosion, and so when his repressed Schmidt decided not to say much of anything it carried a keen kind of hurt. The final scene, where Schmidt broke down in tears, had a special meaning because Nicholson is someone for whom tears come at a cost.

He was "Jack" one more time with Diane Keaton in *Something's Gotta Give* (2003), which is really her vehicle but helped along by his autumnal star power, and then he was too sexual and too comic in his collaboration with Martin Scorsese, *The Departed* (2006). After that, Nicholson basically retreated, but he had dominated American movies for 30 years with his anger and his hedonism.

In his best work, the surface flash of Nicholson's star persona was always undercut by his self-reproaches and his angst. His characters behave badly in spite of the fact that they are just smart enough to know better, and that's what created such dramatic tension with him on screen, particularly in *Five Easy Pieces*. Nicholson is a cleansing figure finally, and scrupulously honest most of the time. He is what some would like an American male to be.

Warren Beatty
Take Off Your Clothes

The legend of Warren Beatty as a compulsive seducer of women far overshadows his sparing filmography. His friend Buck Henry called him a "footage fetishist," a man who in his prime liked to spend years shooting and editing his movies. But when it came to his Don Juan act with any woman at hand, Beatty moved fast.

His serious relationships were all with actresses, most of whom had been nominated for or had won an Academy Award. There was Joan Collins, Natalie Wood, and Leslie Caron. There was the beauteous Julie Christie for a rather long period. There was the insecure but magnetic Diane Keaton. There was Madonna, which was going too far even for him. And finally he settled on marriage with the talented, twinkly-eyed Annette Bening.

Before, after, and in between these main ladies was a forest of conquests, hotly speculated on in the 1960s, '70s, and '80s, that seemingly reached from Mary Tyler Moore to Jacqueline Kennedy Onassis, from Germaine Greer to Joey Heatherton, from Liv Ullmann to Raquel Welch. But the really fascinating thing about Beatty's womanizing, as detailed in Peter Biskind's 2010 biography, is that Beatty was interested in *all* women, not just the most attractive actresses.

He wanted to give a tumble to that shy, slightly overweight girl on the sidelines of a set. He wanted to charm the elderly Lillian Hellman, though maybe not actually go to bed with her (then again, who knows and why not?). He once tried to bed both the diminutive middle-aged film critic Pauline Kael *and* her young daughter. There has never been a serious rumor about Beatty and another man. What seems clear is that he was obsessed with leaving a trace of himself, in any way he could, on every woman he came into contact with. And so there was a kind of poetic justice, and irony, when his first daughter with Bening rejected the female body Beatty had spent his life pursuing and grew up to be a very beautiful and articulate female-to-male transsexual, Stephen Ira Beatty.

Beatty was a football player in high school, and he studied acting with Stella Adler in New York. He was tall (6' 2"), and he liked to hesitate over his lines even from the start when he played Milton Armitage on the TV show *The Many Loves of Dobie Gillis* from 1959 to 1960. On that series, he bragged to avaricious Thalia (Tuesday Weld) that his closet was "sixteen feet long," and his thick voice, thick lips, and fluttering eyelashes made a distinct and not always comfortable impression. Beatty "listens" on that show rather than actually listening, and this might be a character choice, but in this early stage he already seems cerebral and withdrawn, or at least wrapped up in himself.

He was given the big build-up under the direction of Elia Kazan in *Splendor in the Grass* (1961), a psychologically acute and detailed treatment of sexual repression written by William Inge in which the sheer lusciousness of Beatty's good looks and full red lips is taken full advantage of in color close-ups (look at the sensual way he is shot when he closes his eyes in a locker room shower and lets the water pour all over him).

Beatty is laboring in the shadow of Brando and James Dean in *Splendor in the Grass*, and he is most himself when being commanding, as when he orders Natalie Wood's trusting Deanie to get down on her knees and worship him, a scene that carries a very potent sexual charge that, again, is not too comfortable. Beatty's looks and manner give him power, and his performance is mainly about how this power makes him uneasy. (Paul Newman and Robert Redford often behaved in a similar way on screen.) Beatty is an introverted, calculating screen presence in his first movie, preening sometimes yet not quite fully involved, hemmed in by the passiveness of his role, though he is well cast to express relentless priapic pressure and all-pervasive horniness.

Warren Beatty is beautified and sensualized by water in a locker room shower in *Splendor in the Grass*.

He did an Italian accent as the gigolo to Vivien Leigh in *The Roman Spring of Mrs. Stone* (1961), which was based on a Tennessee Williams novel. In his first two movies, Beatty is the stud as imagined by Inge and Williams, gay writers who lusted for but feared men like him. Beatty's Paulo in *Roman Spring* is believably callous, and he was unsympathetic as the selfish and cruel Berry-Berry in *All Fall Down* (1962), which was again written by Inge.

As a male nurse in *Lilith* (1964), Beatty seems like a stereotypical Method actor, taking forever to make a decision about how and when he will say his lines, constantly blinking his eyes to show that he's "thinking," but he is more fully committed to the arty *Mickey One* (1965), where he plays a nightclub performer on the lam. That's an intriguing performance from Beatty because he has to push himself to be a seedy young ham on stage, and this challenge seems to stimulate him.

No one was prepared for what *Bonnie and Clyde* (1967) did for Beatty's career and for American movies in general. Tellingly, Beatty made his first major impact by playing a man who looks like one thing but is actually something else. Faye Dunaway's Bonnie responds to Beatty's looks in the first scenes here as many women did, on screen and off, but when it is revealed that Clyde is impotent, Beatty finds a kind of release in playing his own opposite. It is when he has to imagine something far from himself that Beatty really clicks with a role, and that might have something to do with his training with Stella Adler, who always emphasized the importance of an actor's imagination.

Amid much lady-killing and political campaigning for George McGovern, Beatty gave his finest performance for Robert Altman in *McCabe & Mrs. Miller* (1971), a stone classic in which he gets to play an archetypal bull-shitter and loser. When we first see him, Beatty's McCabe is muttering to himself, "You're not stupid," or something like that (this movie is big on hubbub), and so we know he's insecure as he comes into a town and tries to build it up and be a frontier entrepreneur.

McCabe talks a great deal of nonsense, and Beatty has lots of fun with that. He also subtly shows us, in furtive looks and glances, how McCabe falls in love with the madam Mrs. Miller (Julie Christie) nearly on sight. Beatty is very good at hemming and hawing on screen, at prevaricating, even if in life and on his sets he drove people crazy with this same quality. In one of McCabe's monologues to himself, where he tries to make sense of his large feelings for Mrs. Miller, he cries, "I got poetry in me! I do, but I ain't gonna put it down on paper, I ain't no educated man, I got sense enough not to try!" Beatty hits a really poignant vein here on these lines.

He was a marked man in the very frightening paranoid thriller *The Parallax View* (1974), and then he played the stud hairdresser in *Shampoo* (1975), a project which, like *Bonnie and Clyde*, he had painstakingly developed himself, producing and co-writing it with Robert Towne. Wearing shaggier hair and tight clothes, Beatty has the look now of a man so sexually satiated that it is nearly absurd (especially around the mouth), and so maybe in an attempt to counterbalance this he pushes his "distraction" mannerisms farther than ever before.

Beatty presents himself in *Shampoo* as a passive sex object pursued and pawed over by needy, lustful women. Even though Beatty and George share the same busy sexual life they are very different from each other, for Beatty was famous for his aggressive pursuit of the women he wanted, which was pretty much every woman he met. He only comes fully alive on screen when he is playing something totally unlike his own character.

Beatty moved into direction with the feathery supernatural comedy *Heaven Can Wait* (1978), and then he made the epic *Reds* (1981), a lengthy picture about the American communist writer John Reed, played by Beatty himself, and his lover and comrade Louise Bryant, played by Diane Keaton. There is a very pleasing bohemian atmosphere in the early Greenwich Village scenes set in the 1910s, and out in Provincetown when a triangle forms between Reed, Bryant, and the playwright Eugene O'Neill (Jack Nicholson).

But Beatty tries too hard to be appealing and winsome in *Reds*, and little-boyish. Perhaps because he had played too many unlikable characters in his early movies, Beatty took care in later projects of his own to be sympathetic in a very calculated way. He is goaded into anger in his intense argument scenes with Keaton and uses the effective rough notes in his voice, but it is Keaton who is most impressive in these fights, whereas Beatty deflates into "love me" wistfulness soon after they are over.

He won the best director Oscar for *Reds*, which was recognition of his star status and all the effort he had put into this movie, but *Reds* seemed to exhaust him once and for all. Beatty had made eight movies in the 1960s, including the minor and forgettable *Promise Her Anything* (1966), a comedy made for and with his lady of the time Leslie Caron, and *Kaleidoscope* (1966), where he was a card player.

In the 1970s there were seven Beatty movies, including *The Only Game in Town* (1970), which paired him incongruously with Elizabeth Taylor, *$* (1971), and *The Fortune* (1975), all three of which suggested that comedy was never his forte. In the 1980s, there was just *Reds* and *Ishtar* (1987), a famous disaster of a comedy where Beatty and Dustin Hoffman tried to play middle-aged amateur singer-songwriters, with painful results.

There were four Beatty movies in the 1990s. *Dick Tracy* (1990) was an attempt to keep up with the new Hollywood of that time, and it was colorful but disposable. *Bugsy* (1991) introduced him to Bening and gave him a chance to do one more assured star turn, enlivened especially by a scene of rage where his gangster Bugsy Siegel humiliates a male associate and Beatty pushed himself to reveal a darker side, with histrionically imposing results. There was a lame remake of *Love Affair* (1994) with Bening in which Beatty was starting to be lit very elaborately and carefully, like Blanche DuBois, and for which he bullied a near-senile Katharine Hepburn into making an appearance.

Beatty directed himself in *Bulworth* (1998), a political satire that was somehow both bold and mild, and then he did a disastrous comedy called *Town & Country* (2001) that took an unusually protracted time to complete, even by Beatty's standards. He retreated after that, turning up only for lifetime achievement awards with Bening on his arm, until an attempted comeback called *Rules Don't Apply* (2016), where he played Howard Hughes. Beatty had so often been in close touch with the zeitgeist, but he had waited too long to make his Hughes film, which turned out to be choppy, personal, overly comic, sentimental, and badly out of touch with its time.

Al Pacino
Darkness on the Edge of Town

A great actor needs great parts to play, and Al Pacino had at least two of those: Michael Corleone in *The Godfather* movies and Sonny in *Dog Day Afternoon* (1975). Sonny is a bank robber, a self-described "fuck up and outcast" who is living his life by the seat of his pants and trying to keep his head above water, his big soulful eyes cutely staring helplessly in front of him as things get worse and worse. The hapless Sonny is the opposite of the steely Michael Corleone.

The heroic thing about Pacino's Sonny, finally, is his grace under pressure, even as he gives in to angry exhibitionism while riling up the crowd that has gathered outside the bank. "Kiss me," he says to a police chief (Charles Durning), when he knows he is being tricked. "When I'm gettin' fucked I like to get kissed!" In the explosive moment where Sonny cries, "Attica! Attica!" in reference to a prison riot, he has all of the confrontational physical charisma of Mick Jagger in concert.

Sonny is a Vietnam vet with a mess of a personal life, a man with a wife and kids and a lover named Leon (Chris Sarandon) who needs a sex change operation. After this fact comes out in the press, Sonny exhibits no shame, and the expression on his face even shows a queer, mordant sort of pride. He knows what he feels. He loves Leon; he even had a marriage ceremony with Leon. Like Pacino himself, Sonny approaches everything in a galvanizingly Italian, gutsy, and genuine way.

But Michael Corleone is Pacino's testament part, and his performance in the first 1972 *Godfather* movie is so immensely committed, inventive, and forbiddingly detailed that it dwarfs the rest of his work, even Sonny in *Dog Day Afternoon*, which would be a signature role and performance for just about any other actor. Michael suits the training that Pacino had with Lee Strasberg at the Actors Studio because he is a man who learns to show almost none of his thoughts on his face, just little intimidating glimmers.

In his lesser work from his first star period, Pacino has clearly put copious amounts of thought and imagination into creating his characters, but this preparation often feels more like it is for him rather than for the audience. Like Michael, Pacino is never going to show you much of his internal life, though it is clearly going strong underneath his hooded eyes.

For Strasberg, the process of acting was everything, so that he nearly scorned the results of an actual performance; that was one way he kept so many actors dependent on him, and that was a large part of his destructive influence on acting in the 1950s through the 1970s. Strasberg himself plays the gangster Hyman Roth in the second *Godfather* movie, a benign man, always reclining, speaking softly, so sure of his power that he doesn't need to demonstrate it for more than a split second or two sometimes.

In the first *Godfather* film, Pacino's Michael starts out as a callow, fresh-faced war hero, a college boy, withdrawn, the butt of teasing from his family members, who sorely underestimate him. When he goes to the hospital and realizes that his mob boss father (Marlon Brando) has been left alone and unprotected by guards, Michael is told over the phone not to panic by his brother Sonny (James Caan), and we can see little flashes of fear in his eyes before Michael quickly rises to the occasion, getting a family friend to stand outside with him and pretend to have a gun.

After the men who want to kill his father stop in front of the hospital and then move along, the family friend is a wreck, his hands shaking as he tries to light a cigarette, but Michael finds that his own hands are steady, and Pacino makes this moment defining and thrilling, as if Michael is learning just who he is. When a police chief (Sterling Hayden) roughs him up, Michael takes it calmly, even eagerly.

In the scenes that follow, Michael becomes a coolly justifying monster right before our eyes as he sits in a chair and plans the murder of the police chief, who was out to get his father killed. His family still treats him like a kid who needs protection, but we can see, moment by moment, how Michael is coming into his own, how his big intimidating eyes start to stare people down and even gloat over his own burgeoning sense of power and self-control.

The height of Pacino's performance in *The Godfather* happens in the build-up right before he shoots the police chief and a family rival in an Italian restaurant. Michael goes to the restroom to get a planted gun at the top of an old-fashioned toilet (there is a fraught few seconds when he can't seem to find the gun before he finally grabs hold of it), and he takes a moment to himself and flattens the back of his hair before going back out to sit down. And then, in a few silent moments of excruciating tension, Michael has to decide whether or not to act.

After he does these murders, there is no turning back, there will be no other life but a life of crime for his mob family. With every shift of his eyes, Pacino makes us feel and sense every one of Michael's fears and doubts, and yet there is some steel thread even underneath this reverie that lets us know he won't turn back.

Pacino's eyes briefly roll up into his head before he stands up to shoot, like Garbo in her death scene at the end of *Camille* (1936), and this shows that Michael has morally erased himself in order to do this deed. It's like a whole Dostoyevsky novel in under a minute on a human face, and it is Pacino's achievement, as is the dancer-like way Michael tosses aside the gun after he shoots the men and the great score by Nino Rota rises up to this momentous gesture of abandon.

Yes, the part of Michael is one of the best parts anyone has ever had, the part of a lifetime, and this scene in the restaurant is an enormous opportunity. But just try to imagine some of the other candidates for the part of Michael doing it, try to imagine Warren Beatty or Robert Redford or Ryan O'Neal. Probably the role and the film itself would have carried them, even O'Neal. But they could not have gone as far as Pacino does.

Dustin Hoffman and Robert De Niro could have played aspects of Michael very well, but neither of them could have done the full picture that Pacino does, with all of the charm and attractiveness gradually wiped out by paranoia and the need for vengeance, which poisons Michael's relationships with everyone around him except for his loyal, self-deceiving sister Connie (Talia Shire, who makes as impressive a journey as Pacino does across the three *Godfather* films).

Both Pacino and Brando uncannily seem to age over the course of the first *Godfather* movie, which is something actors nearly never manage to do convincingly, and Pacino smartly cedes the floor to Brando during their one major scene together, just letting Michael listen to his father talk and barely moving his commanding eyes or his face.

In many ways Pacino's performance, the whole arc of his character, is complete by the end of the first *Godfather* movie. In the second film, Pacino has less opportunity as Michael gets locked down into glowering, Machiavellian plotting, though his kiss of death to his brother Fredo (John Cazale) in Cuba is the full-bloodedly large gesture of a great actor.

Less impressive is the confrontation scene Michael has with his wife Kay (Diane Keaton) here, which feels more worked-up and acted than it should, like a scene study class exercise. (Part of the problem is that Kay's character is always poorly written and insufficiently motivated, an afterthought, so that Keaton, who is still a little green in the first two movies, can never quite get a handle on her.)

Pacino is always an isolated figure on screen, listening to others in a dutiful way so that you can see he'd much rather be off on his own glorying in his own emotions (another trait that marks him as a Strasberg actor). Pacino admitted that when he was a kid he used to go home and play all the parts in the movies he had seen, and he confessed to interviewer Lawrence Grobel that he loved to spend ten hours at a stretch playing out roles in Shakespeare plays all by himself in his room.

Women barely interest or challenge him on screen, and it's difficult to even remember some of his leading ladies, from the bland and absorbent Kitty Winn in his lead debut *The Panic in Needle Park* (1971) to the interchangeable girlfriends in *Serpico* (1973) and on to the goosey, talkative Marthe Keller in *Bobby Deerfield* (1977) and the pliant Karen Allen in *Cruising* (1980).

Pacino has his best scenes with men, mainly John Cazale in the *Godfather* movies and in *Dog Day* (they were friends from when they were younger, and Pacino helped him get cast as Fredo in *The Godfather*). The guarded Michelle Pfeiffer in *Scarface* (1983) and the tough and sexual Ellen Barkin in *Sea of Love* (1989) perk his interest, but a Pacino character is always using a woman to feed his own ego, which then moves towards other gratifications. Only in *Frankie and Johnny* (1991), with Pfeiffer again, does Pacino seem like a full-blown romantic, so that when he turns on his full charisma to look at her with longing it feels like an event.

Italian on both sides of his family, Pacino was born in 1940 and lived in the Bronx with his mother until he dropped out of school, and he was homeless for a while in his twenties as he worked a lot of odd jobs and studied acting. Pacino lived with the actress Jill Clayburgh at this time, and her father sometimes sent them money to help out as they struggled to find work. Pacino came up the hard way, and maybe that explains the stealth of his performances, the enclosed quality, the calculation that aligns him with Michael Corleone.

He got a job on a TV show called *N.Y.P.D.* in 1968, acting alongside Clayburgh, where he chose to play his character as a *very* dumb guy. In *Me, Natalie* (1969) he was briefly mean to wallflower Patty Duke, asking her point blank, "Do you put out?" and then casting her aside at a dance. And then he got his first lead in a film, the heroin addict in Jerry Schatzberg's *The Panic in Needle Park*, which was written by Joan Didion and John Gregory Dunne.

He comes charging down the street in that first movie, with a bandana around his head, a street guy, short and shambling, full of life, with dancing feet. The young Pacino has a high, whiny voice that comes right from his nose, but when Schatzberg gives him his first extreme close-up it stops the movie cold because this goofy little guy has the eyes of a movie star, like Charles Boyer, the sort of eyes and attitude that command the screen.

His character Bobby in this movie has all of the practiced charm that many other Pacino characters have, and that Pacino himself has in the off-the-cuff interactions captured in two semi-documentaries he has directed, *Looking for Richard* (1996) and *Wilde Salomé* (2011). But this charm is extraneous, something to be put on, and something to be used as a defense or as a weapon.

In his debut *The Panic in Needle Park*, an extreme close-up reveals Al Pacino's star charisma.

You can see the influence of Brando on Pacino's work in *The Panic in Needle Park* because he just seems to be putting raw, unmediated behavior on screen, direct and seemingly unshaped. In a second movie for Schatzberg, *Scarecrow* (1973), Pacino runs through all of his cutest routines for approval from the lumbering, crass character played by Gene Hackman, but the film's lack of structure finally defeats him.

There's a nasty attempted rape scene that he has to endure in jail in *Scarecrow*, and in *Serpico* he gets shot in the face. As an increasingly angry and dogged police officer offended by corruption on the force in *Serpico*, Pacino showed his gift for moral vanity, and for eccentric clothing that might have pleased Brando: an earring, a floppy hat, various ponchos, and even a walking stick.

After the enormous challenge and triumph of his Michael Corleone and then Sonny in *Dog Day*, Pacino idled a bit, as if to take stock of what he might do. His *Bobby Deerfield* is a neurotic, withdrawn racecar driver, highly conscious, hiding behind sunglasses, an isolated celebrity, filled with disquiet that he refuses to show. This is a movie that presents Pacino at his most repressed and forbidding, cold and brooding and lost in process (he had just given up a heavy drinking habit when he made this picture in 1977).

Whereas English actors of the 1970s like Anthony Hopkins and Vanessa Redgrave leap into action and just do things, Pacino allowed himself to get lost in Method hesitations, preparations, and emotional clutter. In thinking over a part too much, he lost the immediacy and legibility of Michael and Sonny.

Towards the end of *Bobby Deerfield*, Pacino is supposed to do a Mae West impression, and he does it in the half-assed way that his character would when it would be so much more interesting, and more generous to the audience, if he had gradually begun to do Mae full out; surely he was capable of that.

He showed just how bold he could be in *Cruising* (1980) as a cop who goes undercover to catch a murderer in the gay leather underground. Sporting an unflattering perm of his usually floppy, unruly hair, Pacino is all subtext in this controversial movie, giving nothing of his feelings away. When he is first asked by his boss (Paul Sorvino) if he has any experience with gay sex or the leather world, Pacino's face brims with cagy interest, but everything about what happens to him in this movie is made enigmatic by his cloak-and-dagger acting choices. In the scene where he does poppers and lets himself go on the dance floor of a gay club, Pacino displayed his gift for big expressive physical gestures, flinging them out at us in an unashamed way.

By the time of *Scarface* (1983), Pacino had moved in a new direction, perhaps in order to adapt to a different era. Lee Strasberg had died, and now he had another diametrically opposed influence. Speaking about his work in *Scarface* to Lawrence Grobel, Pacino said, "I was very inspired by Meryl Streep's work in *Sophie's Choice*. I thought that her way of involving herself in playing someone who is from another country and another world was particularly fine and committed and … courageous. It was very inspiring."

In *Scarface*, a long, unpleasant, baroque movie, well written by Oliver Stone, with a new level of violence that is gloated over by director Brian De Palma, Pacino moved away from Brando's naturalism and into the sort of hyperbolized impersonation that had once served James Cagney. As tough guy Tony Montana, who has no fear of anyone or anything, Pacino does a thick Cuban accent, and his work, particularly in the first half of the film, is studied and mannered, stylized, a created performance that he gradually sinks into as Tony rises to power.

The character of Tony Montana in *Scarface* isn't a calculating person, as Michael Corleone and Sonny are; it is Pacino himself who is calculating every move of his performance, as Streep was doing in this period, doling out shaped behavior like coins clattering to the floor. And so he comes up against an intriguing problem here.

In the two-shots Pacino shares with Steven Bauer, who plays Tony's best friend Manny, the eye generally goes to Bauer, who isn't really acting at all, over Pacino, who is acting up a storm in this picture. This is a good example of how much the camera soaks up the mere presence of a photogenic guy like Bauer over the flamboyant contrivances that make up Pacino's Tony.

Scarface is impressive in its ugly and absurd way, but it marked a turning point in Pacino's career, the first time where he started to become a comic figure, a cartoon of a man, someone easily imitated. He made a mistake with his next film, *Revolution* (1985), a notable flop where he did a difficult-to-take accent, and he was off the screen for four years, in which time he filmed his own private movie, *The Local Stigmatic*, a 56-minute version of a Heathcote Williams play in which Pacino played a low-level gangster.

His English accent in this picture is again questionable, but Pacino was at his very best, and most chilling, in a long scene here where his character flatters and seduces a well-known actor in a bar by acting exaggeratedly humble until he and his friend cut up the actor's face outside, just to be cruel. There is no other performance by Pacino that so revealed the evil intentions that could lurk under his surface cuteness and charm.

He returned in a sexy thriller, *Sea of Love*, where he was still his magnetic self yet not quite, as if he'd been watered down a bit. Ominously, he offered a cartoon performance in *Dick Tracy* (1990) much like Jack Nicholson's comic book turn as the Joker the year before in *Batman*. When he returned to Michael in *The Godfather: Part III* (1990), it was clear sometimes that he had lost his grip on the character, and there are some moments where he was more Pacino the star than Michael the gangster patriarch in winter.

But Pacino also does some of his finest work in this third and maligned *Godfather* movie, particularly in the very upsetting scene where Michael has a heart attack and calls for his brother Fredo (Pacino really flings himself into this physically in his best 1970s style) and the scene where he confesses his crimes to a priest and breaks down.

These scenes were worthy additions to his greatest performance and most notable character, whereas the last sequence where Michael reacts to his daughter (Sofia Coppola) being shot is too obviously based on the famous silent scream that Helene Weigel did on stage in Brecht's *Mother Courage*, and the final moment, where Michael dies alone and unloved in Sicily, is betrayed by unconvincing old age make-up.

Pacino had played on Broadway in David Mamet's *American Buffalo* in the 1980s, and he played the part of Ricky Roma in the film of Mamet's *Glengarry Glen Ross* (1992). The stylized rhythms of Mamet's dialogue led Pacino further into mannerism, into a kind of show-off acting for its own sake, and this was capitalized on by *Scent of a Woman* (1992), which won him a best actor lead Oscar.

He gets a Bette Davis–like entrance in that movie, barking orders off screen until we see his character, the blind, drunken, suicidal retired army lieutenant Frank Slade, who is pouring himself some Jack Daniels in a darkened room. At 156 minutes, this movie qualifies as Pacino's *Mr. Skeffington* (1944), a silly, corny, implausible vehicle and one-man show that added the nonsense-noise catchphrase "Hoo-ah!" to the acts of Pacino impersonators.

Pacino is convincingly blind in *Scent of a Woman*, and funny with the quips and the dirty talk, and just shameless enough to bring off the scene where Frank tangos with a beautiful woman (Gabrielle Anwar). But when he marshals his full talent for the section of the movie where Frank starts to move towards suicide, Pacino only highlights just how lightweight the film is.

He has always had a gift for woozy emotional fugue states, where his characters get so saturated by emotion that they can barely move, but this mood is too heavyweight for *Scent of a Woman*, which Jack Nicholson might have played just as easily. Nicholson could not have played Michael Corleone (though he could have played James Caan's Sonny) or Sonny in *Dog Day Afternoon*, and Pacino would have had trouble with *Five Easy Pieces* or *One Flew Over the Cuckoo's Nest*, for though he comes from the mean streets he is too much the poet and dreamer for such authentically blue collar parts.

It's hard to imagine Nicholson settling into the rot and drive for power in Michael Corleone without wanting to crack some jokes, and surely he would have flinched from the challenge of playing a desperately romantic man who is in love with a transsexual in *Dog Day Afternoon*. Both resplendent in the 1970s, Nicholson and Pacino were being forced into star turns and easily recognizable gimmicks by the early 1990s.

In Michael Mann's *Heat* (1995), Pacino swerved dismayingly into an over-the-top style that suggested he was doing one of his impersonators (Bette Davis had the same problem sometimes past 1950). He had good roles in *Donnie Brasco* (1997), *The Insider* (1999), and *Any Given Sunday* (1999), but some spark seemed to have gone out of his work. He hit his marks, he thought through his performances beat by beat, and there were times when he could have just been punching a time clock.

Only in a second film he directed, the little-seen *Chinese Coffee* (2000), did some of his invention and humor return. A two-hander, played with Jerry Orbach, about two failed writers in middle age, *Chinese Coffee* stimulated the outcast in Pacino, the loser he might have been if he had never gotten his breaks and his best parts. Like *The Local Stigmatic*, it is a movie that reveals something essential about him.

He had two very challenging roles in the 2000s, Roy Cohn in a TV adaptation of Tony Kushner's *Angels in America* (2003) and Shylock in *The Merchant of Venice* (2004), which he had played on stage. The results were performances that went through the motions in a plodding, methodical way, so that the excitement and danger in Pacino never came close to the surface.

He played Jack Kevorkian and Phil Spector for TV, making Kevorkian modestly sinister and Spector a flake who never seemed quite like a threat. He then played a version of himself in an Adam Sandler comedy called *Jack and Jill* (2011) and further tarnished his legacy with a series of rote crime films.

In *The Humbling* (2014), an adaptation of a Philip Roth book, Pacino played an actor who has lost his appetite for acting. On stage in 2015, he was crucified by public and press for not quite knowing his lines in a poor David Mamet play called *China Doll*. "I was the real thing once," he said in *Danny Collins* (2015), as a singer who sold out to commercial interests at the start of his career. And this was true.

Sonny on the phone to Leon in *Dog Day Afternoon* and Michael in that Italian restaurant in *The Godfather* are certain to endure. Sonny is great extroverted and external work, and Michael is the greatest internal work imaginable. You only need to have one of those roles in a career, and Pacino had two and did things with them that no other actor could have done.

Dustin Hoffman
Midnight of the Method

There is a story about Dustin Hoffman's working methods that practically everyone seems to know, and this is how it goes: on the set of *Marathon Man* (1976), Hoffman stayed up all night because his character was supposed to be sleepless, tormented, and exhausted. Laurence Olivier, who was playing the villain in the picture, is supposed to have said to Hoffman, "Why don't you try acting, dear boy?"

Marathon Man is a scuzzy, lightweight thriller, bloody and nasty, and so it is not really an acting showcase. Olivier presents a chilly surface to us in that movie, cold eyes behind glasses that make them seem bigger, and this works just fine for him until a late scene in a diamond store where the camera catches him moving his eyes around cartoonishly to indicate perplexity and unrest. This is laughably bad work, and it shows just what Olivier thinks of the film.

Hoffman, on the other hand, digs and digs into his character in *Marathon Man* somewhat needlessly, laboring over it and hitting veins of very heavy and unattractive self-pity as he gets tormented by Olivier and others (self-pity will always be Hoffman's biggest vice as an actor). There are moments when he looks actually exhausted in a way that cannot really be acted, and they are effective. So was Hoffman right and Olivier wrong? That's hard to say, because even though Olivier doesn't take his performance seriously enough, Hoffman takes his own work far too seriously given the context of the film and his role in it.

Hoffman was a gentle man on screen. When he first holds a gun in *Marathon Man*, his hand shakes, and when he throws a punch in *Family Business* (1989), he hurts his hand. Yet Hoffman could be vain about his own gentleness, his own liberal piety. The good and distinctive things about his work, his empathy and tenderness with others and his dedication to making each moment real, can turn domineering and heavy-handed at any moment, especially as he got older and more set in his ways.

Olivier was the canonized great English stage actor, and there are plenty of times on film, particularly in some of his later filmed stage work like *The*

Dance of Death (1969), where he presents the externals of a performance with nothing at all going on underneath. Hoffman became known as a Method actor, someone who had studied at the Actors Studio, and as time went on he became notorious as a kind of nightmare Method actor, someone who would hold up production with a stream of questions and doubts; his success in films increasingly destroyed his sense of proportion as a performer. Olivier was capable of major work on screen like his Hurstwood in William Wyler's *Carrie* (1952), and Hoffman was capable of major work, too. How they got to these performances might be said to be their business, but the quality of their best work, and their worst work, is linked to their process, to their method.

Hoffman was born in LA. He was told by his Aunt Pearl that he wasn't good-looking enough to be an actor, and so he concentrated as a young man on character parts in the theater, like *The Journey of the Fifth Horse*, which he played Off-Broadway. In *The Star Wagon*, a Maxwell Anderson play that was filmed for TV in 1966, Hoffman at 29 is trying to play a Walter Brennan-type old man, complete with "old" gestures and a character voice, and he's very false, mannered, and self-important. But soon he would get his chance and make his name, in a way that surely came as a surprise to him.

The part of Benjamin Braddock in *The Graduate* (1967) was written as a "human surfboard," a blond Robert Redford type, a scholar and track star who is about to turn 21. But director Mike Nichols saw that counter-intuitively casting the 30-year-old, worrisome Hoffman in this role would stoke the alienation at the center of the film. Hoffman was one of the first movie leads who was Jewish and not trying to hide that; he kept his own name, and he wasn't aiming to be a WASP like Redford.

This was something new in movies at that time, and his adenoidal style was new, too. He was querulous, a thinker, and not macho at all. Hoffman is the liberal among the major 1970s actors, and his interest in women in all the old romantic and sexual ways is bolstered by an interest in feminism, in seeing a woman as a person in her own right. That, at least, was the image he convincingly projected in his movies.

In his first close-ups in *The Graduate*, Hoffman is disaffected, disconnected, and cloudy-eyed, his face brimming with emotions that are enigmatic both to the camera and to himself. In his interactions with Mrs. Robinson (Anne Bancroft), Hoffman makes Ben's passivity comic while ceding control to Bancroft.

For the lengthy hotel room scene where Ben tries to get Mrs. Robinson to talk about herself, Hoffman has a very distinctive way of drawing her out, gently and cautiously, as if Ben is interested in Mrs. Robinson and Hoffman is also interested in what Bancroft is doing as an actress. He is supporting her in these scenes, to a large degree, and in the second half of *The Graduate*, when Ben pursues Mrs. Robinson's daughter Elaine (Katharine Ross), Hoffman carries the burden of making the film's youth pandering believable.

In the final moments of *The Graduate*, Nichols kept the camera running on Hoffman and Ross as they sat in the back of a bus, waiting as actors for Nichols to call cut. Because Nichols didn't do that, we get to see Hoffman's elated face slowly deflate while Ross becomes purely uncomfortable, and it is interesting to see that her discomfort, which is actual and not really acted, is more compelling than Hoffman's refusal to break character; we can still see some gears turning in his head that say, "What should Ben be doing now?"

Hoffman is still creating a character as an actor whereas Ross has given that up and just wants Nichols to let them stop the take, and she is touching as she does that, whereas Hoffman is all over the place. This is a lesson that acting, no matter how advanced (and Hoffman has always been very advanced in this field) will never trump the presence of a photogenic person like Ross when she has her guard entirely down.

The Graduate made Hoffman a movie star, and he could have played variations on it for a while afterward. Instead, he asserted his character actor bravado and chose to play Enrico Salvatore "Ratzo" Rizzo in John Schlesinger's colorful *Midnight Cowboy* (1969). Hoffman's Ratzo is a New York street bum who is never sanitized for the camera, and he is a triumph for Hoffman, who shows just how convincing and moving the all-out brand of Method acting in this period can be. Hoffman has clearly done an enormous amount of work and research that allows him to disappear into the character of Ratzo, so that Olivier's "Try acting, dear boy," becomes the dismissal of an older man and an older style.

Olivier descends to the depths in *Carrie*, very movingly, but there is still a small area in the actor who is removed from his creation, feeling it, yes, but pulling the strings. Hoffman scorns that sort of removal. He becomes Ratzo for the camera, so that even a whinier voice, a cough, and a limp don't make this man seem stagy or created (all that's missing for this characterization is a hump back, but Ratzo assures us at one point that his father had one from shining shoes all day in the subway).

"I'm walkin' here!" Ratzo cries as he hustles down a crowded street when a car almost hits him, and this was an improvisation from Hoffman. This pure New York moment proves how an actor truly can be a creative artist, unshackled to script or director, if they are willing to really go the distance to become another person.

Hoffman's Ratzo shows that the typical Method scheme of stockpiling information about a character and then doling it out to the audience in a miserly way can work well when a character has things to hide, and particularly when a character has things to hide from themselves. When Ratzo stares at the naïve would-be hustler Joe Buck (Jon Voight) on the morning after he has taken Joe in, it is very hard to tell what he is thinking. His face is armored, because when you live on the streets and by your wits you have to be that way. It's a deadpan look, protective but quietly appraising, and it is ready to glare with contempt like the flash of a knife to scare people.

Joe asks if Ratzo is getting laid, and the Italian-Catholic Ratzo says that this is between him and his confessor. Is Ratzo gay? And if he is, how repressed is he about that? When Joe finally says that Ratzo has probably never been laid, Hoffman's shut down face radiates a world of hurt that is difficult to analyze. There's a puritanical side to Ratzo, but we don't know quite where it comes from, or what he uses it for.

Ratzo and Joe form a kind of marriage, living together and supporting each other all without any real verbal acknowledgment of what they're doing and what they mean to one another. On the way up to an Andy Warhol Factory party, Joe tries to wipe Ratzo off to make him more presentable, and the increasingly ill Ratzo becomes unsteady, grabbing onto Joe's waist in a way that feels both desperate and tenderly affectionate. And yet Ratzo is never quite appealing, in a movie way. His face always has a hunted look, an unsavory look, and his self-pity isn't the kind that makes us want to reach out to him.

Ratzo is distrustful of the camera filming at the Warhol party, and maybe that's all you need to know about him. There is a kind of integrity to this thief and low-life, but it isn't a comfortable kind. When Ratzo dies, sitting in a bus that's taking him to his dream-land of Florida, Hoffman stays with his death stare for an impressively long time, as if he doesn't want to give up being Ratzo, so much so that he doesn't want to give up Ratzo in death, either. This is a great performance that broke new ground, and it does everything that the Method can do when it is properly harnessed.

Hoffman took on another feast of a part in Arthur Penn's *Little Big Man* (1970), where he played a 121-year-old man recounting his long and picaresque life. His deliberately anachronistic persona here was once again that of a neurotic nebbish, stubborn and passive, which allows the film's points to be made; when his character makes love to a bunch of squaws, the women all dominate him sexually.

Hoffman allows his face to open up so that he is the movie's liberal conscience. "Don't you *hate* them?" he asks Chief Dan George, speaking of the plundering white man in his quietest, most sensitive voice. Hoffman revealed in *Little Big Man* that he was capable of working in a different style if it suited the needs of a film, a more meta style that allowed him the freedom to speak directly and honestly about the worst in us as represented by the battle of Little Big Horn.

In *Who Is Harry Kellerman and Why Is He Saying Those Terrible Things About Me?* (1971), Hoffman is at his most open and yielding in his scenes with Barbara Harris. He clearly recognizes that Harris is giving a great performance as an insecure and aging would-be actress, and so he shuts himself down and works as a support for her, retreating and acting only as a feed, subtly reacting to her work and also marveling at it underneath.

His sensitivity was used and nearly exploited in Sam Peckinpah's *Straw Dogs* (1971), where Hoffman scrupulously hews to his own character line, sometimes even contradicting the intentions of the film with his quiet, steady, totally civilized man, a man who winks ironically under the most trying of circumstances.

This is a man who does not want to resort to violence but who does so calmly and methodically when his home is threatened. He is let down by the world and by his wife (Susan George), but he does not react in an angry male way. The look on his face towards the end of this film is like a trusted teacher who says to a favorite student, "I'm disappointed in you." A problematic movie, to say the least, *Straw Dogs* showed that Hoffman was capable of asserting his own sensibility under the least favorable of circumstances.

He took his sexually blocked character from *The Graduate* to an extreme in the Italian *Alfredo, Alfredo* (1972), where his plodding walk and lust-filled eyes start to feel a little stagy. Some of his scenes in that movie are Method real, like a moment where he seems actually tired when his character is tired, but there is an actorly fakeness of created moves and gestures on top of this reality of tiredness, and this is not a good combination.

His glasses got smashed in *Straw Dogs*, and as a prisoner in *Papillon* (1973) he wears thicker glasses that make his eyes look bigger until a guard steps on them. Hoffman was supporting Steve McQueen in *Papillon*, but it is clear that in his own head the movie is entirely about him. His ego was beginning to show.

Lenny (1974), a biopic of comedian Lenny Bruce, seems set up as a vehicle for Hoffman, but he never has the edge or the command of a stand-up comic and provocateur; he seems too nice, and never quite funny, and never really angry. This is a strangely flat performance in the context of his career, with very little going on underneath the surface. In the last third of the film, when Bruce is consumed by obscenity charges and legal problems, Hoffman martyrs himself in a dogged and relentless way that pointed to where his work was now going: into his own narcissistic demands for attention.

He was co-lead with Robert Redford in *All the President's Men* (1976), and this made for a telling study in contrasts between movie actor and Method actor. Redford is an old-fashioned star, reliable and good-looking, and his choices are always completely clear. When he is calling people on the phone and someone picks up on the other line that he didn't expect to hear, Redford legibly reacts so that his face says, "Wow, I didn't expect you to pick up."

Hoffman is far more furtive, with a complex and hidden inner life; if he had done this bit on the phone, he would have had two or three cross-reactions going on at once so that you couldn't tell which was which or what was what. It makes Hoffman the better film journalist here, certainly, trickier and more liable to get what he wants. Whether it makes him the better actor is open to debate.

Hoffman was at his very best in *Straight Time* (1978) as a wary, hardened convict, mustached and emotionally armored, who cannot stand the indignity of being tied to a jerky parole officer (M. Emmet Walsh). This was a part that Al Pacino or Jack Nicholson might have played, but Hoffman makes for a less obvious and altogether more disturbing choice for it. It comes as a genuine shock when he turns against the parole office about 46 minutes into the film; the only warning we get is a steady hardening of his face and posture.

Hoffman doesn't do too much in *Straight Time*, as he had been doing, but scales back until what we're left with is difficult to account for. He doesn't sentimentalize the man he is playing. Hoffman's Max Dembo is a career criminal, filled with coiled resentment. He has his warm side, which comes out in the way he treats his new girlfriend (Theresa Russell), but he carries himself as a man with a grievance, totally at odds with society and with life. Hoffman makes us empathize with Max, but only up to a point. When Max starts robbing banks and jewelry stores, the character retreats from us, so that he is deeply in his element again and lost to most of our conventional emotions of fear and pity.

Straight Time showed just how superlative and unsparing Hoffman could be, but it was neglected in the wake of his two showiest triumphs, *Kramer vs. Kramer* (1979), which won him his first lead best actor Oscar, and *Tootsie* (1982), a farce so well-played and tuned that it feels like one of those flukes, like the first *Godfather* film, where everything somehow works to advantage. Both films featured performances from two emerging major female acting talents, Meryl Streep in *Kramer* and Jessica Lange in *Tootsie*, and both of them received best supporting actress Oscars for their work.

Hoffman is competitive with Streep in *Kramer*, and not always in the most productive fashion. He plays most of his scenes with a child (Justin Henry), and the film dotes on his performance in a way that would feel lopsided if anyone but Streep was playing the role of the wife, who is away from us for most of the movie. But any self-indulgence here might be forgiven for one of the most tender moments Hoffman ever played on screen, in the final courtroom scene where he quietly shakes his head and signals to Streep's wife that he wants to make up with her as much as he can. On the set, Hoffman treated Streep very badly and attempted to rile her up as a person rather than an actress, and this came near to abuse. Streep patiently endured Hoffman's use of the Method as a form of power playing, and she saw her own career ascend and her influence on acting spread as Hoffman's began to slowly decline.

The surprise of *Tootsie* is that Hoffman satirizes his most abiding faults as an actor (self-seriousness, focus on process to the exclusion of all else) while simultaneously showing just how transformative his process could be. As Michael Dorsey, a stubborn actor who has sabotaged his career because of his unyielding demand for truth, Hoffman makes light of his burgeoning reputation as an on-set tyrant and then gives us a demonstration of what makes his talent so worthwhile when Michael starts playing the role of a woman, Dorothy Michaels, to get work on a soap opera. Dorothy gets a separate credit of her own in the end titles, and she deserves it, for she is such a full-blooded, three-dimensional creation that she seems to exist outside of Hoffman's performance and outside of the movie.

Hoffman's interest in women came to its most productive and imaginative conclusion in *Tootsie* because he turns himself into the sort of woman he might be if he were one, and also the sort of woman he would like to be. His Dorothy is his finest achievement, even more so than Ratzo and Max Dembo, because in her Hoffman himself really seems to disappear entirely. It's a performance Olivier might have admired and cheered, but it was achieved from the inside out, and not the outside in; his internal work on Dorothy feeds the external we see of wig and glasses, and her distinctively soft voice.

Hoffman next took on a cherished role, Willy Loman in *Death of a Salesman*, which was filmed for TV in 1985. Alas, his self-pity vice really creeps into his Willy, a small man who calls for attention so flagrantly that the famous line at the end where his wife Linda says that attention must be paid to him feels like a joke; who could possibly neglect Hoffman's diva complainer of a Willy, an insistent man who is such a fussy attention-hog?

Hoffman won a second Oscar for his autistic savant Raymond in *Rain Man* (1988), a role that brought out both his best and his worst instincts. He never sentimentalizes Ray, and this is to be expected. But playing such an isolated intellect, guarded by tics and mannerisms, was a kind of dead end for Hoffman, and an entrée for the striving of his co-star Tom Cruise. Commercial through and through, and barely tolerant of outsiders, *Rain Man* expresses the 1980s just as *Midnight Cowboy* did the 1960s, and just about anyone might see what had been lost in that passage of time.

It's not that Hoffman's work deteriorated from this point on, necessarily, but somehow his opportunities on screen were never stimulating enough to release his full talent. He seemed weary by the time of *American Buffalo* (1996), a film of the David Mamet play that Pacino had originated in the 1980s. Past that point, Hoffman began to look increasingly stranded yet stubbornly committed to holding the screen.

He was billed as "The Conscience" in *The Messenger: The Story of Joan of Arc* (1999), and that odd, superfluous part was indicative of how his films were starting to marginalize him. By the time of *Confidence* (2003), Hoffman had become a kind of late-period Miriam Hopkins–like scene hog, sucking up all the air around him with overbearing, insistent playing that gave no one else a chance to get any word or moment in edgewise.

He was forced to play peacemaker, both on and off screen, in *I Heart Huckabees* (2004), and this revealed the gentleness that was still waiting for someone to make use of it. Hoffman had boxed himself into a corner, and he must share some responsibility for the decline of his career, but surely some better parts might have released some of his former talent and skill.

He supported the poetic young Ben Whishaw in *Perfume: The Story of a Murderer* (2006), but that film didn't give either of them enough scope to make the connection they might have. Hoffman finally got a real chance in the David Milch TV series *Luck* (2011–12), and he responded with his most energized work in years, but the show was cancelled when too many racehorses were hurt and killed while they shot it.

Hoffman made his directing debut with *Quartet* (2012), a film that dotes on Maggie Smith's performance but makes no impact at all. Hoffman had directed a lot of *Straight Time* himself over 30 years earlier. To watch that film and then watch *Quartet* is to see what age can do to a person's talent. *Straight Time* is one of the most unsettling movies ever made about being a criminal and leading a criminal life. In that film, it is made clear that time is running out, for Max Dembo and for everyone around him and for everyone watching the movie.

Hoffman was well suited to the role of the egotistical, failed sculptor in Noah Baumbach's *The Meyerowitz Stories* (2017), but his comic skill was defeated by the garrulous, poorly structured script. He was hit with some serious allegations of sexual harassment in 2017, particularly by the woman who played his mistress in *Death of a Salesman*, Kathryn Rossetter, and this did much harm to his particular legacy, a lot of which had been based on sensitivity to women.

But his best work, his Ben Braddock, Ratzo, Max Dembo, and Dorothy Michaels, secures his place as one of the best actors of his time, and that work should look increasingly impressive after the assorted misfires of his later years are duly forgotten.

Robert De Niro
Born to Lose

In his early films, Robert De Niro was carrying the lessons of Brando's naturalistic work to a kind of violent extreme: all action, all throwing himself into scenes physically. He was uneasy, solitary, a fighter, and a "leave me alone" type of guy on screen. He specialized in characters who were radically alienated from other people and from the world around them, and often he feels like an alien who is diligently imitating certain human behaviors without ever fully understanding what he is doing.

Though he was as dedicated to realism as Brando, his real forefather is Robert Ryan. Like Ryan, De Niro always seems somewhat menacing and intensely single-minded, but in the final reckoning he is unlike anyone else. He never trades on charm (he has very little of that), and he is never purely likable. De Niro is a chilly, near-saintly presence with private standards, and suited to certain types of roles only. But he took his outcasts farther out than anyone else ever has.

He grew up in Manhattan, the son of a gay abstract expressionist painter, Robert De Niro, Sr., and the painter and poet Virginia Admiral. Admiral raised him by herself and did clerical work to support them, and De Niro was known in the neighborhood as "Bobby Milk" because of his pale appearance.

He worked in theater and did his first films for Brian De Palma, playing a voyeuristic filmmaker in *Greetings* (1968) and *Hi, Mom!* (1970). De Niro seems uncomfortable in those De Palma movies, awkward with words and resolutely unfunny, but there is a scene in *Hi, Mom!* when he is impersonating a police officer and talking to himself where his distinctive brand of pure anger was first unleashed.

De Niro broke out in 1973 in two very different roles. As the dying baseball player Bruce Pearson in *Bang the Drum Slowly*, De Niro uses a light Southern accent and has a kind of quicksilver spark underneath his character's dim-wittedness. He is working in a conventional and not particularly well-made male weepie, but there is always something fresh and unexpected going on in De Niro's performance here.

When the pressure of Bruce's illness gets to be too much, De Niro is utterly vulnerable when he says, "I'm scared, hold onto me," to his friend Henry (Michael Moriarty), like a little kid who has learned no guile or guardedness. There is a scene late in the film when Bruce tries to sing and dance with the team where De Niro is at his weirdest and most alien, as if he were trying to catch little rays of something non-human.

In Martin Scorsese's *Mean Streets* (1973), De Niro has the flash part as Johnny Boy, an anarchic street guy, dangerous and anti-social, whose inner excitement comes from an urge for destruction. Scorsese sometimes films De Niro in red light in a bar, and that's apt, because Johnny is a red sort of character, an alarm signal, and De Niro's work is spectacularly fluid here, all legato, and totally un-self-conscious.

Like Brando, De Niro had studied with Stella Adler, and that very much shows in his work. Adler emphasized the physical in performance, famously saying that if you fall to your knees the emotion will come out of the falling itself and hitting the ground. Adler also set great store by extensive research into a role, which De Niro would soon become notorious for.

De Niro is very different from Pacino and Hoffman because he is an Adler actor, not a Strasberg actor. All of his preparation is used as a springboard for the event of the performance itself, so that it is all assimilated and nothing is held back, and none of that work he has done beforehand is shown to us or even visible as work. He is intimidating and scary in the musical number-like fight scenes in *Mean Streets*, especially when Johnny Boy breaks off a pool cue and jumps up on a pool table to defend his territory. De Niro is channeling a life force sort of malevolence here that is charismatic and attractive, seemingly heated yet cold to the touch.

He won an Oscar for best supporting actor for his work as a young Vito Corleone in *The Godfather: Part II* (1974), a big responsibility that De Niro saw as a kind of "mathematical problem." This is a different kind of performance, careful and nearly studied, marshaling a slightly raspy voice to match Brando's voice in the original *Godfather* and a catlike physicality that feels coiled and self-contained. The film makes no large demands on De Niro beyond these surface resonances, but it showed that he had the skill to do many things on screen.

De Niro then took his signature part, Travis Bickle in Scorsese's *Taxi Driver* (1976), an outright Expressionist film with a volatile and instinctive Paul Schrader script. Travis is a Vietnam vet with a nasty scar on his back. He works from 6 PM to 6 AM for six and sometimes seven days a week, and he gets bad headaches, which he notes in his diary. In that diary, Travis writes that he disapproves of "morbid self-attention," yet he is a virtuoso of that sort of thing, a pale-faced, ghostly nowhere man, a void who wants to be a kind of knight in armor in rundown, crime-ridden 1970s New York.

De Niro gives a stark, nearly plain, opaque performance here, never signaling psychic disturbance to the camera but inhabiting it. This is acting that is all interior, most of the time, and yet there also doesn't seem to be any interior in Travis at all. That mole on De Niro's face … is it a beauty mark here, or some other kind of mark? How much of *Taxi Driver* actually happens? All of it, some of it, none of it? Maybe none of it.

De Niro's Travis is like Brando's early work because it is still water, uninflected, never intruded on by the actor himself. Travis lives in a daze, and he is so isolated that he seems disconnected from everything around him, from politics to music to other people. He just "doesn't follow" any of that. He eats Doritos and drinks Coke and watches soap operas on his TV set, yet he doesn't have an ounce of fat on his tight, wiry, military-fit body. There is nothing there inside of him, seemingly, and Travis seems to realize that, so that he finally has to assert that he exists at all through active, physical violence. Nothing is made clear here because nothing is clear to Travis himself. How do you play a void like Travis? By emptying yourself out and letting go of all pre-conceptions.

Surely Pacino, Nicholson, and Hoffman would not have been able to resist sometimes showing us in behavior, in eye movements, in physical movements, what is wrong with Travis, but De Niro gives us no handholds at all. He has stopped making sense, and his famous private moment in front of the mirror, when Travis asks, "You talking to me?" is truly private. It lets no one in. It is for Travis only, not for or from De Niro and not for us, particularly. Again, this is Adler work rather than Strasberg work. This is a character, a creation, and he is weirdly buoyant and sinewy. There is never anything heavy or emotionally saturated about De Niro's work. He is free, and that means being free of the self, and that is what his Travis in *Taxi Driver* is all about.

Strasberg was noted for his private moment exercises where he had actors create an environment where their character, or they themselves, were alone. He wanted his actors to be private in public, on stage or on screen, but he led them too often into their own blocked-off personal traumas. De Niro makes himself a scrupulously clean slate in his best early performances. Nothing of his own is allowed to intrude on the character he is taking on.

Travis Bickle is a hapless person, with so many pieces missing, but he has a certainty about some things. "You're in hell, and you're going to die in a hell like the rest of them," he tells Betsy (Cybill Shepherd), the cool blonde political operative who rejects him after he takes her to a porno theater on their second date. The critic Manny Farber objected to the seeming incoherence of *Taxi Driver* and the character of Travis. He wondered how Travis knows just what to say to Betsy to get his first date with her, and then he wondered how Travis could then make the mistake of taking her to the dirty movie.

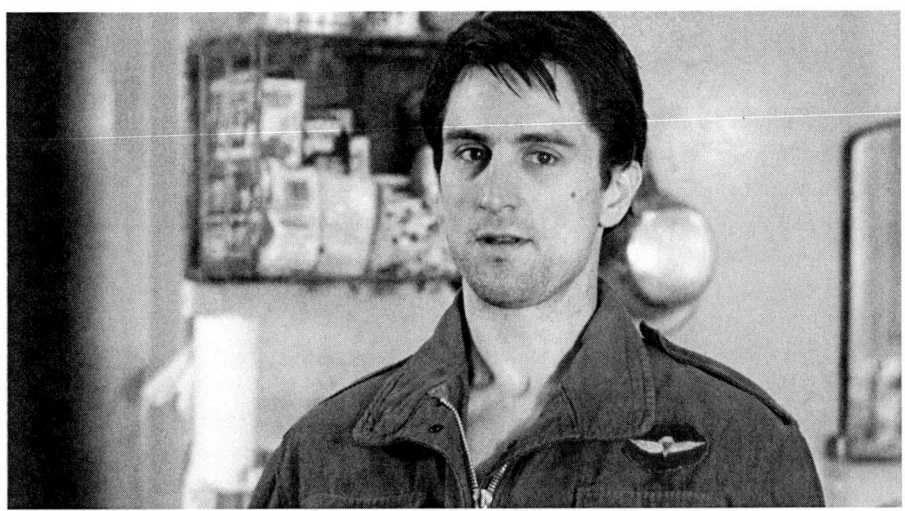

Robert De Niro has a truly private moment as Travis Bickle in *Taxi Driver*.

Travis is an empty vessel who is finally filled by the urge for slaughter in the service of some very vague cause he believes in. Is it vague to him, or just vague to us? It does seem to be vague to him, or at least malleable. He's like a pinball in the machine, bouncing here and there and back and forth, and this film about evil inspired evil in return in life within a man named John Hinckley, which is always the true danger when you take on this type of subject. "Suck on this," Travis tells the pimp Sport (Harvey Keitel) right before shooting him, and that is one moment of clarity that connects Travis's sexual frustration to his final release as a shooter and killer.

Taxi Driver is a nightmare, and pretty far from realism, which is why De Niro's realistic and mysterious performance is still so disturbing. It might be worth noting here that Manny Farber, one of the most vocal and insightful critics of *Taxi Driver*, was in a long-term relationship with De Niro's mother Virginia Admiral, a relationship that De Niro seems to have disliked intensely.

De Niro branched out for Bernardo Bertolucci's epic *1900* (1976), where he was never handsomer under the sensual eye of cinematographer Vittorio Storaro. As the wealthy son of a landowner, De Niro experimented with sex on screen, just as Brando had for Bertolucci in *Last Tango in Paris* (1973), but in far bolder ways.

De Niro really smiles in *1900* and opens his face up to pleasure as he underlines the homoerotic undertones in his friendship with peasant Gérard Depardieu: "Kiss me, my hero!" he cries as they wrestle in an early scene, and Depardieu does kiss him very hard on his mouth. Two hours into this over five hour film, the two friends go to bed with the same woman, and De

Niro even shockingly allows himself to get a hand job on screen, showing just how far he would go in his pursuit of realism.

He does lots of intriguing things in *1900*, especially when he shows off his delicate hands as he lustfully and graphically takes Dominique Sanda in a hayloft. De Niro is only interested in women on screen for sex, but this sexual need of his is a keen one, blunt and forceful. He is trying to give a full-scale romantic performance in *1900*, but always he cannot help adding little sinister touches, little glints of menace. His scenes as an old man in *1900* don't quite work, though he is clearly trying his best, for he was too youthful and energetic yet to reach that far with his imagination.

He then took on the difficult and thankless role of Monroe Stahr, a character based on MGM studio chief Irving Thalberg, in Elia Kazan's film adaptation of F. Scott Fitzgerald's *The Last Tycoon* (1976). De Niro seems smaller and frailer in that movie (he lost weight for it, going down to 128 pounds) and his Monroe is a recessive, gentle man, a watcher and a dreamer. He has fine moments of reverie in the first half of the film, but in the second half the narrative seems to collapse, and De Niro loses his grip on the detached character he is trying for.

He worked for a third time with Scorsese as saxophonist Jimmy Doyle in *New York, New York* (1977), a film that attempted an alienating mix of old and new styles where he went up against Liza Minnelli in many deliberately awkward confrontation scenes that seem inspired by the films of John Cassavetes.

De Niro's Jimmy is a cold and focused bullshit artist, Mr. Relentless, a cynical "actor" in life situations who admits to Minnelli's Francine Evans in their first Meet Abrasive scene that he doesn't have all that much heart. This is a tough, unstable film that seems to shift with each viewing, and the relationship between Jimmy and Francine is one of the most brutally wounding and competitive male-female face-offs in film history.

De Niro is so direct in *New York, New York* that he makes Nicholson, Pacino, and Hoffman look rather rhetorical and definitely cluttered in comparison, yet he boxes himself into a corner here, doing the kind of super-advanced work that is easy to admire but difficult to enjoy or take pleasure in. His privacy and poker face on screen were beginning to seem ungenerous, and threatening.

But then Jimmy Doyle himself clearly plays bebop on his saxophone for himself and for the love of music, not for a crowd, unlike the nearly absurdly crowd-pleasing Francine, whose naked need for audience approval Jimmy views coolly, with light disdain. Jimmy Doyle is like a pebble in your shoe, or a wind on a freezing day. He's a guy Robert Ryan might have understood.

Next De Niro was the shy, closed-off center of a group in Michael Cimino's very painful and very questionable Vietnam war epic *The Deer Hunter*

(1978), and then he famously gained 70 pounds to play the older Jake La Motta in Scorsese's *Raging Bull* (1980), an upping of the ante for character transformation that won him an Oscar for best actor.

This was De Niro's movie from the start, a project that he brought to Scorsese. The near-pointlessness of the ordeal of La Motta's life, and the smallness and sordidness of it, is part of the point of the film, and this stubborn perversity is there in De Niro's work here, too. De Niro himself liked La Motta, and he paints a picture of a man who fears his own softness, his own sensitivity. Jake isn't happy with his "small hands," his "little girl hands," and of course De Niro himself has always had the poetic hands of a violinist, not a boxer, and so this adds to Jake's dramatized masculinity issues.

De Niro's Jake has an ugly, broadened nose even in the youthful scenes, yet his eyes often look at his wife Vickie (Cathy Moriarty) and his brother Joey (Joe Pesci) with furtive tenderness. To guard against this, Jake is a helpless destroyer of beauty and softness, often for complex reasons. When Vickie mentions that a young fighter named Janiro (Kevin Mahon) is good-looking, the hyper-conscious Jake makes sure to destroy his face in the ring (Janiro looks like Montgomery Clift, which adds more resonance to Jake's fears and his inchoate idea of what being a man means).

There is a sense that Jake starts to use his own Othello-like jealousy of Vickie in the ring like a Strasberg-style Method actor would use their own life and emotions for a performance, but by the time he is locked in a jail cell and pounding his head against a wall, Jake has finally reached a place of modest understanding. "I'm not an animal," he cries. "I'm not that bad." That "I'm not that bad" is as touching as De Niro has ever been on screen.

He worked for a fifth time with Scorsese on *The King of Comedy* (1983) as Rupert Pupkin, an autograph hound and would-be talk show host, another nowhere man who talks to himself, and about as unattractive a character as any lead actor has ever played. De Niro's face was changed and broadened after his weight gain for *Raging Bull*; never again would he sport that sleek, hawkish look of his 1970s work.

Rupert has unreal-looking helmet hair and a gross little mustache, and he lives with his mother, a woman we hear yelling at him but never see. He is a loser's loser, a loser that even other losers shun, and this was the end of the line for this type of character for De Niro. (He could take this kind of man no further without trying to portray anti-matter.) There is no pathos in Rupert's situation as sketched in this film. He is an odious, self-satisfied putz, another Mr. Relentless who brings nothing but trouble to the world.

It's hard to know how we're supposed to take Rupert's final comedy monologue, after he has strong-armed himself onto TV by kidnapping a talk show host (Jerry Lewis). De Niro mimics the falsely insinuating rhythms of a third-rate comic, but everything is deliberately off, deliberately un-pleasurable. As in *Taxi Driver*, it's tough to figure out what is real here and what isn't, and De Niro's denial of Pupkin's humanity is finally very creepy in its insistence, though it might be said that Pupkin himself has long since left his humanity behind.

In his 2014 book *Watching Them Be*, James Harvey writes that De Niro's Pupkin and his Travis Bickle are "beyond humiliation" and that they are "superior even to their own lost dignity." Some find this fascinating, others do not. Either way, this is the opposite of the kind of work that might win love or much approval from an audience.

De Niro was an opium dreamer beset by memory in Sergio Leone's alternately languid and brutal *Once Upon a Time in America* (1984), and after that he coasted for a bit before lending his name and aura, and his performing muscle and anger, to Scorsese's *Goodfellas* (1990) and lending his imaginative talent to the very sentimental tearjerker *Awakenings* (1990), which is the inverse of *The King of Comedy*: all pathos. He then worked with Scorsese a seventh time on *Cape Fear* (1991), an unsavory thriller that shows the difference between making personal films in America in the 1970s and trying to make a genre picture in the early 1990s.

De Niro's vengeance-driven convict Max Cady in *Cape Fear* is a cartoon nasty from the start, and like a villain in a slasher movie towards the end, hammy and would-be humorous. The application of De Niro's talent and Scorsese's talent to this particular project makes it all seem rather horrible, and certainly unnecessary. The scene where De Niro's Max bites off the cheek of the charming Lori (Illeana Douglas) feels particularly gratuitous in its viciousness.

In the 1990s, De Niro began to work far more and yet he was truly present far less. He was another unsavory, bullying man in *This Boy's Life* (1993), where he went toe-to-toe with a coltish young Leonardo DiCaprio, and he was the creature in Kenneth Branagh's disastrous *Mary Shelley's Frankenstein* (1994).

He was a watchful figurehead in an eighth collaboration with Scorsese for the very violent *Casino* (1995), and he did a noted scene over a cup of coffee with the increasingly flashy Al Pacino in *Heat* (1995). De Niro himself was becoming increasingly cold, starchy, and distant on camera. His grumpy uneasiness was used for effective shock value in Quentin Tarantino's *Jackie Brown* (1996), where his ex-con Louis unexpectedly kills off the tarty, taunting Melanie (Bridget Fonda) in a parking lot.

After that, De Niro took a plunge into commercial comedy with *Meet the Parents* (2000) and the subsequent sequels, lucrative opportunities for him as a producer and businessman. De Niro chose life and money at this point and willingly sold out his artistry in ways that were as crass as the culture surrounding him.

He worked and worked, doing small films, too, if they could be fit into his schedule, and he's pretty good in *Stone* (2010), a movie that not many people saw, as an old parole bureaucrat whose face shows his severe disappointment with both people and life. This was more like his stripped-down early performances, but in an autumnal key. There were lines and creases on his face now that stayed there whether or not he was grimacing or screwing up his facial muscles into a grin, and there was real authoritative disdain in that older face.

In Glenn Kenny's 2014 book on De Niro, his co-star in *Stone*, Edward Norton, spoke of De Niro's "million-mile stare.... There's a deep sense with him, an ability to convey a very, very powerful, almost unnerving sort of assessment that's going on inside him, of the situation that's taking place." The world did not please De Niro as a young man, and it pleased him even less as an old man.

He is working with Scorsese again on *The Irishman*, where he is set to be digitally de-aged in scenes where his character is young, and this sounds like the kind of cheating that made the overweight section of *Raging Bull* so impressive to some.

No doubt De Niro did tarnish his legacy with all the bad comedies he appeared in, things like *The Big Wedding* (2013) and *Dirty Grandpa* (2016), where he diligently and harshly delivered all of his extremely crude lines. But, as Jake La Motta says in his club act in *Raging Bull*, that's entertainment.

Harvey Keitel
Body Artist

At age 28, Harvey Keitel played J.R., the lead in Martin Scorsese's first feature, *Who's That Knocking at My Door* (1967). He has to carry the burden of J.R.'s ugly reaction when his girlfriend (Zina Bethune) tells him that she has been raped, and he does that because there is something angelic, or striving to be angelic, in his face. But it is in the nude love scene, which was only a commercial necessity for Scorsese insisted on by his producers, where Keitel reveals his full talent.

He is good with his clothes on here, but he's great—complex and uninhibited—with his clothes off. The way this love scene is shot and staged, Keitel and the girl are 50/50 partners, and sometimes Keitel is on his back or on his stomach, allowing himself to be a sexual object for the camera and letting the girl he is with take the lead sometimes. His keen interests on screen are sex and anger, though not always in that order, and his best work managed to meld the two in shocking and incendiary ways.

He was the lead again in Scorsese's *Mean Streets* (1973), where he grounds the film but has to cede, eventually, to Robert De Niro's Johnny Boy. There is a chemistry he has with De Niro here based clearly in rage and actorly competitiveness, and Keitel seems to know that he is losing the battle as that film comes to an end.

Keitel played Ellen Burstyn's violent pick-up and brief boyfriend in *Alice Doesn't Live Here Anymore* (1974), which showed just how far he could go physically and how he could command the space around him in brutal ways, like a geyser going off, or a fire hose. By the time of *Taxi Driver* (1976), Keitel had been demoted to supporting De Niro as a longhaired child pimp named Sport, a fast-talking and odious figure.

In the late 1970s Keitel won a few leads that allowed him to exercise his talent to the utmost and past that. As a demonic officer in Napoleon's army in Ridley Scott's *The Duellists* (1977), based on a Joseph Conrad source, Keitel brought an intimidatingly dismissive physical bravado to the part and caught the nihilism of this unreasonable man and also the existential imperative that makes him lead a life based on feeding his spite for a higher-ranking soldier

(Keith Carradine); he's so committed here that his contemporary New York accent is easy to overlook.

Keitel had a breakthrough as Jimmy in James Toback's *Fingers* (1978), flinging himself into the extremes of the role with a notable lack of caution. Jimmy is a concert-level pianist who plays as if he is in the throes of sexual ecstasy. He is also a debt collector for his low-life father (Michael V. Gazzo), and someone who welcomes physical violence.

Wearing a Caesar haircut, a pink shirt, a white scarf, and a leather jacket, Keitel's Jimmy carries a tape player wherever he goes so that pop songs are the soundtrack of his life, of both his seductions and his beat downs. Keitel physicalizes Jimmy's thrill at being alive, drumming any available surface with his fingers and touching his own head and face with them as often as he can. This part eventually calls for radical bodily commitment and vulnerability, and Keitel exposes forbidden psychic corridors in himself while holding the film together by the tips of his fingernails.

Jimmy is a ladies' man who is equally excited by a hot brunette in a bikini and a schlumpy middle-aged woman crying in the street; he will do or say anything to bed a woman, or get to her somehow. In the scene where Jimmy fails his piano recital audition, Keitel moves directly into a nightmare area of inadequacy and anxiety, and this mood only intensifies as the film goes on.

He goes right out on a limb and shapes all of the extremes in *Fingers*, and on this level, especially when it comes to the sexual demands of the part, he surpasses all of the other major actors of his time. *Fingers* is a companion

Harvey Keitel is both angel and devil in *Fingers*.

piece and rejoinder to *Five Easy Pieces*, taking off from a similar idea but going many places that film would never think to go. In the last shot of the movie, Keitel has reached an animal stage of terror, coiled and naked and ready for anything, but beseeching, too, crying out for relief or help.

Unfortunately, not many people saw *Fingers*, and Keitel suffered setbacks at this point, dropping out of the lead role in Francis Ford Coppola's *Apocalypse Now* (1979), and then having his voice dubbed by another actor for Stanley Donen's sci-fi *Saturn 3* (1980). (Keitel is often uneasy with words and much happier when asked to do physical things, but this dubbing was surely unnecessary.)

He spent the 1980s mainly in supporting roles, often in far-flung and unusual films. Keitel was an inspector in Nicolas Roeg's unsettling drama of sexual obsession, *Bad Timing* (1980), and he played a brooding, red-haired Judas in Scorsese's *The Last Temptation of Christ* (1988). Though his movies were often intriguing in this period, his opportunities as an actor were limited, and his roles often brought out nothing but his bluntness and harshness, his steady, staring, insistent presence.

That changed dramatically in the early 1990s, where in his early fifties he had a string of parts that really suited him. He played a kindly cop chasing *Thelma and Louise* (1991), and he won a supporting actor nomination for his gangster Mickey Cohen in *Bugsy* (1991). Keitel both produced and presided over Quentin Tarantino's first film as a director, *Reservoir Dogs* (1992), and then he took two lead parts that allowed him to go even farther than he had in *Fingers*.

In Abel Ferrara's *Bad Lieutenant* (1992), Keitel allowed himself to be a drug-addled, corrupt cop, snorting cocaine and smoking crack, gambling higher and higher sums, indulging himself in ever-baser ways. He was full frontally nude in an early scene, offering up his thickened but still classically beautiful body to the camera as he did in *Who's That Knocking at My Door*, but more essential here is the far-out state of emotional chaos he is accessing above the neck, in his grimacing face and in the twisted sounds he is making. Keitel is channeling a weird sort of infantile place here shot through with hellishly adult disappointment, and the combination is more than unsettling; it's like something we shouldn't be seeing, a real Lee Strasberg private moment that seems to reveal something uncanny, angelic, and diabolical all at once.

There is a scene mid-way through *Bad Lieutenant* where Keitel's cop pulls over two teenaged girls and takes advantage of his power over them, making one of them show her body to him and the other open her mouth as if she's performing fellatio. Keitel keeps up a steady rap of dirty talk as he jerks himself off to the girls, and it is here above all that he shows how unafraid he is of melding sexual desire with rage, of showing us base human impulses that most actors wouldn't touch with a ten-foot pole.

Keitel does not judge the Sade-ian behavior here, and he goes to this very nasty sexual place on screen as simply as possible and somehow keeps tight control over it technically, no small feat; it is hard to imagine any other actor playing this part as all-out as Keitel does. Jimmy in *Fingers* was torn between street violence and finer instincts whereas the bad lieutenant, who is never named, has flung himself so deeply into an abyss of city debauchery that only his lapsed Catholicism can possibly begin to explain it.

Keitel was fully nude again in Jane Campion's romance *The Piano* (1993), where Campion's female gaze transformed him into a desirable yet forbidding sexual object (when her camera lingers over his lush middle-aged ass this shot practically plays like a musical number). His George Baines has a tattooed face that looks like a sunburst, a fit frame for his burning eyes.

The light accent Keitel does in *The Piano* frees him vocally so that words and body go together for him finally, and his harshness meets its match in Holly Hunter's strange, strong-willed Ada. Once again he plays a man who takes sexual advantage of his power over a woman, but this time a strong love grows unexpectedly out of that situation. If Jimmy in *Fingers* is Keitel's finest hour, then George Baines is his most mature and complete and balanced work, set within an un-ingratiating, uncompromised film.

Keitel kept going after those peaks, playing the Wolf in Tarantino's *Pulp Fiction* (1994) and playing again, just as sexily, for Campion in *Holy Smoke!* (1999). By that time, he had collaborated with Martin Scorsese, Robert Altman, Alan Rudolph, James Toback, Paul Schrader, Bertrand Tavernier, Nicolas Roeg, Abel Ferrara, Tarantino, Campion, Theo Angelopoulos, and Spike Lee. After 2000 he worked for more obscure directors, but his best performances from the 1970s through the 1990s still burn themselves into many of the most interesting films of the period in which he worked and let himself be seen, outside and in.

Keitel was very touching and precise as an agent talking Robin Wright through getting herself scanned for future computer use in the overlooked *The Congress* (2013). In 2014, he displayed his aged upper body in Wes Anderson's *The Grand Budapest Hotel* and showed that his art was a matter of giving himself over to the camera in his darkest moods and in all his stages of life.

Gene Hackman
Keep It Real

No one thought that Gene Hackman would make it as an actor, even as a character actor, and his acting teachers told him as much when he roomed in the 1960s with Dustin Hoffman. He was in his thirties then, and had spent time in the marines as a very young man. As a child, his father had waved goodbye to him, and then he didn't see his father for years, and Hackman said in interviews that this taught him the power of a simple gesture. Hackman had small eyes and a large nose and curly hair that grew sparse pretty early. But he had one thing in his favor: a very expressive and very low speaking voice, an unmistakably barroom voice with a harsh flavor.

Hackman could be an awkward presence. If you look at his acceptance speeches for the two Oscars he won as the cop Popeye Doyle in *The French Connection* (1971) and the sheriff in *Unforgiven* (1992), it seems as if Hackman doesn't feel like he belongs there winning awards and like he doesn't want to reveal too much of himself, and yet his emotion looks deep, and somehow inappropriate, more like a veteran tearing up at a meeting of old war buddies than an actor getting a golden statue. What Hackman brought to the movies was a grainy, un-ingratiating authenticity that felt like it came from the middle of the country, not the coasts. He had very little charm, and he seemed incapable of romanticizing himself.

And yet he did do that once in his late fifties, in Woody Allen's *Another Woman* (1988), and this feels like a revelation of what Hackman could do, or would like to be, if he could get away with it. He only has two short scenes in that movie as a writer named Larry Lewis, a slow-burning literary guy carrying a torch for Gena Rowlands's uptight professor Marion. We first see Larry kissing Marion in an intense, enraptured way, and he insists that she loves him as much as he loves her. This scene lasts a little under a minute, but Hackman is disclosing a whole other persona here, a patient, sensual, extremely confident man of the world far removed from anything else he ever played on screen, partly a fantasy man and partly someone who is imaginable. When he stares down at Marion and speaks of loving her "passionately," Hackman reveals a Eugene O'Neill–like side, a steady and centered romanticism, and some vulnerability, too.

Larry turns up again in a dream that Marion has, and he tells her about his wife and child, and how she inspired a character in a novel he wrote, which she hasn't read. At the end of *Another Woman*, Marion does read the part of Larry's novel that is about her. We see but do not hear Hackman when Larry meets Marion by chance at a concert hall. He goes out to eat with her, walks with her in Central Park, and then he kisses her in an underpass after it has started to rain.

Hackman is powerfully centered and romantic and very attractive in *Another Woman*, and this feels like an event, even if he is in less than ten minutes of this movie. He got an Oscar nomination that same year for *Mississippi Burning*, and he had won popular acclaim for the inspirational sports movie *Hoosiers* (1986), and those were the sorts of parts he usually played in films: conservative, steady, but quick to anger, for Hackman has an unusually deep capacity for anger as an actor. Yet it is Larry Lewis in *Another Woman* that shows the steadfast and disappointed heart in Hackman.

In so many films, Hackman could be seen as an American version of Michael Caine, a blunt presence who imposes himself on disparate material in a domineering way that speaks to some inner insecurity or lack. He played a small role in *Lilith* (1964) with Warren Beatty, and then he got noticed as Beatty's boorish brother in *Bonnie and Clyde* (1967). He was the son to Melvyn Douglas in the earnest *I Never Sang for My Father* (1970), and then he won an Oscar for his Popeye Doyle in William Friedkin's *The French Connection*, so that he graduated to lead roles in his forties all through the 1970s.

Once again he played a boorish man in *The French Connection*, a man who wears a porkpie hat un-ironically as he gets involved in various chase scenes. He was rough as sandpaper here, racist and un-welcoming, but luckily for Hackman this new type of screen protagonist suited the era. Friedkin said that the liberal Hackman had trouble sometimes being as unsympathetic as Popeye needs to be, which speaks to issues of how Hackman would have liked to be seen.

Hackman was monotonously intense in the thankless lead role in *The Poseidon Adventure* (1972), and then he was overshadowed by Al Pacino in *Scarecrow* (1973), in spite of a strange extended scene for balance where his character does a striptease in a bar. He then gave his best performance as the repressed, religious, isolated, and increasingly paranoid surveillance expert Harry Caul in Francis Ford Coppola's *The Conversation* (1974), where he tells a younger lover (Teri Garr) that he is 42 rather than 44.

That's a juicy part in a closed-off, arty film where Hackman wears glasses and a mustache like character badges as he slowly reveals Harry's disquiet and his eventual unraveling. Hackman proved here that he was best and most creatively tense when he was holding his emotions, and especially his anger, back. Real or personal emotion is important to Hackman, for he studied at the Actors Studio and would often use his own feelings to fuel his work.

Hackman was unexpectedly funny as the blind man in one scene in *Young Frankenstein* (1974) and then he was a tough, embittered, philistine detective in *Night Moves* (1975). That was his peak, and afterward he was a comic villain as Lex Luthor in the *Superman* movies, where he did a double act with Ned Beatty as his bumbling sidekick. He's fairly funny in those pictures and his rocky voice is at its most resonant, and there was a welcome sense of him enjoying himself, even if Terence Stamp clearly stole the second film with his General Zod.

Hackman was at his most assured and subtle as the gold prospector in Nicolas Roeg's campy and highfalutin *Eureka* (1983), a rare movie where he really believes in himself as the humane center of a narrative. *Eureka* is often absurd, but Hackman's performance is unerringly precise and detailed and believable, and it hinted at what a romantic he could be. In the many movies that followed, Hackman was not above yelling his way through confrontation scenes when he played authority figures, but he showed a more appealingly warm side as the director who comforts Meryl Streep in *Postcards from the Edge* (1990).

He got his second Oscar for his very tough lawman in *Unforgiven*, a fine if predictable performance, and he did seem most comfortable in conventional material. When he puts on a dress at the end of *The Birdcage* (1996), there is nothing funny or suggestive about it—he merely looks like a man in late middle age who is uncomfortable in women's clothing.

The father figure in Wes Anderson's *The Royal Tenenbaums* (2001) functioned as a capstone to Hackman's career, and he was very good in that film, even if he was a bit miscast. Hackman's patriarch is something of a rogue, and his performance is maybe a little too low-down for the fey material. The man he played in *The Royal Tenenbaums* should probably be more whimsical and more unpredictably dangerous (it was likely more a role for someone like Gene Wilder). But Hackman felt and thought his way through the part with diligence and intelligence, and after 2004 he walked away from his career as an actor and wrote novels in his retirement, but they were not the sort of literary novels that Larry Lewis writes in *Another Woman*.

Albert Finney
Married People

In his heyday as a young actor, Albert Finney was more devoted to the theater than to movies. He replaced Laurence Olivier in a production of *Coriolanus*, and he appeared on stage at the National Theatre all through the 1960s and 1970s, notably in Strindberg's *Miss Julie*, Samuel Beckett's *Krapp's Last Tape*, Christopher Marlowe's *Tamburlaine*, and as Hamlet and Macbeth. Finney received Tony nominations for his performances in *Luther* and *A Day in the Death of Joe Egg* in the 1960s, and he turned down the role of Lawrence of Arabia for David Lean after an elaborate four-day screen test when he didn't want to sign a movie contract that would have restricted his ability to choose his parts and return to the stage.

He made his screen debut in a small role in *The Entertainer* (1960), which starred Olivier, but he soon took a lead in *Saturday Night and Sunday Morning* (1960) as a working class factory hand. "Don't let the bastards grind you down," he says in voiceover, as he smokes a cigarette after his shift is done. "What I'm out for is a good time," he says. "All the rest is propaganda." Finney is sweaty here, slightly piggy, and filled with heavy rebellious hostility for the world around him. He is one of the key so-called "angry young men" of this time, oafish, but with just a touch of the apprehensive poet in him, and with a marked capacity for hedonistic pleasure (mainly drink and women).

That film and performance still feels fresh because Finney was breaking decisively with the sort of external British acting based in technique practiced by Olivier, John Gielgud, and Ralph Richardson. Look at the way he listens to others in *Saturday Night and Sunday Morning*, and the subtle fluctuations of thoughts and feelings on his face. This was intricate and sensitive work, influenced by the American Method actors like Brando and Clift.

Smiling, semi-whimsical charm alternates in Finney here with nasty boyish impulses, and nothing ever feels worked up or shaped. Finney exists un-self-consciously on camera, never pushing or showing, or showing off, but his sheer presence feels massive and naturally authoritative, solid, unbreakable. He is a little like Jeanne Moreau in that his naughty, wolfish smile utterly transforms his sulky face.

That toothsome, Mr. Charisma smile was put to use again as *Tom Jones* (1963), a big hit that won the Oscar for best picture. He handled the asides to the audience in that movie and any wench at hand with aplomb, and it was proof of his range and his ability to be likably goofy, proof that he was a scamp, a rogue, and a sex symbol, particularly in the notorious scene where he lustily bites into his food with a very willing lady (Joyce Redman).

A remake of *Night Must Fall* (1964) didn't come off, and he spent a year travelling the world with a girlfriend rather than capitalize on his success. This rebelliousness and wanderlust kept him off screen until 1967, when he was felicitously paired with Audrey Hepburn in Stanley Donen's *Two for the Road*, a swooningly romantic movie about a troubled marriage that was lifted aloft by a Henry Mancini score and told in bits and pieces in different time periods.

The combination of the naturalistic Finney and the stylized Hepburn in *Two for the Road* is unlikely, and that's partly what the film is about. They fell for each other off-camera as they made it, and he liberated her so that Hepburn looks at him with rapturous love on screen until Donen cuts to Finney looking at her with "yes, this will do for now" consideration that gradually turns to panic and guilt. "During a scene with her, my mind knew I was acting but my heart didn't, and my body certainly didn't!" Finney said in a later interview. "The time spent with Audrey is one of the closest I've ever had."

He starred in and directed *Charlie Bubbles* (1967), a would-be surreal tale of a successful writer and his alienation and ennui that revealed Finney's own discomfort with his own success. He hid himself away sometimes, and in the 1970s he did very few movies. Most notable was his Hercule Poirot in *Murder on the Orient Express* (1974), a bit of old-fashioned impersonation where he doled out a heavy Belgian accent and wore dark hair and a dark mustache, so that he was practically unrecognizable as himself. He approached this part with a zest that sometimes feels a little strenuous. It was the first signal that there was something of a dominating ham in Finney.

But then in the 1980s Finney did his finest work on screen in four films that demonstrated his range and what he was capable of when he had a meaty role that fully engaged him. He gave perhaps his best or most impressively wounded film performance in *Shoot the Moon* (1982), another movie about an unhappy marriage. As George Dunlap, a writer who leaves his wife Faith (Diane Keaton) and four young children for another woman (Karen Allen), Finney starts the film at a deep depth of exhaustion, nerves, and pain and only burrows deeper and deeper into the disaster of this man's life.

In the primal scene where George forces his way back into the family home to try to give his oldest daughter Sherry (Dana Hill) a birthday present, Finney reaches such a desperately un-civilized, childish, nearly nihilistic state of mind that we can feel him being hurt by it, as if he himself is panic-stricken

Destructive male anger erupts from Albert Finney in *Shoot the Moon*.

and gasping for air as he taps into masculine rage that insists on making a tough situation far, far worse than it already is. His George Dunlap is that raw, and that personal.

George pushes Faith out the door and locks her out of the house, and finally he starts beating Sherry when she won't accept his present, but then the power dynamic shifts so that he is sitting on the stairs and looking like a beaten child himself when Faith comes rushing up (looking fierce and punitive) to cradle Sherry. George just walks slowly away from this disaster he has created, and then he starts to run to his car.

At the end of *Shoot the Moon*, when George has pledged himself to Faith and her new boyfriend (Peter Weller) to be reasonable, Finney accesses that same irresistible and waste-laying unreasonableness we saw in George in the confrontation with Sherry as he walks away from his old house, waving stiffly so that we can feel the flux of his feelings, and how he is teetering once again on the brink of "don't do it!" destruction.

This was major work, way out on a limb, and it marked Finney as one of the finest and most deeply searching actors of his time. Next he turned on a dime and did the musical *Annie* (1982), playing bald plutocrat Daddy Warbucks in an enjoyably hammy, cartoon style, sometimes taking on the vocal cadences of his director John Huston and going toe-to-toe with Carol Burnett at her comic best (watch the way he licks his fingers when she splashes him with bathtub gin in their musical duet, and the game delight he takes in his light hoofing in the finale).

Finney then played a half-mad old Shakespearean warhorse in *The Dresser* (1983), a character based on the theater actor Donald Wolfit, a real red meat part. Finney flings himself into this man's deterioration, showing us how acting for so long and so hard has left him exhausted and bereft. "Another blank page," he says helplessly, as he finally starts to make up to do King Lear.

Finney sometimes plays in a distinctively older style here, with strategic hints in his lingering cello vocal delivery of John Barrymore, and he reactivates this old style so that we can see the color and the fun and the expressivity of barnstorming Shakespearean acting. He followed this bravura performance with another one as an alcoholic diplomat on his last legs in John Huston's *Under the Volcano* (1984), carrying the heavy burden of that film as best he could. "I choose hell," he says at one point, his eyes staring down into an abyss. "Hell is my natural habitat."

In the 1990s, Finney had his misfires, like a poor updated movie of *The Browning Version* (1994), but he made a strong showing as the gangster chief in *Miller's Crossing* (1990), and he was poignant as the gay bus conductor in *A Man of No Importance* (1994), and suitably callous as Dr. Sloper in *Washington Square* (1997). He supported Julia Roberts to her Oscar for *Erin Brockovich* (2000), and then worked sparingly, for his was a sparing and remarkably varied film career.

His talent was best served in his two marriage films, his Mark Wallace in *Two for the Road* and his George Dunlap in *Shoot the Moon*, both uncommonly painful and honest performances that also drew on that tenuous charm he was often so squeamish about showing us and his on-screen spouses.

Finney was a man of appetite on screen, and not shy about crowing over that, or being youthfully sly, but he was so deeply in touch with dismay and disgust with himself and the world that his best work could have the force of an earthquake, so that when he was done there was nothing left but rubble.

Anthony Hopkins
High, Wide and Handsome

To my mind, Anthony Hopkins is the finest actor of his time, the male equivalent of Vanessa Redgrave, equally lyric, equally daring, just as unpredictable and dangerous, but this only seemed clear to me after exploring his work for television in the 1970s and 1980s, particularly his Pierre in the 1972–73 BBC series of Tolstoy's *War and Peace*. He is able to develop this character over 20 episodes (which run to 14 hours or so), bringing him from youth to middle age. His young Pierre is fidgety, sweet, exposed, inappropriate, nervous, and reckless, and on this basis Hopkins creates one inspired scene after another.

Hopkins's tumult of emotions feels very Russian in this *War and Peace*, and he is very much at home in an unusually extreme drinking scene where Pierre and an officer have consumed many bottles of liquor. Hopkins himself had a drinking problem in this period, and so he intimately understands what an extreme intake of alcohol can be like; he makes Pierre both flighty and sodden at once.

Hopkins is superlative in the scene where Pierre can't stop laughing as his father is dying, and especially in the scene where he simply *cannot help* voicing an unpopular political opinion at a party. He dynamically physicalizes the push and pull of a man helpless to resist his own impulses and his own complex character. This is Hopkins's best performance, and maybe the most inexhaustibly varied performance ever given by anyone, a whole world of beautiful, damned, reckless choices, filled in with lovely little moments of wistful dissatisfaction, too.

Hopkins's Pierre holds many contradictions. He is cowardly, but he fights a duel when pushed to the brink of his patience. "I hate my life," he tells a religious man, with such speed and casualness that he knocks the wind out of you with this simple statement. Hopkins is still young and hungry in *War and Peace* (he was in his mid-thirties), and so his talent really blazes forth at this opportunity, and the part of Pierre suits him perfectly; he must have identified strongly with him to be as good as he is in this series, for nothing else would explain such heated work of this caliber.

Anthony Hopkins gives one of the most multi-faceted performances of all time in *War and Peace*.

During the war section, Pierre gets hit by a bomb, and he makes for a clownish figure on the battlefield. When a callous general tells him that his friend Andrei has been killed, Hopkins puts his hand out as if he wants to stop the words, like a sensitive child. By the end, Hopkins's Pierre is watching men being executed and is almost executed himself, but the executions stop in the nick of time for him, and so he knows that life is all a matter of chance. This BBC *War and Peace* is not exceptional in and of itself. It's the typical costume plowing through of a classic that they generally did, and the other actors are so far from Hopkins's super-high level of performance as to be drably comic, but that contrast makes his achievement all the more precious.

Hopkins was born in Wales in 1937. A poor student, he was bullied by other kids and belittled by his grandfather, but he took heart from a meeting with his idol and compatriot Richard Burton at age 15. He served two years in the British army and then trained at the Royal Academy of Dramatic Art.

In 1965, Hopkins cheekily auditioned for Laurence Olivier at the National Theatre with a speech from *Othello*, which Olivier himself was performing at the time. Aware of what he had in front of him, Olivier let Hopkins join the company and become his understudy. When Hopkins went on for

Olivier in *The Dance of Death*, Olivier remarked that Hopkins took the role "like a cat with a mouse between its teeth." Hopkins went on to play Macbeth, Coriolanus, and Petruchio in *The Taming of the Shrew* on stage in the early 1970s.

He made a feature film debut as a gay and conflicted Richard the Lionheart in *The Lion in Winter* (1968), but neither this nor his reasonable Claudius to Nicol Williamson's *Hamlet* (1969) gave more than hints of what he had in him. In the TV movie *Lloyd George* (1973), Hopkins showed the influence Olivier had had on him, delivering a mannered, stagy performance filled with "make things happen" authority unconnected to deeper thought or emotion. He does so much "acting" here that we can barely hear the words he is saying.

His two filmed TV Chekhov productions from 1970, of *Three Sisters* and *Uncle Vanya*, show that he is straitjacketed still by the "singing" technique of the British actors around him, where words are delivered only for show. It's clear why he wanted to go to America, finally, for some pulp and a breath of fresh air, away from this deadly embalming of the classics.

After his breakthrough in *War and Peace*, he was a formidable Torvald to Claire Bloom's sensual Nora in a film of Ibsen's *A Doll's House* (1973), and he played in *Equus* on stage in America, but he showed his full talent in two disparate films for television made in 1976. In a lengthy remake of *Dark Victory* with Elizabeth Montgomery in the old Bette Davis part, Hopkins seems suggestively more like a mad doctor than like a smooth bedside manner leading man, favoring a blank look that reads as impatience or need for a drink, and he shows here that he has the turbulence and the unrest of a great actor.

When he falls in love with Montgomery in *Dark Victory* and moves in to kiss her, Hopkins looks like he's going to vomit because he is so scared of what he is feeling, a fabulous and colorful choice. Montgomery is bland in her role, and this TV movie would hold no interest whatever without Hopkins, but he is so inspired here that he makes his real, connected emotions matter in a dense, loaded way. Hopkins is so in touch with what he's doing in this movie that he makes meaning out of life; he makes it clear that we as humans have been here and that there is something more to life than just this reality we experience. That's how good he is in *Dark Victory*.

He played the German kidnapper Bruno Hauptmann in *The Lindbergh Kidnapping Case*, catching exactly the eerie calm and the evil of a sociopath with some part of his humanity missing, and once again he gave a great performance with no help at all from the TV movie and the actors surrounding him. Hopkins brings a fullness and a specificity to all of his silent reactions in court at Hauptmann's trial, seeming mentally stressed and physically restless. When he speaks, Hopkins also exactly catches Hauptmann's huffy German superiority, and when Hauptmann is to be executed Hopkins has stripped himself down to a bare minimum. He won an Emmy for his work here.

He was briefly riveting in the horror movie *Audrey Rose* (1977), but in feature films in this period only *Magic* (1978) allowed Hopkins the scope to create a memorable performance as a deranged ventriloquist with a dirty id who is possessed by a murderous dummy. In that movie Hopkins is like a religious applicant whipping himself further and further into states of madness, unconcerned about control or technique, truly an actor for the screen at last, all traces of Olivier's surface rhetoric gone.

Something in him was freed by the chance to do trashy but vital genre material, and he was especially encouraged by the chance to be macabre (not to mention the chance to love and make love to Ann-Margret). He is an actor here who is radically in the moment, yet his moments come out of symphonic emotional chaos, with all kinds of competing currents and patterns, until his dummy has forced him to get down on all fours like a dog and Hopkins accesses a purely animal place.

Hopkins tussled in a hot tub with Bo Derek in *A Change of Seasons* (1980) and was the kindly, empathetic doctor in David Lynch's *The Elephant Man* (1980), and then he won a second Emmy for his diabolically mannered Adolf Hitler in *The Bunker* (1981), which is back to a more theatrical Olivier model of playing, but no less impressive for that.

His Hitler has dead eyes sometimes (his face keeps going slack and blank and there is obviously something severely wrong with him). He looks depressive and glazed at first, but then he gets the shakes, and Hopkins starts to find and channel the depths of this man, as if there are wars being fought inside his head, all disconnected and shot through with illness, distress, stubbornness, and a core of stiff-backed evil.

When he whips himself into a froth about "Jewish Marxism" here, Hopkins relies on some very weird work with his hands that is nearly German Expressionist, maybe, and at a certain point in *The Bunker* he finally seems to be acting too much, chewing on too much, thinking too much through, but of course playing this role is such an impossible task, and he isn't helped on any level by the poor TV production around him.

Hopkins's weakness sometimes is that he instinctively goes for pathos and sympathy, and this is why some of his villains are so uncomfortably grasping and muddied. Like some of Olivier's work, Hopkins's Hitler shows that there is sometimes a fine line between the boldness of great acting and the boldness of very bad acting, so that it's perilously easy to wander into both, moment to moment, when you are aiming so high.

He played St. Paul for TV in *Peter and Paul* (1981), coasting on the rhythms of his voice so that we can barely hear what he says but just how he says it. That same year he did *Othello* for TV, where he started off strong but seemed too small physically, and of course a white actor in this role in 1981 is just hopeless (he's not as black as Olivier was in the 1960s but merely tan).

He grabbed at pathos as Quasimodo in *The Hunchback of Notre Dame* (1982) on TV, but then he conquered a difficult late Ibsen play, *Little Eyolf* (1982), for the BBC opposite Diana Rigg.

He faced off against an elderly Olivier as Captain Bligh in *The Bounty* (1984), where his conception of the role is vague and he mainly gives his performance with his voice. And he confirmed his appetite for all-out trash with an appearance in the Jackie Collins TV miniseries *Hollywood Wives* (1985), where he tells Stefanie Powers, "When you have no taste, you can do anything."

He overacted wildly as Count Ciano in *Mussolini and I* (1985) for TV, and then he attempted to give a major performance of wounded male spite in *The Good Father* (1985) but was defeated at every turn by the poorness of the film's editing. On stage at this time, he played at the National as King Lear in 1986 and in *Antony and Cleopatra* with Judi Dench in 1987.

As the spy Anthony Burgess in *Blunt* (1987) on TV, Hopkins looks beefy and stumped by the old-time aesthetic homosexuality he is asked to portray (he just can't seem to get his mouth around a man who keeps saying, "My dear...") but in *84 Charing Cross Road* (1987) he found his most winning commercial mode: repressed romance in the manner of *Brief Encounter* (1945). This was a signal that the mature Hopkins would always be at his best when asked to be restrained or held back in some way.

The Oscar win for best actor for his Hannibal Lecter in *The Silence of the Lambs* (1991) finally allowed Hopkins to break through to movie stardom in his fifties. It's difficult now to see that film and that performance fresh because it has been copied, parodied, and referenced so many times. Hopkins himself has said that it wasn't a difficult role once he got the contemptuous and hushed but grating voice down, and there is maybe a little of Olivier still in his instincts here, but shot through with his own danger and wildness.

The evil but childish eyes of Dr. Lecter, waiting, expectant, and finally alien, are certainly a haunting image, but the conception of a genius killer is still a movie cliché he cannot finally transcend. Hopkins's Hannibal was a real coup, and it opened the world to him, but maybe his Bruno Hauptmann had been a more truly penetrating and detailed portrait of a murderer.

The Oscar and acclaim made Hopkins extra-ravenous for work, so that the following year he moved from his cold Wilcox in *Howards End* to a role in a Barbara Taylor Bradford TV movie called *To Be the Best* without batting an eye (though he does play that in his sleep). Most everyone thinks that Hopkins's finest feature film performance is as the consummately repressed butler Mr. Stevens in *The Remains of the Day* (1993), and they aren't wrong.

For this role, juicy but very difficult, Hopkins used the pianissimo voice of John Gielgud, and he played the many scenes where Mr. Stevens cannot show what he is feeling with virtuoso skill, like an opera singer acing a Mozart aria. Hopkins must distinguish for us when Mr. Stevens is not showing what he is feeling to others and when he is not allowing himself knowledge of his own feelings, and he does that with awe-inspiring skill. He will throw away key lines like "I prefer to keep things as they are" as if they were so close to this man's sheltered heart that Mr. Stevens must toss them off or the words will burn him alive.

Hopkins's interpretation of the role is dark in hue, and tough, and not sentimental. Mr. Stevens is self-deceiving and complacent, and fearful, but there is something small and pure in him, which is only revealed in the scene where fellow servant Miss Kenton (Emma Thompson) tries to take a book away from him and discovers that it is a "sentimental old love story." The look on Hopkins's face as she says this is both boyish and girlish at once, helpless, beseeching, yet also begging her to stop, because he cannot stand to be touched in this private place even though part of him longs for it.

This is a full-scale tragic performance, with many notes unerringly played (look at the split-second flashes of anger in his eye movements when a diplomat visiting the estate he works for humiliates him over his lack of political knowledge). When Miss Kenton tells Mr. Stevens that she has had a proposal of marriage, Hopkins freezes his facial expression as if Mr. Stevens has been briefly struck dead before managing to go right on with his servile routine. This is a performance that proves that such British grace under pressure can be wrong-headed and not at all admirable, and Hopkins is unsparing in showing the price that Mr. Stevens pays for always keeping his head in the sand and doing what he feels to be his duty.

He was at his best again as C.S. Lewis in *Shadowlands* (1993), especially in the scene where the armored Lewis breaks down and all-out cries with a young boy at the end. And then he took on an immense challenge: playing a hyperbolized *Nixon* (1995) for Oliver Stone, which involved impersonation and trickery on a marathon level. He did honorably playing this dishonorable, pathological figure, particularly in the scenes of Nixon's breakdown in the White House at the end, which he steers into Shakespearean territory. Hopkins gets the creepily disconnected smile of Nixon just right as well as the sweating paranoia and the rabid self-pity.

In *The Edge* (1997) there is a shot of a half-eaten ham and then a cut to Hopkins, and that just about sums up his career at this point. He did fine, pinpoint work as John Quincy Adams in *Amistad* (1997), and then he took on the large and risky task of playing *Titus* (1999) in Julie Taymor's film of Shakespeare's *Titus Andronicus*, a role that was one of Olivier's signature parts on stage in the 1950s. He is good but restrained in that film in comparison to his dominating co-star Jessica Lange, as if his prodigious exertions over the years had finally left him a bit tired-out.

After that he reprised Dr. Lecter a few times and took on many roles in mainly genre fare. In 2007, he wrote and directed *Slipstream*, a druggy movie shot in a late-1960s stream-of-consciousness style, and none too good. He was often at his best unexpectedly in small films like *360* (2011), but he could do nothing to save his *Hitchcock* (2012) from being a travesty. He had exhausted himself, but the achievement in his best work is inexhaustibly vital.

Unlike his American counterparts, Hopkins has never taken his own craft too seriously in interviews, and when he taught acting at UCLA he stressed clarity of speech and articulation and was very much against naturalistic muttering. Though he has been critical of Olivier sometimes, he is in the Olivier tradition, but with scarier emotional colorations. Hopkins had been in a great tumult of anger and self-loathing as a younger man and was very hard to know or control, but that lifted somewhat as he aged. He learned not to take life itself too seriously, for he had always preferred the life of his imagination.

He played the elderly Shakespearean actor known only as "Sir" in a TV movie of *The Dresser* (2015) with Ian McKellen, which placed him in the tradition of all the great theater actors who had come before him. (He could do spookily accurate impressions of Olivier and Gielgud in interviews, almost as if he were channeling them.) This was clearly Hopkins's finest latter-day performance: truly wild emotionally, yet infused with an exhausted sort of kindness in the last scenes that he had never shown before as an actor. Hopkins's Sir seems a far more talented performer than the second-rate ham played by Albert Finney in the 1983 movie of this play, a man more deeply in touch with the suffering of others.

Hopkins did a *King Lear* for the BBC in 2018, and he began on a distracted and ruined note in the first scene that left him nowhere to go as the play progressed. He had backslided here to the "shouting to keep the attention of the audience" style that Olivier had taught him, and there were times in this *King Lear* when he was so vocally purple that he evoked memories of John Barrymore. This was not a modern Shakespearean performance. It was very grand, and grandstanding, and it showed that Hopkins did finally want to secure himself within the modes and techniques of the past.

As an older man, he began writing music and making vividly colored paintings with a Gauguin feeling that he called "dreamscapes," and dreams have been important to him. On his Twitter account on May 30, 2017, Hopkins wrote, "Dreams are free, and so often can have no logical or linear development. For me they contain a deep form of rebellion against reality."

Daniel Day-Lewis
In Character

Known as an outlandish Method actor who wants to live his roles, the very beautiful Daniel Day-Lewis has won three best actor Oscars, for *My Left Foot* (1989), *There Will Be Blood* (2007), and *Lincoln* (2012), yet he works sparingly. Not counting some early bits, he made seven films in the 1980s in substantial parts, five in the 1990s, and just four in the 2000s. And some of these movies are minor and oddball, like the bewildering *Eversmile, New Jersey* (1989), in which he keeps exclaiming, "But I'm a dentist!"

Day-Lewis was the son of poet Cecil Day-Lewis, and he was involved in a tempestuous love affair in his youth with the equally intense Isabelle Adjani, who favored going mad in period clothing in most of her films. As a boy he can be seen scraping a car with a key in *Sunday Bloody Sunday* (1971), which provides an alarming first glimpse of him, androgynous and menacing.

As a young man he had bits in *Gandhi* (1982) and *The Bounty* (1984), and he did a TV series called *My Brother Jonathan* (1985) where his extraordinarily romantic good looks were displayed at length. He has a conventionally written scene in that series where he has to confront a group of men, a Robert Donat–style set piece where he must tell them off, and Day-Lewis is still green here, unable to fully connect to the emotion he needs.

But he became a star that same year in two strikingly contrasted roles: as the skinhead Johnny in *My Beautiful Laundrette*, daringly touching his tongue to the neck of his lover Omar (Gordon Warnecke), and *A Room with a View*, where he was the pompous Cecil Vyse, a man rejected by his fiancée Lucy (Helena Bonham Carter).

If you look at these performances closely, Day-Lewis is sometimes coasting on his natural charisma and authority, the blessing of his looks, but he had a gift for making certain moments really land, like the way he swigs champagne in *My Beautiful Laundrette* and then dribbles it sensually into Omar's mouth, and the way he sits down on a staircase to tie his shoes in *A Room with a View* after he knows that he has lost Lucy. Day-Lewis can't quite transcend the limitations of those roles, but he showed he had a spark beyond his own surface looks.

Daniel Day-Lewis (right) flaunts a gay love affair with Gordon Warnecke in *My Beautiful Laundrette*.

Using a light Czech accent and letting his hair grow long and fluffy, he played the intellectual libertine Tomas in the extremely erotic *The Unbearable Lightness of Being* (1988), catching his character's wolfish, predatory manner and his good humor and how he is slowly trapped by his love for the innocent Tereza (Juliette Binoche). Day-Lewis felt later that this movie had been a mistake because he was too young for the role and also because he disliked the unreality of a Czech character not speaking Czech. He is like an American Method player like Montgomery Clift here, chewing more than he bites off, opaque yet loaded, and very sexy and sexual, repeatedly telling beautiful women to, "Take off your clothes." Day-Lewis is an actor who has often been drawn to and interested in sex.

This interest suffuses his Christy Brown in *My Left Foot*, a performance with few precedents. Because of Brown's cerebral palsy, which leaves his face and body uncontrolled, the usual ways of judging, and giving, a performance have to be jettisoned. Day-Lewis asks the very tough questions here, starting with a profound level of empathy for this embattled man and then going very far with that empathy for his particular suffering.

In the restaurant scene where Christy declares his hugely intense and unreasonable love for his teacher Eileen (Fiona Shaw) only to be told she is going to marry someone else, Day-Lewis's rage is so concentrated, so heightened, that the other actors and the camera itself seem to be in some kind of jeopardy, because what the camera is recording is not shaped and not nice and not even acted, really.

This scene ends with Christy slamming his head on the table and then pulling the tablecloth off with his teeth, so that the brutalized Eileen cries, "Bastard!" in response. There is no distance here. As in the rest of the performance, Day-Lewis starts at a level of emotion that would scare and exhaust most actors and just takes it further and further, so that it's intolerable, nearly, a vision of agony and feeling trapped, of thwarted appetite (for Christy's needs and lusts are enormous).

Day-Lewis's Christy wants everyone in that restaurant to know exactly what it is like to be him at this moment, and there is nothing poignant about that, finally, because he is being aggressive and punishing them with this knowledge, yet this punishment, this upsetting scene in a restaurant, is only a tiny fraction of the pain he has had to feel his whole life. This is work that takes off from Charles Laughton's best 1930s film performances, and Day-Lewis has often spoken of his admiration for Laughton.

Any actor could have won an Oscar playing Christy. It's an Oscar part. But Day-Lewis works wonders with it, making Christy a tough, combative, self-pitying, self-critical, charismatic, murderous, and extremely attractive man. His performance in *My Left Foot* is his one real unmitigated triumph on a small list of uneven or at the very least questionable work.

Day-Lewis had played on stage as a young man in *Another Country,* as Romeo in *Romeo and Juliet* for the Royal Shakespeare Company, as Dracula, and as the Russian poet Mayakovsky. But when he played Hamlet in 1989 at the National Theatre, he had some sort of breakdown during the scene where Hamlet talks to the ghost of his father. The story became that Day-Lewis thought his own father was talking to him, and he couldn't handle that; he ran off and dropped out of the production, and he has not acted on stage since that time.

He put on muscle and learned how to live off the land and do woodwork for his role as Hawkeye in *The Last of the Mohicans* (1992), where he won the hearts of a generation of women with his heartfelt declaration, "Just stay alive, no matter what occurs.... I will find you!" to Madeleine Stowe. He played the closed-up and repressed society man Newland Archer in Martin Scorsese's careful adaptation of Edith Wharton's *The Age of Innocence* (1993), and then he worked again with Jim Sheridan, the director of *My Left Foot,* and got another Oscar nomination for his Irish prisoner in *In the Name of the Father* (1993), where once again his intense emotional commitment to a role left the rest of the film looking very modest in comparison. (He supposedly wanted the crew to rough him up a bit to get him in the proper mood for the interrogation scenes.)

It was at this point that Day-Lewis began to withdraw himself from circulation, only taking roles once in a great while, with years in between credits. He played John Proctor in an adaptation of Arthur Miller's *The Crucible* (1996), and he married Miller's daughter Rebecca. After an unexceptional third film for Jim Sheridan called *The Boxer* (1997), the extremely sensitive Day-Lewis went away for five years to make shoes or do woodwork or something along those lines.

He returned for Martin Scorsese's *Gangs of New York* (2002), totally overshadowing Leonardo DiCaprio as Bill the Butcher and offering an overbearing and stagy one-man show in the midst of a disappointing film—this was the kind of acting that called attention to itself to an excessive and unpleasant degree. He did a small, little-seen film directed by his wife called *The Ballad of Jack and Rose* (2005), where he had aged handsomely. Two years then passed before he won his second lead Oscar for Paul Thomas Anderson's *There Will Be Blood* (2007).

Fourteen minutes go by without any dialogue as we watch Day-Lewis's Daniel Plainview digging for oil and establishing himself as fully equal to the elements. When we finally hear his voice, it becomes obvious that Day-Lewis has modeled his speaking tones here after the absurdly courtly delivery of the director John Huston, who himself made a movie about men versus land: *The Treasure of the Sierra Madre* (1948). This vocal choice is a big risk. It proclaims that Day-Lewis is leaving any attempt at naturalism behind and putting together a performance based on artifice and bigger-than-life style. It also proclaims that the influence of a figure like Robert De Niro on Day-Lewis's work has been replaced by the memory of Olivier.

The voice Day-Lewis uses in *There Will Be Blood* never feels organic; it feels and sounds like an actor doing a voice. As such, this is actually the kind of work that had seldom been seen since the days of, say, Paul Muni in his 1930s biopics. And because this kind of acting hadn't been seen in such a very long time, and because Day-Lewis was obviously putting so much visible effort into it, his Daniel Plainview impressed many people.

Day-Lewis is also sometimes attempting to do the kind of stylized work that James Cagney did in the 1930s, but the seams are always showing. *There Will Be Blood* is a portentous film, obscure and awkwardly structured and edited, straining for significance but short on inspiration. (Another problem is that Paul Dano, who plays Ely Sunday, Plainview's preacher antagonist, is monotonously one-note in his role.)

But there is a section of this movie where a man calling himself Henry (Kevin J. O'Connor) claims to be Plainview's half-brother and comes looking for work. Around a campfire, Plainview confides in Henry, telling him about his hatred of people and his competitiveness, and Day-Lewis's work improves when playing opposite the simple, focused, naturalistic O'Connor. He returns to the Method style he had started his career with, but then in the scene where Plainview realizes that this man is not a relation, Day-Lewis does a kind of 1920s-silent era expression of heightened rage right before shooting Henry in the head.

When he looks at the diary that Henry took from his actual brother, Day-Lewis is very moving in his hard-man, late-night distress. This Henry/O'Connor part of the movie lasts about a half hour, and it contains very fine work from Day-Lewis. A charitable eye might take his performance in *There Will Be Blood* as a kind of anthology of acting modes reaching backwards and forwards, but there is no strong unifying thread holding them together; they are like costumes put on and taken off too hastily. Alas, the film ends with an absurdly forced and broad semi-comic confrontation scene between Day-Lewis and Dano, and this only underlined the aimlessness on view, and the vague reaching for meaning.

Day-Lewis squinted and squirmed his way through the musical *Nine* (2009), and then he got his third Oscar as Abraham Lincoln for Steven Spielberg. He was still far too beautiful to be a really convincing honest Abe, but Day-Lewis worked hard at his character's folksy digressiveness, and this effort plus the hallowed nature of the part itself led him to victory.

He uses a light, high, Walter Brennan–like sort of voice in *Lincoln*, and again most of his work is so old-fashioned that it wouldn't be out of place in a 1930s biopic, or a Hal Holbrook one-man show. All his earlier interest in sexuality had been utterly drained away by *There Will Be Blood* and *Lincoln*, which is shot in such relentless chiaroscuro lighting in darkened rooms that Day-Lewis is sometimes just a worked-up voice from the shadows, talking loftily and ponderously.

He announced that he was retiring from acting, but not before playing fashion designer Reynolds Woodcock in Paul Thomas Anderson's rather strange *Phantom Thread* (2017), which functions as a sort of screwball melodrama. Woodcock is a control freak and also a very angry child-like man with Oedipal issues, and Day-Lewis was at his personal best again for this picture. His face brims with the suppressed emotion of a lifetime when Woodcock deals with his forbidding sister Cyril (Lesley Manville) and his new girlfriend Alma (Vicky Krieps), who knows just how to break him down.

Anderson said that Day-Lewis did some un-credited writing on *Phantom Thread*, and this most likely shows in some of the more Pinter-esque dialogue between Woodcock and Cyril and also in Woodcock's obsession with his dead mother. If it does prove to be his last film, and that is far from certain, *Phantom Thread* is a fittingly eccentric and romantic way to close out an acting career that sought to make a large impact with a small amount of credits.

Jeff Bridges
Straight No Chaser

The son of actor Lloyd Bridges and the brother of actor Beau Bridges, Jeff Bridges has been one of the most steadily reliable screen presences from the 1970s to today, in movies of just about every type. Open-faced, natural, sexy, all-American, Bridges excelled in roles as decent and not particularly bright guys as a younger man, and as he got older he gained in color and assurance, going from the freshest of male ingénues to a grizzled character actor-star.

He most resembles the underappreciated Joel McCrea in his un-flashy giving himself over to the camera from youth to old age (though his films aren't as good as McCrea's films for Preston Sturges and Hitchcock and King Vidor). Many of his characters are guys who aren't going to make it or who never made it, guys who have to accept that they are not going to have worldly success.

Bridges took acting seriously enough to go to New York as a teenager and study at the HB Studio with Uta Hagen, and he also served in the United States Coast Guard for seven years. At age 22 he got an Oscar nomination for best supporting actor for his Duane in Peter Bogdanovich's *The Last Picture Show* (1971), and he got another nomination for his sidekick to Clint Eastwood in *Thunderbolt and Lightfoot* (1974). In both of those movies he was blithe and un-self-conscious, and unafraid to look bad, goofy, dumb or silly.

He met the demands of a difficult part in the faithful Eugene O'Neill adaptation *The Iceman Cometh* (1973), but his most characteristic early performance was as a promising young boxer in John Huston's stark *Fat City* (1972), where he is judged "soft in the center" by older boxer Stacy Keach. Bridges then worked mainly in mid-range commercial projects, to all of which he brought his enthusiasm, honesty, and physical expressiveness. In the 1980s, he started to mature and take chances. His voice lowered, his body settled down a bit, and life started to add texture and depth to his look and his manner.

His callow characters of the 1970s gave way to men who were familiar with compromise, like the man he plays in *Cutter's Way* (1981), an evasive guy who is always walking away and shrugging things off but also aware of his shortcomings. In his thirties, there was a severe, cranky, unforgiving look that could settle on Bridges's face, so that he showed what could lie on the underside of his shaggy dog-like good nature.

Bridges got an Oscar nomination for best actor for *Starman* (1984) as an alien who takes on the physical form of Karen Allen's dead husband. That was a performance of charm and romantic sweetness, funny in its birdlike mannerisms as his starman adjusts to life on earth, and then touching when he falls in love—in his alien way—with Allen, before going back to his own planet (he leaves her with a baby to remember him by).

He extended his range as a devious man in *Jagged Edge* (1985), and he provided tactful support to Jane Fonda in *The Morning After* (1986) and tried his hardest in *Tucker: The Man and His Dream* (1988) to be an exuberant operator and entrepreneur. And then he was at his mature best, resigned, worldly wise, and admirably restrained in his contempt for his milieu as a lounge pianist in *The Fabulous Baker Boys* (1989), where he played with his brother Beau.

Bridges gave maybe his finest performance as a man who lives through a traumatic plane crash and feels untouchable afterwards in Peter Weir's very unsettling *Fearless* (1993). In that tough and unusual movie, Bridges showed how much he had grown and matured in the 20 years since he played Dwayne in *The Last Picture Show* and the soft boxer in *Fat City*. Now he was a man who could seem so sour as to be almost sinister, and so when his former boyishness tried to emerge on his weathered, softened face the effect could be

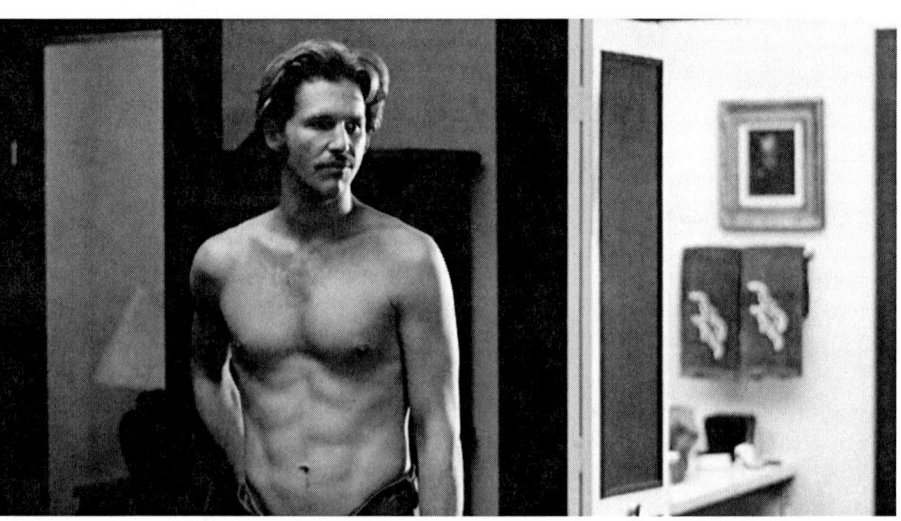

Jeff Bridges is morally questionable in *Cutter's Way*.

very sad. Bridges had become the kind of actor who could make difficult roles look as easy as falling off a log.

He stood in the shadow of Barbra Streisand's ego in *The Mirror Has Two Faces* (1996) before taking his best-known part, The Dude, an archetypal pot smoking old hippie for the Coen Brothers in *The Big Lebowski* (1998). Bridges gave himself over to that role to such an extent that it blended with his own off-screen image, and into a good-humored sort of Zen attitude. The Dude, unlike some of his other characters, is not at all a difficult role, and so Bridges just serenely inhabits the rhythms in the Coens' verbal comedy sequences and scores his many laughs (while also gracefully letting John Goodman's volatile Vietnam vet dominate in some scenes).

He got another Oscar nomination playing the president in *The Contender* (2000), where he transcended some boilerplate writing and managed to move and fidget a lot without ever being mannered; emotional directness was always his core value as a performer. As the years went by, and he became increasingly beloved, Bridges let himself age physically in a way few actresses would or could have allowed themselves. He also attained modest Renaissance man status with a 2003 book of on-set photographs and some forays into making music.

His movies were less rewarding in his later years, and he was given a best actor Oscar for the very modest *Crazy Heart* (2009) as a tribute to his skill, stamina, and self-effacing talent, but he was far better in the Coens' *True Grit* (2010) as Rooster Cogburn, a part that once won John Wayne his own career tribute Oscar. Bridges was the image of old-time law and order in *Hell or High Water* (2016), and he had earned that uncomplicated veteran status.

Nick Nolte
Crucified

No matter what his age or the crumbling state of his characters on screen, Nick Nolte always kept in touch with a pure little boy within himself, so that he sometimes seemed like a lovable blond toddler stuck inside the massive, doughy frame of a rogue and a shit-kicker, a hulk and a volatile bar brawler (he named his son Brawley).

He came up the hard way, and his very unstudied, uncommonly direct work on screen shows that Nolte was battered by life, and by himself, but he would stay on the ropes and never go down for the count. He's always something of a mess, a bruiser, a hunched-over caveman, and sometimes it seems as if you can smell him from the screen, as if he likes to sleep in his clothes and then just keep going on rot-gut bourbon, like many a Midwest man's man in a beat-up brown leather coat.

He was born in Omaha, Nebraska, in 1941, and he was a jock in school, where football couldn't quite keep up with his already prodigious drinking. Nolte, whose middle name is King, was arrested in 1965 for selling draft cards, a serious offense that kept him out of the Vietnam War. Nolte had a charismatic mother who always sought to protect him, and she set a contrary and independent example that he followed for the rest of his life.

In his 2018 memoir *Rebel*, Nolte paid tribute to the many lively and free women he knew all his life, including a first wife with whom he had an open marriage (it was her idea), and a second wife he nicknamed "Legs" who was averse to wearing underwear and always searching for a good time. As a young man in Hollywood, he was approached by the notorious agent Henry Willson, who offered to make him a star like Rock Hudson or Tab Hunter in exchange for a session on the casting couch. Nolte was at Willson's house to discuss things when the agent entered in a robe and cried, "Hello, cuddle bunny!" The young Nolte was quickly out the door.

Though he read Stanislavski and took his work very seriously, there was no Actors Studio for him; he went into modeling for a bit, and he audited classes with Stella Adler and Sanford Meisner. Nolte also did a lot of regional theater and lots of television before breaking through at age 35 in the much-touted TV miniseries *Rich Man, Poor Man* (1976), where he was the bad boy son Tom Jordache, a big lug, a rebel, and a boxer.

Nolte goes large and obvious in a lot of that series, but he showed a softer side in the romantic scenes he shared with Fionnula Flanagan, who played a careworn but sexy Irish servant. Even here his voice was rumbly and low-down, though far from the Jason Robards, Jr., rasp it would become.

He might have gotten stuck on TV shows, but Nolte was able to make the move to features. He was offered the role of Superman, and his response was, "If I can play him as he truly is, a schizophrenic, I will do it." He couldn't compete with Jacqueline Bisset in a wet t-shirt in *The Deep* (1977), but he soon got better parts. Nolte brought a surprising sense of irony and complexity to Ray Hicks, a Vietnam vet and drug runner in *Who'll Stop the Rain* (1978), where he meets the cerebral Tuesday Weld on the same worried territory.

Nolte seemed more his age in that movie than he had as Tom Jordache, and this look of experience was key to unlocking his talent. His anger, which was already formidable, comes from a place of deep unrest and disenchantment with the world, and it somehow manages to be both boorish and semi-intellectual.

Nolte's Ray is a reader of Nietzsche, and he is tired of being ordered around by what he deems "inferior people." When a potential drug buyer slaps him, the look Nolte gives this guy is purely murderous in a startling way. He had a rich vein of savagery in him, and he wasn't afraid to access it (what a Kurtz he could have made in *Apocalypse Now* {1979}).

Nolte followed this with another major performance as the continually battered football player in *North Dallas Forty* (1979), an energetic, sleazy, detailed film with a hard-to-place tone in which the mustached Nolte was alert and physically imposing. He was still sexy here but starting to decay, and he lets us see the wear-and-tear of life on his character and the depth of feeling he can barely hide in his small, blue, little-boy eyes.

Football is a nasty business in this picture, crushing bones, bodies, and spirits, and Nolte surveyed this particular landscape with rueful, held-back power, memorably and ironically raising his arms in a Christ-like pose at the end, which is freeze-framed for the credits. Nolte himself chose and developed *North Dallas Forty* as a screen vehicle for himself, and it showed just how personal he wanted his work to be.

Nolte was well cast as Beat generation icon Neal Cassady in *Heart Beat* (1980), where he was restless and complex and effortlessly cool but let down by the limitations of the film. There's a memorable moment he has when Neal is entrapped for smoking marijuana by a black guy who is just trying to get by; when the police pull them over and Neal realizes he was set up, Nolte just takes it in and looks at this guy sitting next to him and offers him another toke off the reefer.

Something like that is the essence of cool, and it comes from the inside out with Nolte. He doesn't need to posture or strike attitudes, or work anything up. He is just a bulky, shambling guy on screen who is in touch with deep-down, complicated thoughts and emotions that make his face ripple like the surface of water. Nolte has the ability to exist in the moment without any self-consciousness, so that his work feels both weighted and always unfolding fluidly.

He was a match for the edgy Debra Winger in *Cannery Row* (1982), and he had a hit opposite Eddie Murphy in *48 Hrs.* (1982), which is really Murphy's movie. Nolte was a leading man for Katharine Hepburn in the macabre comedy *Grace Quigley* (1984), and she was not happy about his drinking on the set. When Hepburn told Nolte that she had heard he was "falling down drunk in every gutter in town," he replied, "I've got a few to go yet." His cocaine use during this period was also prodigious, and he was fond of pulling elaborate pranks and gags with his male buddies.

He crawled out of the gutter for Paul Mazursky's farce *Down and Out in Beverly Hills* (1986) as a street bum who revitalizes a repressed and affluent family. Nolte brought a much-needed reality and also a powerfully direct sexuality to that movie, so that it was believable that he might sway every member of the household with his stop-you-cold blue-eyed stare. "I didn't bathe for a couple of weeks," Nolte said, about preparing for this role. "I never want to wash a character off, so to speak, at the end of a day's shoot. There's an important feeling I get from a certain amount of dirt."

In John Milius's *Farewell to the King* (1989) Nolte was a longhaired leader of natives, believably unhinged, who wants "guns so they can't take the freedom away." And then he took another of his major parts, the abstract expressionist painter Lionel Dobie in "Life Lessons," the Martin Scorsese segment of *New York Stories* (1989).

At 48, Nolte had aged again, and his voice had gone down to a more gravelly place, low and then lower. As Lionel, he wore glasses and tired reddish hair, and a beard that had some white in it. He was bedeviled by the song "A Whiter Shade of Pale," diegetically and non-diegetically, and by an upcoming art show he wasn't ready for (a procrastinating habit with Lionel), and also by a woman played by Rosanna Arquette.

Nolte's Lionel bestows a murderous smile on a younger artist who has just slept with Arquette under his nose, and he exhibits both sorrow and pride in his ability to sublimate his feelings directly into his work on canvas. There are times here where Nolte stares way, way off into somewhere or something, and his stare is staggering because we have to wonder just what he is accessing and just what he has access to.

These deep looks on Nolte's face are like thunderbolts that strike to the core, like natural disasters. He has an animal aspect, sometimes, predatory,

Nick Nolte confronts formidable demons in the "Life Lessons" segment of *New York Stories*.

and then all too human, as if Lionel is too smart to not realize just what a cycle of ever-diminishing personal returns he's caught up in (when Nolte's Lionel realizes this fully, he puts his hand to his face and the hand is covered in green paint, and somehow this is the ideal jungle-like image for him).

In *Everybody Wins* (1990), Nolte tried his best to keep up with Debra Winger at her most mercurial but finally looked as confused as Humphrey Bogart does in *Beat the Devil* (1954), bedeviled himself by the film's shiftiness and the risky camp style Winger applies to her temptress part. "You've been tryin' to go north, south, and powder your nose all at the same time, but not with me, baby!" he finally howls. But then he transformed himself to become Captain Michael Brennan in Sidney Lumet's *Q & A* (1990), a dark-haired, corrupt, racist, mustached cop in wrinkled clothes.

Like Lionel, Mike has a gut, but he has a very different physicality and manner: big and blustery and barroom performative. This is a performance more shaped for the camera than was usual for Nolte at this time, and it is mannered because Brennan is a liar, a monster, and a very mannered guy. He is a predator of transgender streetwalkers, and we see him strangle two of them. Nolte aligns these murders with Mike's seriously twisted sexuality, which is based in self-loathing and a sense of violence as release.

In 1991, Nolte got an Oscar nomination for his Tom Wingo in Barbra Streisand's *The Prince of Tides*, and this marked a brief period where he was a real bankable lead actor, crowned "the sexiest man alive" by *People* magazine at 50. He was back to blond for Tom, rough and sensitive and needing to be saved.

Nolte physicalizes Tom's evasive discomfort in the early scenes of *The Prince of Tides*, but this is a movie that proves that first-rate acting can only muddy the waters when contending with a disjointed script and uncertain direction. Nolte is memorably subversive when he cries, "And that's what I like about the south!" with hands out in a "show biz" sort of way after Tom makes a whopper of a confession about childhood trauma to Streisand's therapist; she tells him he's just covering his pain, which of course makes him quickly break down and weep, for both his inner and outer child. Nolte was on firmer ground as the compromised lawyer in *Cape Fear* that same year, his morality getting eroded by Robert De Niro's venomous stalker bit by bit until he is left with his face full of a howling kind of nothing at the end.

Nolte went big with an Italian accent in the extremely depressing *Lorenzo's Oil* (1992), and biggest of all in the scene where he learns just how ill his young son is after researching the illness at a library, flinging himself down a staircase like a bat out of hell and banging his head (bam bam bam) on the steps as he goes down, his face contorted by enormous agony; that film showed just how elemental and non-naturalistic Nolte could be if he had enough support.

He ran afoul of Julia Roberts on the set of *I Love Trouble* (1994), but he was very intense and imaginative as Thomas Jefferson in *Jefferson in Paris* (1995), laboring to catch a complex character with no help at all from the film itself. He was the stud plumber Lucky in *Afterglow* (1997), tending to women's needs but still attached to wife Julie Christie, and then he took his last really challenging role: Wade Whitehouse, a cop with a toothache in snowbound New Hampshire in Paul Schrader's bleak *Affliction* (1997), for which he was again nominated for an Oscar for lead actor (he lost to Roberto Benigni for *Life Is Beautiful*, a notably asinine decision from a group not much noted for getting it right).

The divorced Wade has a bad temper, and his young daughter keeps rejecting him. Standing like a sentinel at a school crosswalk, Wade's arms are up in a crucifixion pose that is far from Nolte's ironic taking on of that image at the end of *North Dallas Forty*. He stands there with his head resting on his shoulder, and his face looks disturbingly emptied out, as if he's being struck by some kind of paralysis.

When he says goodbye to his daughter at his mother's funeral, Wade makes a conventional waving movement at first and then throws his hand down dismissively, a powerful expression of his self-loathing and lack of hope. Wade has a mean streak that he inherited from his drunken father (James Coburn), and Nolte's perpetual little boy look comes in handy in the scenes Wade has with his dad, so that you can see what he was and what he is, sometimes simultaneously.

When Wade finally takes dentistry into his own hands and pulls his infected tooth out with a pair of pliers, Nolte's face is reddened and livid with pain, his blue eyes swimming in the redness, and when he finally gets the tooth free with the pliers his face slowly goes back to normal as he wipes away the blood from his mouth. (When I saw *Affliction* at the Angelika Film Center in Manhattan, the whole audience gasped when Nolte pulled the tooth out with pliers, and one woman in the back let out a high-pitched scream.)

Nolte fronted smaller, wayward films after that, and he took supporting roles in larger pictures. He did two more for Alan Rudolph, the lamentable *Trixie* (2000) and *Intimate Affairs* (2001), where he is married to Tuesday Weld and holds forth to a sex study group about how he once copulated with a female donkey.

He was arrested for reckless driving under the influence in 2002, which led to a soon-notorious mug shot with flowered shirt and wild-man hair, but in the documentary *This So-Called Disaster* (2003), a film about the rehearsals for a Sam Shepard play, the seasoned Nolte revealed himself to be as earnest about his work and his craft as any starry-eyed theater student.

He started to be cast as a figure of fun, a craggy-voiced old timer with a hair-trigger temper, as in *Tropic Thunder* (2008). That same year, he did the strange documentary *Nick Nolte: No Exit*, where he was seen interviewing himself about his life and career. Then again, self-confrontation had always been his thing in his best work, but in his later years he was often supporting Robert Redford, an old-time matinee idol and a far more soothing presence.

Sean Penn
By Himself

Armored with major talent and all the studied machismo of a man who knows his full worth, Sean Penn is an actor who often seems dismissive of acting. It is something he can do so well and so easily that, like Marlon Brando, he has often spoken up for other causes and things he felt were more mature, and he has directed four very somber, rather awkward movies that feel too consciously serious and gnarly, whereas in his best acting he shoots up as high as anyone has ever been, nearly effortlessly, but sometimes with the self-importance and domineering style of a Dustin Hoffman.

Like Brando or Vanessa Redgrave, Penn is so advanced as an actor that he sometimes gets impatient, and there are many film performances where he shows up and does just the bare minimum, with one or two scenes acted full-out just to show that he can, that he has it in him. Yet who else would have been capable of the extremity of his performance in the barely seen *This Must Be the Place* (2011), where he plays a burned-out rocker?

The choices Penn makes for this movie in regard to voice and manner couldn't be more risky: his Cheyenne speaks in very high, absent tones and is always blowing a stray piece of hair from his face. He dresses in a Goth style, all in black with long black hair and lipstick, and Penn can be very funny as he sketches in this space case; his work here is so specific that he seems to be exactly mimicking someone he has known, met, or observed.

There is a scene in this film where Cheyenne cracks open, where he confesses his life-ruining guilt when two kids killed themselves after listening to his gloom pop, and Penn brings the level of emotion here to an almost intolerable height (his scene partner is the musician David Byrne, who is playing himself). There's something so brutish about Penn's talent in a scene like this, which very few other actors would have gone as far with as he does. It's unclear, even, if he should have gone so far outside the framework of his characterization for this "big scene." A lesser actor than Penn might have been less impressive in the role of Cheyenne, but more simply touching. So little is simple with Penn.

The son of actors, Penn grew up in Los Angeles, and he made his first impression as a member of a male ensemble in *Taps* (1981). His amiable stoner Jeff Spicoli in *Fast Times at Ridgemont High* (1982) showed a comic talent that Penn has kept mainly hidden or dormant. He gets big laughs with Spicoli's delayed reactions and arbitrary impulses, and the little giggle he does in the back of his throat—at age 22, Penn was already carefully shaping behavior like a veteran theater actor. Spicoli is said to have been "stoned since the third grade," and Penn finds the sweetness in that, and the muted belligerence, too.

He dominated the gloomy *Bad Boys* (1983), where he went to prison, and then he was a drug dealer and addict who becomes a spy and spits at his own reflection in a mirror in *The Falcon and the Snowman* (1985). Penn used a nerdy voice in that movie and put together a complex, shifty characterization that sometimes leaned towards the showy side, as if he were playing a John Cazale beta-male on Dustin Hoffman–steroids.

He was one of the few players of this time who was building on the work of Hoffman, Pacino, and De Niro, a star character actor who made few concessions to what might be attractive or appealing. Most of his characters are losers, some amiable, some not at all. His talent was in being able to go so way out on a limb with different voices and mannerisms without ever being absurd or unbelievable, and when you look at just how far he can go with these things, this is no small feat.

Penn married the pop star Madonna in 1985 and spent four stormy years married to her in the glare of her publicity, which led to trouble with the law when he assaulted invasive paparazzi photographers. He appeared with his wife in the notoriously poor *Shanghai Surprise* (1986) and worked sparingly, emerging in Brian De Palma's *Casualties of War* (1989) to go all-out as a soldier in Vietnam who recklessly and willingly indulges the very worst in himself. It was on the derivative and gloomy *State of Grace* (1990) that he met Robin Wright, who would become his second and long-suffering wife in 1996. Wright, a real beauty with lots of acting talent herself, would come to be one of Penn's best screen partners.

He destroyed his own looks for the role of the cokehead lawyer in *Carlito's Way* (1993), wearing extremely unflattering curly hair (long in back, sparse on top) and round glasses, playing the sort of role that John Cazale probably would have played opposite Al Pacino had he lived. Penn then got an Oscar nomination for his killer on death row in *Dead Man Walking* (1995), a virtuoso performance with all the requisite pity and terror, and then some.

At first Penn's character Matthew Poncelet is insolent with Sister Helen Prejean (Susan Sarandon), mean as a snake, with his pompadour hair and his ugly goatee, filled with the stink of barrooms and narrow attitudes. But gradually Poncelet is made to see the wrongness of his own macho overcompensations, which led him to murder a pair of teenagers with another man.

When he confesses to the sister, his eyes flash with the remorse of a panicked little boy, and he is seen as a martyr on a cross as he dies of a lethal injection. Sarandon has the more difficult role here, but Penn is scrupulously naturalistic, sometimes to a fault, and he earns the high level of emotion with which he ends the film.

Penn did a kind of tribute to John Cassavetes in *She's So Lovely* (1997) opposite Wright, who matched him dare for dare, and he played with her again as another coke addict in an adaptation of David Rabe's play *Hurlyburly* (1998). He then offered one of the very best male performances in a Woody Allen movie as a selfish jazz guitarist in *Sweet and Lowdown* (1999), which is Allen's take on *La Strada* (1954).

In *Sweet and Lowdown*, Penn gave size, color, and specificity to what might have been just a notional role in the hands of someone else. His Emmet Ray is a self-important, even weaselly guy who is always second-best to the jazz guitarist Django Reinhardt until the suffering his self-destructive behavior brings briefly makes him a major musician, and Penn sells this romantic notion toughly and convincingly.

He got another Oscar nomination for his Emmet, and then another one for *I Am Sam* (2001), where he extravagantly played a mentally handicapped man like an explorer mapping unknown territory. The choppily edited film itself is sentimental, but Penn never is. And then he won his first Oscar as the grieving father in Clint Eastwood's *Mystic River* (2003), a film that was widely overpraised when it came out.

Penn likely clinched the award for an operatic short scene where he fights against a group of cops to get to his dead daughter, and of course he had been nominated several times already for very strong performances (in retrospect, this award most certainly should have gone to Bill Murray for *Lost in Translation*). He was excessively mannered in *Mystic River*, but in *Milk* (2008), which won him a second lead Oscar, the macho Penn did one of his best transformative performances, locating a wide-eyed gay guy within himself and then uninhibitedly letting that gay guy loose.

Penn was publicly upset when he saw Terrence Malick's *The Tree of Life* (2011) because so much of his work had been cut. He had been used there as a kind of model or alienated figure in a landscape, like the actors in Michelangelo Antonioni pictures, but *The Tree of Life* is still the finest film he has ever appeared in, and this pointed up the fact that Penn's best performances were always in movies that weren't up to the high level of his work.

Curiously, Penn is an actor who can't transcend poor or gaudy or pedestrian writing (which he has often been given) as much as separate his own characterization from the words he is saying. He has barely ever acted in the theater, or had roles that might have really challenged his talent. Instead, he has been content to give a dozen or so great performances in parts that are usually just pretexts for his creativity. When the writing in his films is really bad but Penn is going at it with all his might, the effect of separation can be almost campy, though never quite.

River Phoenix
Only Once

Dead at age 23 of a drug overdose outside of the LA club the Viper Room on October 31, 1993, River Phoenix never really got a chance to do what he might have done as an actor, but he left some indelible hints. His filmography is small. He doesn't really have a classic film, either, though his Mike Waters in *My Own Private Idaho* (1991) is a classic performance, in touch with madness, morbid humor, and bottomless hurt.

Phoenix's Mike Waters has been a touchstone for some actors and enormously influential, so much so that James Franco, the Joyce Carol Oates of moody current actor-directors, put together an homage out of outtakes from the film called *My Own Private River* (2012). In letting us see some scenes that never made it into the film, like a wondrous tracking shot where Mike eats what he can at a grocery store and grabs food items like a hungry animal, more detail was added to Phoenix's achievement.

Phoenix moves very poetically as Mike (like Ben Whishaw does in his own best work), as if he hears some music all his own. So much of his performance was improvised here, so that this is his movie more than it is a movie by its director Gus Van Sant, who has never come close to matching the best Phoenix footage in *My Own Private Idaho*. In another unused scene, Mike has sex with a girl on top of autumn leaves and under a looming bridge (she is on top, and his booted legs move spasmodically with effort and pleasure). They have an improvised talk, and he removes a spider from her head without missing a beat.

In *My Own Private River*, we are allowed to see the scenes from *Idaho* in long master shots unmediated by cuts, so that the outlines of Phoenix's performance expand and stretch much further. In his un-edited conception, Mike is both more damaged and more aggressive than he wound up in the finished film, and far more derisive and vulgar with Hans (Udo Kier), his German performance artist john. He is also somewhat more heterosexual in the scenes that never made it into the film, and not just in the sex scene with the girl, who is seen in the finished film at a table in a restaurant (Mike's loaded look at her there carries more weight with knowledge of their deleted scene under the bridge).

River Phoenix is the ultimate in morbid and sexy self-destructiveness in *My Own Private Idaho*.

"I've got you, bro," Phoenix's Mike says to his friend Scott (Keanu Reeves) in another *Idaho* outtake. Phoenix gives Reeves a masculine pat on the neck before going into a truly nutsy improv with some imaginary person behind him (both here and in the finished film, Reeves looks like he full well knows how he is being over-shadowed by Phoenix). In these outtakes, Phoenix is trying to add lightly macho touches to offset the famous campfire scene, which he wrote himself, where Mike confesses his love to Scott.

Phoenix was very beautiful, of course, with his James Dean–like hair and his perfect little pointed nose and beautifully proportioned body, and he had a soft but resonant voice so that he could seem both totally vulnerable and commanding at the same time, and in too much pain to stand it much longer. He did not smile easily. And he seemed to have things on his mind that he could not share or speak about.

Ethan Hawke, who worked with Phoenix as a child actor, told Phoenix's biographer Gavin Edwards that the performance Phoenix gave as Mike Waters in *My Own Private Idaho* reminded him of the Daffy Duck cartoon where Daffy drinks gasoline and gunpowder and swallows a match and then explodes to impress an audience before floating away. Bugs Bunny tells Daffy's ghost it was a great trick. "I know, I know, but I can only do it once," Daffy's shade replies. "I thought that about *My Own Private Idaho*," Hawke said. "We got to watch River light himself on fire. And he did. And he was somebody really worthy of being competitive with."

Dermot Mulroney worked with Phoenix in Peter Bogdanovich's *The Thing Called Love* (1993). "His eyes made him the focus of energy in every scene, the centrifugal force so strong you didn't even try to duel him for control," Mulroney said. "The off-center eye read as madness, and the other read as pure sanity. In close-up, from one side he was the guy next door, and from the other he was absolutely insane." This angel/devil split was rich terrain for Phoenix as an actor.

He was born River Jude Bottom in 1970 to two hippie parents who were members of a cult called the Children of God, which encouraged incest and child sexual activity. River said in an interview that the sexual experimentation, in whatever confusing form it took, lasted from ages four to ten. At four he was also forced to go out and beg in the street for his family and later sing (and proselytize for the cult), and if he didn't bring back enough money they wouldn't eat that night.

The family left the cult and went to Hollywood, where River was expected to be the main breadwinner as a child actor and was represented by agent Iris Burton. "Kids are pieces of meat," Burton said. "I've never had anything but filet mignon. I've never had hamburger. My kids are the choice meat."

Phoenix never had any education, and did little socializing with other kids outside his family, so it was hard for him when he got his first job on the TV show *Seven Brides for Seven Brothers* in 1982; when the guys in the cast teased him, he would burst into tears. (On that show, his character says a resounding "no" when he is offered pot to smoke.) Phoenix himself was a vegan from the day he and his siblings saw fishermen spearing fish on a dock.

Phoenix was dyslexic, but no one bothered to diagnose or help him with this, even though he starred in an afterschool special called *Backwards: The Riddle of Dyslexia* in 1984, where he already has a wary, dismayed, adult face and has sweet little moments of being sassy and softly feminine. He played a math tutor to Michael J. Fox's Alex P. Keaton on the TV show *Family Ties*, and he was a high-voiced little dork in Joe Dante's *Explorers* (1985) opposite Ethan Hawke. "I saw him practicing his character's walk in the parking lot," Hawke said. "Uncommon behavior for a thirteen-year-old."

He was impressively grounded in the TV movie *Surviving* (1985), where he was egged on emotionally by Ellen Burstyn, an actress who knew a prodigy when she saw one. "Oh God, yes, he was so special," Burstyn said during our interview when I mentioned Phoenix. "He was just a darling boy and a new and young talent, you know, that was just beginning to blossom. That was a tragic loss. Did I recognize his talent? Oh *definitely*, oh yeah."

Phoenix proved his range by playing a little tough guy from the wrong side of the tracks in *Stand by Me* (1986), though he did reveal his sensitive side by the end. (He was such an uncommonly blunt child actor, never winsome or ingratiating.) In *A Night in the Life of Jimmy Reardon* (1988), Phoenix looks too young to be playing his ladies' man part, and he's so uncomfortable that he does stilted work, but he was far better than *Little Nikita* (1988) deserved, especially in the scene where his character confronts his parents.

"Is River Phoenix a star?" asked Hal Hinson in his *Washington Post* review of *Little Nikita*. "Perhaps not. But his hair is. *Little Nikita* would be nothing without River Phoenix's hair. It's the most engaging, the most watchable thing in the film. It has body. It has character. It even has drama. In other words, it has everything that's missing from the rest of the picture."

But that same year he got an Oscar nomination for supporting actor for *Running on Empty*, a Sidney Lumet drama in which the pain and anger roiling beneath Phoenix's beautiful prince face sometimes seemed to overwhelm both him and the modest context of the movie, especially in the scenes he shares with his real-life girlfriend of that time, the magnetically tough Martha Plimpton.

Phoenix was noted for wanting to become the character he was playing, which bled into his off-screen life. "After *Dogfight* (1991), I remember thinking he was being a real jarhead asshole," said cinematographer Bobby Bukowski, who was his friend and sometime lover. "It took a month for him to become sweet again."

Dogfight is a special case, a kind of screwball drama based initially in an extremely nasty situation (Phoenix's Eddie Birdlace takes Lili Taylor's Rose to a contest where the marine with the ugliest date wins prize money). He made a notable transformation to play the marine in *Dogfight*: stiff-backed, nearly unattractive, with close-cropped hair, and he is straight-ahead and very angry here, with a tiny bit of decency trying to break through. In the soft-voiced, sensitive Lili Taylor, Phoenix found his ideal acting partner, for *My Own Private Idaho* is really a one-man show.

Phoenix did everything he could to give the performance of his curtailed life as Mike in *My Own Private Idaho*, living the role as much as possible and stamping it with his control. The lengthy scenes in that movie involving Keanu Reeves and Bob (William Richert), a Falstaff-ian street mentor, fall flat and distract us from Mike and what Phoenix is doing with him, and this is a source of frustration that must be dealt with in *Idaho*.

Reeves is uneasy with Phoenix on screen, which works best in the campfire love scene. Originally it was written by Van Sant as Mike hitting on Scott because he is bored and horny, but Phoenix re-wrote it as an impassioned confession of love, so momentous that it unbalances the rest of the movie.

Phoenix's Mike is one of the key dangerous cinema boys, narcoleptically falling asleep when life gets to be too much for him, but ready to bare his fangs or throw his hat into the ring with a quiet declaration of love. This is very romantic and self-destructive work, right down to the scene where Mike is putting his face down in broken glass in the street (this is seen more clearly in *My Own Private River*).

In Sam Shepard's *Silent Tongue* (1993), a dirty-faced Phoenix has his own little one-act play going, mainly around a campfire, but without Reeves's Scott this time. He sang in Peter Bogdanovich's *The Thing Called Love* (1993) and was brooding and intense in Jordan Catalano plaid. Phoenix, who was heavily into drugs when he shot this movie, still has his striking kind of aggressive softness, romantic, awkward, with a slice of cruelty in it, or hostility. His intensity is of the burn-out variety; there is nowhere to go with it but down.

As he prepared for what would be his final film, the unfinished *Dark Blood*, Phoenix told his director George Sluizer that the only time he felt security was when he was acting. "Myself is a bum!" he cried. "Myself is nothing!" He had trouble with all the lines he had been given to say, and he was also having trouble with his character, a kid who is just called Boy.

"In my opinion, that was made more difficult by the director constantly telling him how he would play it," said his co-star Judy Davis. "Whether he should be angrier, loonier, whatever. It was a difficult part because it could so easily be absurd. He had the most dialogue in the film, huge speeches; he kept trying to cut the lines down. Any change freaked the director out. River said to me one day, 'Maybe I should give up acting.'"

But he needed to make money for his extended family. From the time he was four years old, Phoenix didn't exactly have a choice in that matter, though he was trying to break away from them at the time of his death. He'd been told that the location for *Dark Blood* was a favorite for UFO sightings, and so sometimes Phoenix would lie down and cry out, "Take me, I'm ready! What else is out there?"

Phoenix had been doing hard drugs on and off for a while, but Sluizer said he was clean on the set of *Dark Blood* (Davis felt otherwise). At one point, he said to his other co-star Jonathan Pryce, "Somebody's going to die on this film." Phoenix had trouble with the prickly Davis, too, who was having her own far worse problems with Sluizer.

During a hiatus in shooting, Phoenix left for Los Angeles, and one night he went to the Viper Room with his girlfriend Samantha Mathis and his brother Joaquin and sister Rain. He brought his guitar because he wanted to play on stage, but he was told there were too many musicians scheduled, and so he took a seat.

A guitarist friend came up to his table with a cup and said, "Hey Riv, drink this—it'll make you feel fabulous." Phoenix took the cup and downed it all in one gulp. It was a dissolved speedball, a mix of cocaine and heroin.

Phoenix knew immediately that something was wrong. "What did you give me?" he shouted at his friend. "What the fuck is in it?"

Phoenix took a Valium to try to calm down, but soon he vomited on himself and on the table and slumped unconscious in his chair. It was 12:45 AM when he fell unconscious in his own vomit. Mathis called Phoenix's assistant. At 12:55 AM, Phoenix woke up, and he asked to be taken outside for fresh air.

His brother Joaquin helped him walk outside, and by 1 AM Phoenix had collapsed on the sidewalk and was having convulsions. Mathis began banging her head against a wall in frustration. At 1:10 AM, Joaquin called 911, and at 1:14 AM an ambulance came, but it was too late. By 1:51 AM at the hospital, Phoenix was pronounced dead.

Joaquin went on to a substantial career of his own, mainly in gloomy films where he could be an "unpredictable" sort of savant, best of all in James Gray's *Two Lovers* (2008). Leonardo DiCaprio took on many of the roles that Phoenix probably would have played had he lived, and surely Phoenix would have played them with more poetry and more kindness.

George Sluizer eventually cobbled together an 86-minute version of what remained of *Dark Blood* with his own narration filling the gaps, and it played some festivals in 2012. The reconstruction of *Dark Blood* ends with a death scene for Phoenix's character Boy where Boy leans back and dies.

This is one of the most realistic death scenes in cinema history: Phoenix's eyes and mouth open and you can see and feel when the life has left him, as if his face is just an empty envelope left on his bed. This is what someone looks like when they die, and no other actor has come as close to imagining it as Phoenix does here in one of the last scenes he ever shot.

Denzel Washington
The Duke in His Domain

American movies still have a long way to go when it comes to offering worthy opportunities to our best African American performers. Sidney Poitier was a pioneer and standard-bearer in the 1960s, and by the 1980s and '90s, there were several major performances by black actors. There was Harry Belafonte in Robert Altman's *Kansas City* (1996), where he held the screen in the most dynamic possible way in long takes as a gangster who loves to talk. And there was Angela Bassett's Tina Turner in *What's Love Got To Do With It* (1993), clearly one of the boldest and most complete and searching biopic performances, an achievement that was bolstered by the intense and sinuous style of Laurence Fishburne's Ike Turner.

No one who has seen it will ever forget the scene late in that film when Fishburne's Ike comes to threaten Bassett's Tina in her dressing room with a gun as she attempts to make a comeback without him. The stand off between Bassett and Fishburne in this scene as they stare in the mirror at each other takes on a kind of elemental and universal size, which is what the best acting always seeks to do. It stands in, finally, for all women who have to stare down abusive men seeking to confine and degrade them. (Notice how pathetic and lost Fishburne's Ike begins to seem as that encounter goes on and then reaches its conclusion.)

Taking the torch from Poitier, Denzel Washington worked steadily until he became the premiere African American male star of his era. Great looking, sober, steady, and intimidating until he smiles warmly, Washington has the authoritative presence of an old-time American male movie star of the 1930s or '40s, and he is a conservative figure, a religious man, the son of a Pentecostal minister.

There is usually no fuss with Washington's acting, no insecurity, and his focus and concentration on what he is doing in a film is commandingly total. He is an ideal camera actor because his face can call up any emotion with a kind of diamond-cut exactitude, and this surety of his is a quality to gain both audience trust and respect with. Washington has the on-screen presence of a lion, royal and not inclined to look kindly on foolishness, and so his moments of playfulness land so delightfully precisely because they're so rare. He has not often had notable dealings with women on screen, but it was that very reticence and withholding of that aspect of himself that made him so elusively attractive.

His mother sent him to a prep school when he was 14. "That decision changed my life," Washington said in 1999, "because I wouldn't have survived the direction I was going. The guys I was hanging out with at the time, my running buddies, have done maybe forty years combined in the penitentiary. They were nice guys, but the streets got them."

Washington went to Fordham University in Manhattan and studied acting, and he performed the leads in Eugene O'Neill's *The Emperor Jones* and in *Othello* while at school. He made his feature debut in a comedy with George Segal called *Carbon Copy* (1981), but this was an anomaly in a career that quickly became more noted for serious and socially conscious drama.

All through the 1980s he played Dr. Philip Chandler on the TV show *St. Elsewhere*, and then Washington got an Oscar nomination for best supporting actor playing South African freedom fighter Steve Biko in *Cry Freedom* (1987). He is a presence to be reckoned with in that movie, but his character is martyred and neglected in comparison to Kevin Kline's white journalist.

Washington had a more substantial role as a proud and defiant soldier during the Civil War in *Glory* (1989), which won him the Oscar for best supporting actor. In the scene where his character gets flogged and we see the whip marks on his back from past floggings, Washington's face holds memorably strong and steady even when a single tear slides out of his right eye. This is a close-up that mingles sorrow with unbending righteous dignity, and it is one of Washington's most impressively layered moments on screen.

In *For Queen and Country* (1988), Washington played a former British soldier who gets involved with a white woman (Stella Gonet), and that movie was stiff and restrained like some of Poitier's more buttoned-up 1960s pictures. But as a trumpeter in Spike Lee's *Mo' Better Blues* (1990), Washington was allowed to cut loose and thrive in the midst of lively, well written ensemble scenes played out in long takes with challenging black female co-players like Cynda Williams and Lee's sister Joie.

Washington then took on the intimidating task of being *Malcolm X* (1992) for Spike Lee. This is an epic movie, over three hours long, where he had to show us the drastic changes that took Malcolm from street hustler to a controversial leader of his race in America. Washington has some trouble in the film's first hectic hour with Malcolm's youthful vigor and restlessness and anger; these are things that lie outside of his range. But once Malcolm puts on his glasses and joins the church of Islam, Washington's performance dramatically improves and focuses, particularly in the scenes he shares with Angela Bassett, who plays Malcolm's wife Betty.

There's too much flashy cutting from Lee during the speeches here, but Washington makes an impact with them anyway, displaying the kind of leader charisma that cannot be acted or faked. (Watch the scene where a young white girl asks his Malcolm what she can do for his cause and he says, "Nothing," in a very firm way that can brook no response.) Washington, like Malcolm, has the air of being somehow blessed or chosen, or special in some way, and this has to do with his looks but also with his steady bearing, and his single-minded intensity. This intensity of his can run the risk of being monotonous, and it needs heroic parts on a large scale to feed on.

In the three films he had in release in 1993, Washington was a support to white stars, most troublingly as the lawyer to Tom Hanks's dying gay man in *Philadelphia* (1993). Press interviews for that film, and his publicized advice to the younger Will Smith not to kiss a man on screen in the movie of *Six Degrees of Separation* (1993), made his own religious conservatism clear.

In the mid-to-late 1990s, Washington came into his own as a movie star and lead in films that often had a military or sports background. He worked two more times for Spike Lee in far more conventional stories, and he did five films with the action director Tony Scott, who favored such busy and rapid cutting that any performance choices Washington made tended to get lost.

In *The Hurricane* (1999) he played a boxer unjustly sent to prison, and he held up with all the victimized contempt of Burt Lancaster in *Birdman of Alcatraz* (1962). He won an Oscar for best actor as a rogue cop in *Training Day* (2001), a film in which the bad behavior of his character so went against the grain of Washington's own character and image that it was immediately understood and acclaimed as an acting feat. There were more action movies after that before a return to acted "flaws" in *Flight* (2012), where he played a drunken pilot.

Washington then directed himself opposite Viola Davis in a film of August Wilson's great play *Fences* (2016), which he had played with Davis on Broadway to acclaim. He tried to look his age and seem broken-down enough for this part, but at age 61 (nearly ten years older than the age of the character he was playing) he still often felt like a matinee idol, especially when he smiled.

Washington did full justice to Wilson's heady words, particularly in the first hour or so of the film, before ceding his authority to the estimable Davis in the second half. His performance was maybe more dutiful than inspired, but he was a real star grappling with profound material, and that was enough to make this film an event. Washington honored Wilson's achievement and basically got out of the way of the writing while also seeking to lift it aloft with his star charisma, and he racked up another Oscar nomination for *Fences* and another one for *Roman J. Israel, Esq.* (2017), where once again "character flaws" let us know that he was practicing his craft.

Viggo Mortensen
Set Apart

It wasn't until he was well into his forties that the mysterious and creative and lethally beautiful Viggo Mortensen started doing leading roles in movies consistently. Born in New York, he drove trucks and sold flowers in Europe for a while before coming back home and going into acting. He was glimpsed only briefly as an Amish man in *Witness* (1985), where he seems a little self-conscious but takes command of the camera when he smiles in a way that reads as dirty-minded.

Working his way up, he finally got the lead in Sean Penn's first try as a director, *The Indian Runner* (1991), a somber, pretentious movie about two brothers in which Mortensen was the wild one. He had a restrained kind of daring in that film that was snakelike, un-ingratiating, and very sexual, and there were also times when he seemed a little like a robot imitating human behavior, which maybe signaled the influence of Robert De Niro.

Mortensen stole *Carlito's Way* (1993) with just one set piece scene as the weak Lalin, a former gang member in a wheelchair who is caught trying to record a conversation with Al Pacino's Carlito. When he is found out, Mortensen's Lalin memorably whines, "It wasn't even turned on!" several times and tries to play on Carlito's sympathy, showing him the diapers he has to wear and crying, "I shit my pants every day, I can't walk, I can't hump, you know!" This is the sort of juicy small part that gets you noticed, even if the half-Danish Mortensen is peculiar casting for a Latino character.

He worked steadily throughout the 1990s, making the camera stop to gawp at him as he smirked and wore a mustache and flashed incongruously "vulnerable" blue eyes while he tormented Demi Moore's soldier in *G.I. Jane* (1997). He donned period costume to play an intense Caspar Goodwood in *The Portrait of a Lady* (1996), and his own paintings were used for *A Perfect Murder* (1998), where he was well cast as a lover-turned-killer. Director Gus Van Sant leered at his nude body as he turned off a lamp in *Psycho* (1998), and then Mortensen made his first real impact as the lover of Diane Lane in *A Walk on the Moon* (1999), where he accessed the kind of steady, sensitive sexual attentiveness many women in the audience longed for.

It was in the three *Lord of the Rings* movies, though, from 2001 to 2003, that Mortensen became a star and a sex symbol, without having to do much more than look solemn and heroic and manly in an old-fashioned way. With fame came the revelation that he was a Renaissance man, a poet and musician as well as a painter, and a publisher who used some of his *Rings* money to put out books by little-known writers he admired.

It was in 2005 that David Cronenberg assessed that eerie removal in Mortensen for their first major film together, *A History of Violence*, a half Hitchcock, half Anthony Mann tale of identity and murder where all the disparate parts of Mortensen finally came together into one disturbing picture: family man, killer, and sexy beast, eerily calm and not remotely trustworthy and all the more exciting for that. Cronenberg's cool, probing scrutiny allowed Mortensen to be one of the most faceted screen presences of his time.

Mortensen then picked up an Oscar nomination for best actor for his second film with Cronenberg, *Eastern Promises* (2007), in which he gave his finest and most physically daring and committed performance as the Russian gangster Nikolai. Sexually insolent, and animated by morbid humor, Nikolai is a real wise guy and hard ass. When tasked with disposing of a corpse, he matter-of-factly says he is going to break its fingers. "You might want to leave room," he tells his superior, before blithely putting his lit cigarette out on his tongue. In the second half of the film, Mortensen's extraordinary near-50-year-old body was put on display and then put to the test in a violent sequence where he is naked and attacked by two men in a sauna bath and has to defend himself.

In his third Cronenberg film, *A Dangerous Method* (2011), Mortensen shifted to scene-stealing support as an authoritative, above-it-all Sigmund Freud, but his humorlessness was exposed by *Captain Fantastic* (2016), an absurd espousal of extreme left-wing attitudes that Mortensen played with an entirely straight face. He was rewarded with another Oscar nomination, but his work with Cronenberg is what will last.

Christian Bale
Transparency

Christian Bale gave what is still his finest or most well rounded performance at the age of 13 in Steven Spielberg's *Empire of the Sun* (1987), an epic movie, novelistic in scope, that he basically carried by himself. His character Jim is supposed to age from 12 to 16, but Spielberg keeps Bale in the part in the second half of the picture for emotional continuity, and maybe also because Jim's growth could have been stunted by lack of food in a Japanese POW camp.

Bale has a transparent face that shows anything he is feeling and thinking, and his performance is fresh and nuanced from the first time we see Jim singing in a high soprano voice at school. Bale gets across Jim's intensity and boredom here, and his slightly bratty privilege in subsequent scenes, but once he lets go of his mother's hand to pick up his toy airplane, this little British colonialist boy has to show his mettle and survive war and abandonment for years, talking and fighting his way through many difficult situations.

Jim's natural bossiness helps him to stay afloat and active, whereas someone who was older and softer might have folded at any one of the tests he faces throughout this movie. He is tough and managing, doing whatever he has to but never losing his humanity like the heartless Basie (John Malkovich), a scavenger Jim finally has to reject.

Jim is someone who thrives under pressure, but Bale himself was less able to cope. Born to British parents who pushed him into show business, he chafed against responsibilities to them, and he wondered if he wanted to continue acting after the press attention for *Empire of the Sun* took its toll on him.

He did smaller parts and then took a lead in a dud musical, *Newsies* (1992), but he won devoted fans throughout the 1990s who called themselves Bale-heads and devoted many fan sites to him in the early days of the Internet. He was sweet as Laurie in *Little Women* (1994) and then sour as Edward Rosier in *The Portrait of a Lady* (1996), and he was the slow brother who gets blown up in *The Secret Agent* (1996). Bale then gave a fluid, open, erotic performance in *Metroland* (1997) as an ordinary man who had once wanted to be extraordinary, and the camera soaked up all the pure emotions and thoughts that would emerge on his face.

As the journalist in *Velvet Goldmine* (1998), Bale was without vanity, giving himself up to fanlike inadequacy and masturbatory seclusion before he is ushered into one great night of sex with his idol (Ewan McGregor). In the little seen *All the Little Animals* (1998), Bale again played a mentally slow boy and did it with very appealing simplicity, his face an open book. He was Demetrius in *A Midsummer Night's Dream* (1999) and then Jesus on TV in 1999 before he took on the challenge of being the soulless yuppie Patrick Bateman in *American Psycho* (2000).

Bale goes big in *American Psycho*, using a throaty, hollow voice and American accent that sometimes sounds like Tom Cruise. (Director Mary Harron said in an interview with *Black Book* that Bale had seen Cruise on the David Letterman show and had been fascinated by Cruise's "very intense friendliness with nothing behind the eyes.")

When Patrick does his killings, which are later revealed as fantasies, Bale goes all out, pushing himself to imagine the splurging anger and relief this man feels when he axes a hated rival (Jared Leto) in the face. Bale got his body into maximum condition for this role, so that the sight of him doing yoga in tightie-whities made him a sex symbol regardless of the film's satirical intentions.

In his work from *Empire of the Sun* to *American Psycho*, which took him from his teenaged years to his late twenties, it seemed like Bale had it in him to become a major actor in drama, comedy, and romance, but things didn't turn out that way. He lost 60 pounds and got down to a skeletal frame for *The Machinist* (2004), and this masochistic weight loss was all that performance was about in a minor film. (Surely Bale was taking the influence of De Niro in *Raging Bull* fatally far here.)

Worse, he lent his intensity to a series of gloomy Batman films where his self-serious, Method approach seemed either wasted or incongruous. In 2009, a recording was released of Bale yelling at a crewmember for moving while he was doing a take for *Terminator Salvation*, and this was widely distributed and mocked. The recording showed that he had a serious anger problem, which had already been revealed when he had a bad fight with his mother and sister in a hotel room in 2008, so bad that police were called.

By the time of David O. Russell's *The Fighter* (2010), for which he won an Oscar for best supporting actor, it had become clear that Bale had devolved into a very different sort of actor from what he had been in the late '80s and all through the 1990s. He lost weight again for that Oscar part, and his playing was hyped-up, flashy, pushed, and obvious.

Bale was self-conscious in his second film with Russell, *American Hustle* (2013), using external signifiers to give his performance as an overweight con artist. He wandered around Los Angeles without compass or sense for Terrence Malick's *Knight of Cups* (2015) and was rewarded with another Oscar nomination for best supporting actor for his work in *The Big Short* (2015), where he again offered up tics and effort as a numbers cruncher. This was all a sad decline from the naturalistic excellence of his beginnings, but he is only in mid-career, and other changes may occur for him.

Leonardo DiCaprio
Bad Influence

As a teenager and young adult in the 1990s, Leonardo DiCaprio captured a generation of young girls who went to see *Titanic* (1997) over and over again to savor the jolt of his feminine beauty and his raucous, Tom Sawyer–like, boyish energy. He was slender and his face was delicately pretty, yet his personality was hard-charging and daring and a little nasty. There was a cruel and demanding streak in his performing character, enough so that he could memorably stand up to Robert De Niro in his first notable movie, *This Boy's Life* (1993), challenging the lauded older actor on a purely physical level and winning that fight.

Even better, DiCaprio won a richly deserved Oscar nomination for best supporting actor as the mentally handicapped Arnie in *What's Eating Gilbert Grape* (1993), an improvisatory landmark, boldly imaginative and detailed and very physical (look at the way he uses his hands so expressively), founded on an otherworldly laugh and gurgle that was reminiscent of Mickey Rooney's Puck in the 1935 movie of *A Midsummer Night's Dream*.

DiCaprio's Arnie is a full-blooded creation that uses the boy's handicaps as only a starting point for an exploration of purity and impurity, instinct and lack of control, impishness and dirty fingernails. Not once does DiCaprio ever fall back on pathos or on vulnerability or helplessness, not even when Arnie's exasperated brother Gilbert (Johnny Depp) punches him. DiCaprio's Arnie is a force for liberating chaos and disruption, a boy who shows up the formal hypocrisy of people who think they have themselves under control. This is a great performance, as fine and vivid a portrait of being young as has ever been offered in a movie.

DiCaprio himself had started young. Before his voice changed, he appeared on the TV sitcom *Growing Pains*, where he resembled the androgynous young 1970s-era Jodie Foster. After coming to prominence with *This Boy's Life* and his Arnie in *Gilbert Grape*, DiCaprio had a good death scene, sprawled out in the dust of a street and clinging insistently to life, in the western *The Quick and the Dead* (1995), and then his bad boy, unruly side was emphasized in *The Basketball Diaries* (1995), where he played the heroin-addicted Jim Carroll.

In both of these pictures he had access to lots of raw emotion, and the poetic physicality to go with it. DiCaprio was so striking in this period because of all his contrasts, because of the harshness of his voice, which sounded like it had just changed and lowered (the hormonal charge propelling his body), and the sweetness of his face in repose, which was always getting attractively ruined and unsettled by his dirty thoughts and impulses, his bad and unwholesome ideas, his prankishness.

DiCaprio seemed born to play the French poet Rimbaud in *Total Eclipse* (1995), but the film was stilted and cautious, and he was uncomfortable depicting the homosexual love affair with Verlaine (David Thewlis) and with the heightened language. But then he had a hit as Romeo to Claire Danes's Juliet in Baz Luhrmann's hyped-up *Romeo + Juliet* (1996), where he was the ultimate teen heartthrob, beautiful and intense and insistent, emotionally aflame. In *Marvin's Room* (1996), all of the histrionics of De Niro, Meryl Streep, and Diane Keaton could not keep him from stealing all scenes from them with his mere unconvinced, boyishly carbonated presence.

DiCaprio reached his youthful apotheosis in the mega-hit *Titanic*, the kind of period-defining success that can kill as well as enrich. He was glorified and exploited by that epic movie, which positioned him as a figurehead for girls who made him the object of a mass fantasy that depended on the death of his character. DiCaprio in *Titanic* was made for pining over and remembering, not for settling down with.

In the new century, when he was not yet 30, it was clear that DiCaprio had drastically changed. He worked a lot for Martin Scorsese and got helplessly upstaged by Daniel Day-Lewis in *Gangs of New York* (2002), where he seems gloomy and blocked, and then he failed as Howard Hughes in Scorsese's *The Aviator* (2004). It was as if all of the emotional valves of his 1990s talent had been shut down, and now he was working grimly and simplistically, furrowing his brow and then furrowing it harder to express his discomfort and effort.

Steven Spielberg's *Catch Me If You Can* (2002) used this new, stagnated DiCaprio to advantage, making his displeasure and evasiveness the subject of the film, but he was merely strenuous in *Revolutionary Road* (2008) and Scorsese's *Shutter Island* (2010), where he was reduced to indicated, frozen distress.

DiCaprio was undone by the woeful sentimentality of *J. Edgar* (2011), in which there were only the briefest reminders of his former vitality. He worked hard as the villain in Quentin Tarantino's *Django Unchained* (2012), and then his steady collaboration with Scorsese finally paid off in the exuberant, unsettling, and controversial *The Wolf of Wall Street* (2013), where some of his 1990s mojo was again in evidence as high-finance crook and figurehead of debauch Jordan Belfort.

DiCaprio really tapped into a comic demon in himself for this picture about the depravity of high finance, and he was again elemental, unappeasable, a cheerleader for greed, whipping his employees into a religious frenzy; this is a nightmare Tom Cruise part that Cruise himself could never have acted so well or so uninhibitedly, so freakishly.

In the early scenes of *The Wolf of Wall Street*, DiCaprio is careful to show us that Belfort starts out as a kid with a modicum of conscience, but he gleefully dispenses with his good boy qualms as he builds his company and unscrupulously rakes in dollars, which he uses to buy copious amounts of drugs and prostitutes.

Scorsese got into trouble with this movie because his viewpoint is neutral and because DiCaprio shows all the fun that can be had while going straight to hell, using that side of his public persona that kicked in after *Titanic*: the serial dater of models and the king of various party scenes. His romantic image of the late 1990s is also inverted here because Jordan is a bad and inconsiderate lay and philanderer, quickly banging hookers and barely able to make an effort with his trophy wife (Margot Robbie).

DiCaprio's re-activated talent is particularly unhinged in *The Wolf of Wall Street* in an inventive and extended comedy set piece at the top of the third hour, an eight-minute, Jerry Lewis–esque tour-de-force where Belfort is debilitatingly stoned on Quaaludes but must get out of a country club and drive to his associate Donnie (Jonah Hill) so a business deal won't be ruined. DiCaprio was at his uncontrolled best here, daring and charismatic but basically unsympathetic, and the Quaalude scene showed just how skilled he could be at physical comedy.

He finally won an Oscar for *The Revenant* (2015), a movie as endurance test where that furrowed brow of his was attacked by a bear and the elements and a grueling shoot that was mentioned many times for publicity. His performance in that picture was nowhere near his Arnie, his Romeo, or his Jordan Belfort, but DiCaprio was being rewarded, finally, for sheer survival, even though he was only 40 years old.

Then again, Mickey Rooney had some tough years after his own initial youthful success at MGM in the late 1930s and 1940s, and the comparison to DiCaprio holds because some players are dependent on youth. Rooney never lost that mad spark of inspiration through many years of unworthy credits, and it's likely that DiCaprio will uncover his own talent from time to time if he can throw off the burden of heavy drama and actorly self-consciousness.

Michael Fassbender
Angel Eyes That Old Devil Sent

In Steve McQueen's *Hunger* (2008), the story of Irish freedom fighter Bobby Sands, Michael Fassbender was essential to the narrative, but the film is shot in such a way that it keeps us at a distance from him. That's a movie where the emphasis is not on Fassbender's face but on his tormented body being dragged and tossed around by prison officials in the same curiously voluptuous fashion that marked Brad Davis's semi-porny imprisonment in *Midnight Express* (1978).

In 2009, Fassbender played a jaunty film critic in Quentin Tarantino's *Inglourious Basterds*, and he wasn't allowed to dominate that movie, though he did show flashes of wit. It was only in Andrea Arnold's *Fish Tank*, which was made that same year, that Fassbender really took the screen with his full charisma in his very first scene.

Teenaged Mia (Katie Jarvis) is dancing in her kitchen to a rap video on a small TV. Her moves are shy, even a little scared; she would like to be sexy. When Mia turns around, she realizes that she's being watched by Fassbender's Conor, her mother's new boyfriend. "Don't mind me, girl," Conor says. "Carry on. I was enjoying it."

He's shirtless, and his face wears an extremely attractive lightly intrigued look. Conor has noticed Mia in a private moment, and so he knows all about her all at once, and Fassbender's expressive eyes show lots of things to her all at once. There's sexual desire, but it's defused by his tender amusement, as if to say, "Just who are *you*, miss? You're sort of special or weird, aren't you?"

Conor strolls away from the door out of the shot and asks Mia if she'd like some breakfast, and Arnold cuts to Conor at the kitchen cabinet looking over at Mia. His blue jeans are as far down his hips as possible, and there's no roundabout way to say this: Fassbender has probably the most beautifully small, tapered, elongated male waistline since Montgomery Clift broke Olivia de Havilland's heart in his tailored suits in *The Heiress* (1949).

"I'm a friend of your mother's," Conor explains, in a low, light Irish accent. "You dance like a black," he says, in the same careful, low tone. Arnold cuts to Mia looking confused. "It's a compliment," Conor tells her, and Arnold frames Fassbender so that the light from the kitchen window falls into the two Venus dimples in the small of his back.

He makes coffee, and Arnold shows Mia starting to let herself notice how Conor is putting his body on display for her; she even shows us a shot from Mia's point of view that mimics the girl looking him up and down. Conor knows what he's doing. He's giving Mia a look at himself, and Fassbender is doing the same thing for the camera in the smart, near-comic way that Jessica Lange let us look at her body in *King Kong* (1976).

Fassbender's blue jeans seem to move up and down his hips in the various shots as if he were doing some kind of kitchen sink burlesque act. The camera loves him. Conor leaves, finally, and Mia watches him walk up the stairs. It only lasts a minute or two, this scene, but Fassbender walks into that kitchen an actor and he walks out of it a star.

Fish Tank is a flawed movie because it sets up Fassbender's Conor as deeply appealing and compassionate and then tries to shoehorn him into an uncaring, near-villainous role by the end. Arnold shot the film chronologically and she only showed parts of the script to her actors as they went along; this was a bad idea, particularly for Fassbender. He's under a disadvantage because he's played the character one way throughout and then he has to try to reveal sinister motives and feelings that he hasn't been able to prepare us for.

Fassbender himself credits his first break to François Ozon, who gave him a prominent role as an artist in *Angel* (2007), but that's a disaster where he has to play most of his scenes opposite Romola Garai, and she's busy giving a thoroughly miscalculated comic performance. Fassbender played leading man to a baby cub in *A Bear Named Winnie* (2004), and he had a minute or so dancing in the TV movie *Wedding Belles* (2007) that rivaled the kitchen scene in *Fish Tank* for sheer "the camera loves every move I make!" showing off.

Fassbender played in four movies in 2011, and it was clear in all four of them that he was in charge. He is Irish and German, which makes for an odd combination. To be stereotypical, the Irish side is for the romantic leads, for Mr. Rochester in *Jane Eyre*, brooding in front of the fire and eying Mia Wasikowska's Jane with his limpid, curious blue eyes. Fassbender has a thin mouth, a large forehead, and a strong jaw-line, and he might be non-descript or maybe even cruel-looking if it weren't for those rare eyes of his, which follow fellow actors around unwaveringly and take to the camera like heat-seeking missiles.

Fassbender seems to have an open face, but that's not quite true; he keeps his face "open" until he's ready to showcase what he's feeling and thinking. He is an economical performer with no actorly fuss in his work, and no mannerisms as yet. He knows that he just needs to show up to hold the screen with his eyes and the movements of his graceful, neatly made body.

The methodical German side of him is more in evidence in David Cronenberg's *A Dangerous Method*, where he plays straight man to Viggo Mortensen's Freud and spanks Keira Knightley's power bottom analysand. That commitment to sexual deviation finds full expression in Steve McQueen's *Shame*, which feels like the first real Fassbender vehicle in that it hinges entirely on him and his minute facial reactions and (especially) on the constant workout of his body walking and running through space.

Shame begins with a shot of Fassbender staring up at the ceiling, his body covered by blue sheets. McQueen holds the shot just long enough for us to wonder what Fassbender's Brandon is thinking, but the matching combination of the actor's ice cold blue eyes and the ice cold blue sheets is more than sufficient on a purely visual level to hold our attention. Craft and thought have been put into *Shame*, and it's handsomely shot in widescreen by Sean Bobbitt, but the film would be nothing without Fassbender, who gives himself entirely over to the idea of sex without intimacy as a joyless compulsion.

Fassbender had been naked in movies before, and he's naked in *Shame*, but so is Carey Mulligan as Brandon's needy sister Sissy and Nicole Beharie as Marianne, an office co-worker whom Brandon tries to seriously date. The nudity is not salacious, and it's in the service of a theme that isn't supposed to be sexy, but McQueen's *Shame* is like Mary Harron's *American Psycho* (2000) in that it will probably be enjoyed more for its surface pleasures than for any easily disregarded critique of those pleasures.

Brandon's boss David (James Badge Dale) is a married man who aggressively pursues other women at bars with Brandon but fails because he's so charmlessly pushy and hapless. When David almost instantly succeeds in hooking up with Brandon's sister Sissy, it's very painful for the dandyish Brandon because it somehow confirms his own self-loathing that his sister would sleep with this jerky, lowbrow guy.

But this is complicated by the most striking moment in Fassbender's performance in *Shame*. He's watching David flirt with Sissy. Those icy eyes turn to his boss and focus for a moment, and it's clear that Brandon sort of likes David, or feels some furtive affection for him, but then his eyes cloud over with barely controlled anger.

Fassbender might be a major new film actor mainly because of how expressive his face is; he can just hold it stock-still and keep his eyes open and every feeling and thought he has is reflected back to us. And his rage comes from a genuinely dangerous place. There are lots of actors who yell at scene partners and try hard to work up anger but it doesn't really land. When Fassbender yells at Mulligan in *Shame*, he's so forceful that you would think she would *stay* yelled at, but the sad thing about Sissy is that she's unreachable.

Shame is a grim movie, and it's persuasive most of the time in its carefully molded way, but the natural reaction is to laugh a bit at its conservative despair and just enjoy the show of Fassbender walking around naked in "sex again!" circles. Whether or not you believe in sex addiction, Fassbender makes a case for it while also making a case for himself as an actor with such natural charisma and authority that he might make anything persuasive.

He played the slave owner Edwin Epps in the brutal and necessary *12 Years a Slave* (2013), where he never softened his commitment to the vileness of his character. He was awkward and self-conscious for the first time in *The Counselor* (2013), surely one of the worst films ever made, and then his face was barely seen in *Frank* (2014), and this seemed to express Fassbender's discomfort with his newfound fame and all the jokes and references to his nude scenes in *Shame*.

The films he has made since then have begun to show some of his limits as a performer. Fassbender was a vocally monotonous *Macbeth* (2015), forcing his voice down too low so that it killed all verbal clarity, but then he was ideal as *Steve Jobs* (2015), playfully pitching his voice higher and handling all the reams of Aaron Sorkin dialogue with aplomb. He was at his sexy, self-loathing, physical best in Terrence Malick's unfairly maligned *Song to Song* (2017), which had been shot around the time of his first exciting emergence as an actor circa 2011. But *The Snowman* (2017) was another embarrassing failure where Fassbender was given the unfortunate character name Harry Hole.

Fassbender is most engaged when he can be a little more than human, coolly sexy and remote, even robotic, like a youthful Terence Stamp. It seems clear that he is a key actor of his age. What he does with that status is still very much an open question.

Ben Whishaw
Diamond in the Rough

There are certain rare actors who give off a sense of touching fragility, as if they are beautiful hothouse flowers that aren't meant to last. Robert Donat was like that, and Margaret Sullavan, and Gérard Philipe in France, and River Phoenix in the early 1990s. Fey, bone-thin, with a resonant speaking voice reminiscent of both Donat and John Gielgud, Ben Whishaw is another of this delicate band of players, these perishable actors who are not like others.

Whishaw is gay, and he was closeted in the press until 2014, when he came out about his marriage to the Australian composer Mark Bradshaw. He had met Bradshaw on the set of Jane Campion's *Bright Star* (2009), where he played the poet John Keats, who died young. Whishaw is a romantic figure with a poet's heart and charge, and in spite of the comparisons I have made there is no one really who sounds like him or moves like him.

Whishaw was born in Bedfordshire, England, in 1980, and his parents separated when he was seven; he has a non-identical twin brother. Very shy, Whishaw started to perform in plays as a teenager. At the age of 15 he garnered attention in an adaptation of Primo Levi's *If This Is a Man* at the Edinburgh Fringe Festival.

He made his film debut as a soldier in *The Trench* (1999), where he puts a hand on another soldier's knee in a friendly way and gets rejected: "Bugger off, you!" the other soldier cries. He appeared in a short film called *Baby* (2000) in which he was a faun-like boy masturbating alone in his room and thinking about men he saw naked in a locker room (he showered naked with them) and a girl in a swimsuit. At one point in *Baby*, some jeering girls hit him with large inflatable penises.

For his first lead film role in the very unpleasant *My Brother Tom* (2001), Whishaw was victimized and shy and naked again, playing an outcast who has been forced to sexually service his father. In that movie he is a freak and a nature boy, and his behavior is truly unpredictable, unlike, say, the self-consciously "unpredictable" mode of Joaquin Phoenix's work from this time.

Whishaw seems to be doing Jerzy Grotowski theater exercises in the private scenes he plays in a forest here (he was studying at the Royal Academy of Dramatic Art during this period and breeding cats to go along with his very cat-like eyes), and when he tries to dance conventionally he has no rhythm, which is charming.

At one point in *My Brother Tom*, when his friend Jessica (Jenna Harrison) touches his face, she stops herself and says their relationship isn't sexy enough for her, that it's too gentle. "Sexy?" Whishaw asks, unable to understand this distinction between love and sexual power dynamics. It was clear here that Whishaw was ideal for old-fashioned romantic material.

At age 23, Whishaw did a notable *Hamlet* for Trevor Nunn at the Old Vic, one of the few occasions when this role was cast with an age-appropriate actor. "I thought I was just going up for a small-ish part, Osric or something," Whishaw told the *Evening Standard*. "But by the end of the first audition I'd picked up that Trevor might be thinking of me as Hamlet. I found that audition kind of grueling and emotionally tough. I felt quite exposed. I phoned a friend and said I didn't think I could do the part if I were offered it. Of course, my friend just said, 'Shut up.'"

When they were rehearsing *Hamlet* and he was also playing some small roles at the National Theatre at night, Whishaw went to Nunn and said he couldn't cope with the strain, but Nunn kept him on track. He reportedly played Hamlet with huge intensity, through lots of tears and sobs and mucus flying everywhere.

"This is the kind of evening of which legends are made, one of those rare first nights that those who were present are never likely to forget," wrote Charles Spencer in the *Telegraph*. "No theatre has boasted a more illustrious line-up of Hamlets than the Old Vic, among them Gielgud, Olivier, Burton, Guinness, Redgrave, O'Toole and Jacobi. Last night, twenty-three-year-old Ben Whishaw spectacularly earned his place in such distinguished company. Whishaw, with his light, tremulous voice, painfully thin body, and the kind of cheekbones that will have adolescent girls swooning in the stalls, presents the most raw and vulnerable Hamlet I have ever seen."

"He has all the gangliness of adolescence and the unbearable pain of a once bright and happy scholar who returns home to find that his family has imploded and nothing makes sense any more," Spencer wrote. "No wonder that this inadequate prince finds it so hard to revenge … he is also the most lovable of Hamlets. During the soliloquies he genuinely seems to be confiding in us, the audience, with a rare, bruised candour that catches the heart. 'Oh that this too too solid flesh would melt' is delivered through tears and snot and I have never heard 'To be or not to be'—during which he contemplates knocking back a bottle of sleeping pills—spoken with such freshness and depth of feeling. You seem to be hearing it for the first time."

Whishaw played Keith Richards in the obscure *Stoned* (2005) and then he got his first real lead role in a prominent picture, *Perfume: The Story of a Murderer* (2006), one of the silliest films ever made, a 147-minute boondoggle where it is said of Whishaw's character, "His phenomenal gift of smell was a gift given to him and him alone!" He was used for his striking looks as an Arthur Rimbaud figure addressing the camera in an American accent in Todd Haynes's *I'm Not There* (2007), and then he was stripped naked and abused again in the TV series *Criminal Justice* (2008).

In the misbegotten 2008 film of *Brideshead Revisited*, Whishaw was the victim of both society and the clarified script, where his Sebastian is made to give Charles (Matthew Goode) a kiss that gets rejected. Fine as he is here, Whishaw did not erase any memories of Anthony Andrews's stubborn, erotic, decadent drunkenness in the 1981 British TV miniseries version of this material.

He was well cast as Keats in *Bright Star*, bringing his full romanticism to the reading of the poetry and offering the camera the lovely "catch me if you can" look that had made the career of Gérard Philipe. Whishaw was well cast again as Ariel in a Julie Taymor film of *The Tempest* (2010), but that picture made him too much of a special effect.

Whishaw played on the New York stage in 2010 in *The Pride*, where he had some electric scenes with Hugh Dancy, who looked rather substantial and butch next to Whishaw's physical frailty. It was at this point that his press got awkward. Whishaw was asked if it was difficult to play a gay role in *The Pride* when a journalist just assumed that he was heterosexual, and this question was later deleted from the online version of the interview.

Whishaw did a lyrical *Richard II* for PBS in 2012, playing it like a Gielgud for the 21st Century, feline and discriminating in golden robes, painfully aware, stripped naked emotionally, making us feel, in a shivery way, that even some of Shakespeare's highest flights of poetry cannot comfort Richard one bit as he loses his crown and kingdom.

And yet Whishaw does full justice to the poetry, too, and his voice is every bit as beautifully resonant and expressive as Gielgud's was in this role. He steers clear of the aesthetic snobbery and mournful self-pity of Gielgud's interpretation of this inadequate king and emphasizes a more modern helpless and weak and ruined quality, making Richard like a beloved child star brought low in adulthood.

Whishaw played the unkempt, tactless Freddie Lyon in the TV series *The Hour* (2011–12), an attempt at a British *Mad Men* that doesn't show him off to best advantage. He is unflatteringly photographed in *The Hour* and made to bemoan his "unmemorable" face, but surely Whishaw's face couldn't be more distinctive, with those cheekbones and cat eyes and saturated-red lips and that low hairline to the unruly mop of abundant jet-black hair on his head.

He played the nerdy/cute Q in the James Bond film *Skyfall* (2012), where he sometimes seems to be flirting with Daniel Craig's Bond, and then he did the short film *Beat* (2013), a key piece of Whishaw-ephemera that consists only of him moving uninhibitedly and instinctually down streets as eccentrically as possible; he begins this journey in movement with some perplexity and then ends it in weird euphoria after a guy beats him.

On stage in London in 2013, Whishaw played the psychotic Baby in *Mojo*, and photographs show that he was moving around in that production just as strangely and originally as he did in *Beat*. Whishaw was the voice of a bear in the film *Paddington* (2014), another assignment that exactly suited his special sensibility.

At this point Whishaw was finally out of the closet, and so he felt emboldened to do a very erotic gay sex scene in the first episode of the series *London Spy* (2015). Whishaw plays Danny, an aging, romantic club kid who meets the handsome and mysterious Alex (Edward Holcroft) and sets about courting him.

They go to a beach, and Whishaw does charming physical business, pinwheeling and jumping from one riser to another as Danny says, "Not that I'm presuming you're seduced by me … that's a … process ongoing." When they make love, the willowy Danny tops the substantial and muscular Edward, a scene that goes against sexual expectation in an unusual and stirring way.

Poetic vulnerability is Ben Whishaw's strong suit as he addresses the camera for the mini-series *Queers*.

Whishaw is so important because he is a fully contemporary and new sort of figure as an out gay actor. He has had better opportunities on stage and on TV than in movies, but as a British performer that has often been a tradition, as it certainly was for Vanessa Redgrave and for Laurence Olivier later in life. In feature films the same year as *London Spy*, which depends on him, Whishaw got only small and thankless roles in *Suffragette* and *The Danish Girl*.

Whishaw is at his best when he is a little more assertive and prickly as well as poetic and romantic. Though he was miscast when he played John Proctor in *The Crucible* on Broadway in 2016, especially in moments where he had to physically dominate women, Whishaw dug deep into himself to hurl out a grievous and wounded last scene with his mucus flying everywhere, which he sweetly and determinedly tried to keep off his fellow actors while acting the hell out of his role at the same time. In his courtesy and gentleness, Whishaw has the basis for bringing many fresh sorts of moods and men to the stage and the camera, and of course that's what the camera is greedy for.

Whishaw excelled in the Stephen Frears series *A Very English Scandal* (2018) as the emotionally unstable former lover of nasty British politician Jeremy Thorpe (Hugh Grant), and he was often very funny here, especially when his character was being a little ditzy. That same year, he played Brutus in a stage production of *Julius Caesar*, and so his range keeps expanding. No other modern-day acting career is quite as pleasurable or as unexpected as this one.

Jane Fonda
The Search

Bree Daniels, the self-destructive call girl played by Jane Fonda in *Klute* (1971), is a talented but thwarted actress. Bree has channeled her talent into performative-based prostitution, which she finds exciting in the moment but then deadening. After servicing one client and wielding her sexual power over him as much as possible, Bree sits alone in her apartment smoking a joint and suddenly finds herself singing a familiar church hymn. Her sense of guilt numbs her, and her deepest hope is to be "faceless and bodiless ... and be left alone." She seems to be on the road to suicide.

You cannot discuss Bree Daniels without discussing Jane Fonda, for *Klute* is an actress's movie (it is also the movie of a cinematographer, Gordon Willis, and a composer, Michael Small, both of whom do memorably atmospheric work). At a 2005 signing for her autobiography *My Life So Far,* I asked Fonda what she thought happened to Bree after *Klute* ended. "Oh," she said, hesitating dramatically. "That's a tough question." She paused for a moment. "I don't know what happens to her, but I know that she gives up hooking, I know that," she insisted.

The daughter of Henry Fonda, a gentle man on screen but a rigid and un-giving patriarch off screen, Fonda spent her life trying to get his attention even long after he was dead. When Fonda was 12, her mother Frances committed suicide by cutting her own throat, and this suicide bedeviled and frightened and drove Fonda into ceaseless activity. As an actress in *Klute*, she went right to the source of the demons that killed her mother. Fonda's performance in *Klute* is a kind of exorcism, and every scene is filled with extreme emotional danger for her.

In her early years as an actress throughout the 1960s, Fonda appeared in a series of films that highlighted and sometimes degraded her nervy sexuality. She was nubile, sometimes opaquely cerebral, and often very uninhibitedly horny on screen, and this horniness is something that emanates from her as both something genuine of her own and something offered up to men.

In essence, Fonda had the worst of both worlds as a young performer: tame sex comedies in the Doris Day mold (*Sunday in New York, Any Wednes-*

day) and some barren French films typified by the voyeuristic movies she made with her first husband Roger Vadim. She is busy, broad, and insecure in *Cat Ballou* (1965), and in Otto Preminger's *Hurry Sundown* (1967) she is eclipsed by Faye Dunaway, who owns her own neurotic emotions in a way that makes Fonda seem skittish, blocked, and a little trite by comparison.

Fonda is committed to acting and to trying to act well in these early films, like a student who does lots of extra credit for class, but her effort is too visible. She showed unmistakable promise and glimpses of a disturbing sort of emotional turmoil, but the quality of her work fluctuated erratically in these 1960s movies, often from scene to scene. Fonda is clearly a follower of the Lee Strasberg version of the Method in that she always rushes right for the most colorful emotional breakdowns within scenes rather than exploring more ordinary and calmer registers of feeling, which is partly why she is never really funny in any of the many comedies she made.

Fonda is more assured but still slightly too intense by the time of the slick comedy *Barefoot in the Park* (1967) and the shag-carpet sci-fi sex romp *Barbarella* (1968), where she is very engaged and aware but somehow lacking in dimension, as if defining herself solely through her own sexual appeal and needs had closed off other areas to her. Her blithely perky Barbarella is an odd creation, nervous and present yet also somehow absent and hidden.

In her memoir, Fonda obsessively insists that her whole life has been spent in trying to please various men. She had a Zelig-like ability to morph into what was most acceptable to those around her; most actors do. But Fonda's mutability was so extreme as to be comic, hellish. She played Daddy's girl, sex kitten, political radical, bland liberal, exercise queen, Southern trophy wife, Christian social worker, and finally earnest blogger and geriatric sex symbol.

But most of those Fonda personas will fade. Bree, looking over all these disparate women, would simply snarl at her creator, "Fuck it." Underneath Fonda's increasingly desperate searches for meaning lies the profound, exhilarating negativity of her two best performances: her hardened loser Gloria, a prospective actress trapped in a 1930s dance marathon in *They Shoot Horses, Don't They?* (1969), and Bree in *Klute*.

Fonda's Gloria is the sort of person you move across the room to get away from, or like someone on the street spewing random venom. She is obsessed with protecting herself, staying tough, knowing the score, and she's finally convinced, just like Bree is, that Central Casting has everything rigged before you even show up. Gloria is a great part, but Fonda has to advance into very frightening and layered psychic territories to play it full out, and she was ready for this rebellion and this impressively bleak rebuke to American lies and hypocrisies.

"This was the first time in my life as an actor that I was working on a

The nether reaches of exhaustion and nihilism are explored by Jane Fonda in *They Shoot Horses, Don't They?*

film about larger societal issues, and instead of my professional work feeling peripheral to my life, it felt relevant," Fonda wrote in her memoir. Her Lee Strasberg training had prepared her for a challenge like this, and Fonda did everything she could to make sure that she was living this role rather than only or just acting it, and this was a sign of the times. *They Shoot Horses, Don't They?* is a harbinger of all the 1970s movies to come with anti-heroes and anti-heroines who are swallowed whole by a corrupt system, which is represented in this particular picture by Gig Young's odious emcee.

It could be said that the part of Gloria is playing Fonda rather than the other way around, and that was another harbinger for the triumph of Strasberg's version of the Method all through the 1970s. Fonda takes full advantage of the lowness of her speaking voice for the first time in *They Shoot Horses, Don't They?*, and the emotional and physical torture of the dance marathon itself melts all of her tensions and inhibitions so that she can inhabit woozy, far-out emotional states without any sense of push or strain.

When the formerly armored Gloria is reduced to tears over a torn pair of nylons, the wound Fonda inflicts on the audience goes deep. Gloria advances steadily towards death, but she needs Michael Sarrazin's blankly decent dance partner to shoot her and put her out of her misery. Fonda had trouble playing this last scene at first, but she finally reached the distant and stripped-down plateau where she needed to be. Fonda's Gloria is one of the major film performances of this time, but with Bree Daniels she went even further into exploratory destruction and self-destruction.

Fonda did research for *Klute* and met with some call girls and madams in New York, and she felt that none of the pimps took notice of her. Panicked, she phoned her director Alan J. Pakula and told him to re-cast the role of Bree with Faye Dunaway, but he calmed her down and she started to very seriously meld with Bree, who was very much her own creation. (In the film's credits and some other sources, Fonda's character is listed as Bree Daniel, but in the film itself and sources like the *New York Times* she is Bree Daniels—perhaps Fonda went for the plural because she, like Bree, contains multitudes.)

During the shooting of *They Shoot Horses, Don't They?* and *Klute*, Fonda stayed at the studios where they were shooting because she didn't want to break her identification with her roles. When crewmembers on *Klute* hung an American flag on the door of Bree's apartment, which was meant to impugn her patriotism, Fonda refused to be intimidated. Her attitude, which is also Bree's attitude, was "Fuck you."

Marlon Brando is still lauded in some quarters for his confessional, partly improvised performance in *Last Tango in Paris* (1973), and some even see it as a pinnacle of the actor's art. Fonda in *Klute* goes just as far as Brando in *Last Tango*, but her own performance is more controlled and less indulgent.

Fonda is putting out her own sexual and personal insecurities on film in *Klute*, especially in her improvised therapy session scenes, but she is using Bree as her conduit, whereas Brando blatantly and verbally uses his own history to inform his character. Not many can remember the name of Brando's character at the end of *Last Tango* (it's Paul). No one who has seen *Klute* can forget Bree Daniels, who is first heard speaking in a very low, taunting voice on a recording made by one of her clients, a killer who stalks her throughout the film.

Fonda wrote in her autobiography about the metamorphosis of her speaking voice. In her 1960s films, it was finishing school thick but high and somehow disembodied; by the time of *Klute* it was rich and throaty. She was actively bulimic for most of her adult life, and all that vomiting is bound to affect the throat, among other things, eventually. (In one of her memoir's few daring moments, Fonda admits that the act of purging is "somewhat orgasmic.") Whatever the cause, Fonda's voice in *Klute* signals that this is a whole different kind of performance we're about to witness: dark, moody, filled with rage and gallows humor.

We first see Bree in a line-up of models at an audition. The camera pans past the girls and Bree is asked to show her hands. She does so, and when the casting directors pass her by, we can see the anger in Bree's face as it reflects outwards at the world around her, which she'd like to attack and destroy, and then inwards, where she can attack herself to her heart's content. After this fresh humiliation, she stops by a payphone to get a client, a commuter, and with this client she'll attempt to get her own back.

In the commuter's hotel room, Bree strikes a powerfully sexual pose on a couch, her legs crossed to show off the slit in her skirt; this whole scene has an uncomfortable cinéma vérité feel to it. "We could have a good time for $50," Bree says, nodding her head, her voice challenging and very husky. "If you wanted something extra it would be a little more."

After bringing up business like this, she leans in and bites the cloth of the client's shirt, and this is meant to be "sexy," but all we feel is her rage. When he whispers to her his special request, she laughs and purrs, "Oh, that's so exciting!" And then she says, "But it's going to cost you more," with the tone of her voice barely changed. We see both her mastery of men and her deep contempt for them.

Then comes the famous moment: "Oh, my angel!" she cries as the john wimpily humps her (we never learn what his special request was). Bree moans and takes a quick peek at her watch as she keeps on moaning, and there's no real break in the action. If Fonda had wanted to get a bigger laugh, she would have made the movement of looking at her watch more staccato. Instead, she takes the riskier, more realistic route, showing that you can have two disparate things going on at the same time without switching from one to the other. Again, she wasn't playing this part, she was living it. "In retrospect I see parallels between myself and Bree, a woman who felt safer hooking than facing true intimacy," Fonda wrote in her autobiography.

Bree walks home with yellow flowers, somewhat satisfied and validated as an actress, as an artist, which she is. She lives next to the (William F.?) Buckley Funeral Home, and we are allowed to drink in the grittiness of the early 1970s New York streets and the clutter of her urban apartment. Fonda improvised the hymn that Bree sings as she smokes her pot, a key part of her character that Pakula, to his credit, left in.

When private detective Klute (Donald Sutherland) knocks on her door, Bree immediately reacts defensively, just as Fonda's Gloria does for most of *They Shoot Horses, Don't They?* In the next scene, she has to put up with another man who might help her career, a fool who doesn't listen to her. Bree looks at this man with vulnerable longing, smiles at him, and then drops the mask completely, puffing out her lower lip in colossal anger at her own neediness.

Klute stays with Bree as she comes down from a drug high, and he begins to get through to her, to love her, and she starts to love him. But Bree won't have it. In her next two therapy scenes, she talks about her love for Klute and how all her instincts tell her to destroy the relationship. She can't relax and longs for the comfort of being numb again.

Fonda uses her hands very expressively in these therapy scenes, and when the second one ends, her hands cover the lower half of her face as she stares, quite palpably, into an abyss: nullity, death. Fonda is looking at these things as an artist, and showing them to us directly, and Small's saxophone love theme cannot ameliorate the dread Fonda has caught. Bree may give up hooking, as Fonda suggested, but this won't solve her problems.

Fonda won a best actress Oscar for *Klute* and then spent several years working to end the war in Vietnam, stridently, notoriously, blunderingly, bravely. For many people still, Fonda will never be anything more than the treasonous "Hanoi Jane," the woman who foolishly sat down on a North Vietnam aircraft carrier in the early 1970s as if she were about to shoot down American planes. Fonda apologized for that misjudgment for the rest of her life, but it was no use. Her always-blatant sexual attractiveness made her an irresistible scapegoat and target for Vietnam veterans who needed to place blame somewhere other than the Nixon administration.

She made some adventurous film choices after her Oscar win for Bree: *Tout va bien* (1972) for Jean-Luc Godard and a version of *A Doll's House* (1973) for Joseph Losey, but she seems very distracted and angry in the Godard film, which she felt she was forced into, and her Nora in *A Doll's House* is a strange mixture of Old Hollywood presentation, debutante pluck, and Actors Studio prop handling. There was a gap after that, but in 1977 she returned with two films, *Fun with Dick and Jane*, a commercial comedy, and the prestigious, vague *Julia*, in which she strenuously played Lillian Hellman. In the western *Comes a Horseman* (1978) she looks so habitually worried that when she manages to smile it feels like an event.

Fonda entered a period in the late 1970s and early 1980s where she produced her own movies and always played dim characters getting radicalized. Her consciousness was raised about the Vietnam war in *Coming Home* (1978), the nuclear issue in *The China Syndrome* (1979), workplace sexism in *Nine to Five* (1980), and high finance in the underrated *Rollover* (1981), a financial flop directed by her *Klute* director Alan J. Pakula in which Fonda has a vivid but rather un-likably hard kind of sexual glamour that is far more intriguing than the soft ditziness she had purveyed in some of her other late '70s features.

Rollover ended her run of successes after she secured an Oscar for her father with the very sentimental *On Golden Pond* (1981), and the results on screen in this period for Fonda suggest that her mind was on things other than acting. She had seemed like a major emerging actress for a brief period from 1969 to 1971, but her work after *Klute* was often tense, closed-off, and anxious. Her father Henry was noted for his stark, plain, unadorned performances, clean and sharp as a knife or a flame in his best films like *You Only Live Once* (1937) and *The Wrong Man* (1957). The hyper-conscious Fonda never had his kind of assurance, but that's partly what her best work is about.

Fonda was famed in the 1980s for her tireless aerobics workout videos, which usually lasted an hour but seemed exhausting after only five minutes.

She won an Emmy for *The Dollmaker* (1984) on TV, a performance of some serenity and tact within the body of her work, and she picked up one more Oscar nomination for her campy has-been actress in *The Morning After* (1986), but this was small beer after Bree. Dissatisfied, eternally restless, she retired from acting in 1990 and didn't act again until after her divorce from media mogul Ted Turner, whom she later said needed a babysitter more than a wife.

After she published her memoir in 2005, Fonda fitfully returned to performing in a series of poor comedies, and her nerves had gotten worse with the years. In her seventies and beyond, Fonda still insisted on her peacock sexuality and on displaying herself, going in for lots of judicious plastic surgery to look as smashing as ever. The results were impressive, in a way, but also unsettling. (Random insightful Facebook comment: "She's had everything lifted except her self-esteem.") As always, Fonda knew how to draw attention to herself and would do just about anything to keep it.

She appeared on Broadway in 2009 in a very modest vehicle called *33 Variations,* she was cruelly lit as an aged actress in Paolo Sorrentino's *Youth* (2015), where she gamely spewed some crude dialogue, and she was reunited with Robert Redford for the mild *Our Souls at Night* (2017). Her most characteristic latter-day effort was her own website and blog, www.janefonda.com, where she over-shared in classic Jane Fonda style, compulsively taking photos at parties and events and dinners and family gatherings while ceaselessly and gamely engaging with her commenters, even the mean-spirited ones.

For all the tacit bragging about her lifestyle and its fullness, the effect of Fonda's blog was one of emptiness, of searching, of fear of death and meaninglessness. The blog was her final engaging with her time, and it says just as much about Fonda as Bree did. Fonda's life was often high comedy. Bree Daniels is high tragedy. It is Bree who haunts us.

Faye Dunaway
Touched to the Quick

Towards the end of Emir Kusturica's eccentric *Arizona Dream* (1992), Faye Dunaway aces an extraordinarily difficult scene that was cut when the movie had its brief release in America. She plays Elaine Stalker, a flighty, demanding, childlike middle-aged woman who dreams about flying and who wants to go to Papua New Guinea. Elaine has been having an affair with the much younger Axel (Johnny Depp), and she feels neglected.

Axel drives up to her house and sees a blindfolded Elaine whacking a large hanging bag with a stick; she needs something like this to *do*, somewhere to put all her outsized energy, and the volatile Dunaway intimately understands this need. When Axel tries to talk to Elaine, she puts up a defense against him because her pride has been wounded, and so she tells him to go but she wants him to stay. At a tremulous height of emotion, Dunaway physically dramatizes this furious "Go!" and "Stay!" push-and-pull in a way that builds and builds the scene higher and higher, like a house of cards.

Most actors are blocked and stymied by tension and nerves, but these things are the very wellspring of Dunaway's creativity. She personalizes all of Elaine's fears and insecurities in this big tense confrontation with Axel in a very Actors Studio kind of way, helplessly exposing herself and making much out of it and dragging Depp right up with her (part of the thrill of this scene is how stimulated Depp is by Dunaway and how he is clearly working very hard to match her intensity, in a way that matches up with what his character is trying to do).

Elaine has mental problems and she is supposed to take medication for them, and she is off her meds, and Dunaway locates all kinds of unusual states of mind here having to do with a sort of revved-up exhaustion. Elaine's birthday is imminent, and she is terrified of losing her attractiveness and losing the young and cute Axel. She hurls her fear in his face, she tests him, she forces him, nearly, to reject her so that he won't leave her. "I want you to go!" she tells him on her front porch and then immediately moves in for a passionate kiss. Go! Stay! It is in that dramatic tension between "Go!" and "Stay!" that Dunaway operates best, and this can be comic, as it is deliberately in

Network (1976) and not as deliberately in *Mommie Dearest* (1981), the film where she notoriously went too far.

"Nothing is going to be OK!" Elaine tells Axel in *Arizona Dream*, and in that moment nothing can convince her otherwise. "You think I'm old, don't you?" she asks him, after he has kissed her and almost succeeded in allaying her enormous anxiety. Is he ashamed of her? She doesn't want his pity! Axel, she says, should be with someone sweet and young and beautiful like himself. As tyrannical as Elaine can be (she is sometimes a wicked stepmother figure here), there is something sweet about her, about the way she smiles sometimes in her furtive, shy way.

Elaine might, or might not, have killed her late husband Mr. Stalker. The film doesn't judge Elaine. It just sets up a canvas for Dunaway to create on, and she goes all-out and all over the place, as only she can. And she's operatic in this confrontation with Depp, with its visual hint of Blanche DuBois thrown on the bed by Stanley Kowalski, and cleansingly honest, and deeply touching. Finally Axel and Elaine are smacking each other and then they are down on the floor and she is crying and he is cradling her, and they have worked things out momentarily.

Dunaway's distinctive talent has always been based on how quickly she can go to extremes, leaving other players in the dust. Continually looking daggers with her basilisk eyes, pledged to old-fashioned glamour, clothes, and hairstyles, she was a fragile and neurotic figure for the 1970s, but so insistent about her own fragility that she almost seemed to use it as a weapon, as Elaine does with Axel in *Arizona Dream*. Born in rural Florida in 1941, Dunaway was moved around a lot as a kid and she felt abandoned when her father left their family. She went to New York and started working in the theater, went into analysis, and had a brief affair with comedian Lenny Bruce.

Her breakout role on stage was *Hogan's Goat* in 1965, and from there she was cast in her first films, Otto Preminger's *Hurry Sundown* (1967), *The Happening* (1967), and the movie that made her a big movie star, *Bonnie and Clyde* (1967), where her 1930s look with beret set off a fashion trend and made her an icon of the 1960s. Her Bonnie is capricious and vital, and the first sign of Dunaway's impatience, her edginess, her exciting unease. She had a hungry quality that seemed sexy (hungry for what?), but director Arthur Penn said that this was because Dunaway fasted to get as thin as she wanted to be and "this contributed to a sizable degree of irritability."

In *Bonnie and Clyde* she was every small town girl who wanted to live it up, however briefly; think of the sexy and loving way she looks at Clyde (Warren Beatty) right before they are both shot up by gunfire. Dunaway became known for her temperament, her drive, her ambition, and underneath there was loneliness and insecurity, which animated her work and gave it force, heart, and color. She made being jittery and paranoid into an acting style and even a tacit moral viewpoint, and this exactly suited the times she was living and working in.

Dunaway was overdressed and "sensual" playing chess with Steve McQueen in *The Thomas Crown Affair* (1968), like a little girl playing in her mama's clothes and hoping to be pleasing, but that was not her dominant mode in this period. She is so tightly wound on screen and seemingly hunted that sometimes Dunaway radically detaches from the words she is saying and starts to run ahead of them, or behind them, or against them, like a jazz musician, taking the oddest pauses.

This racing, disconnected quality could be made to suggest mental breakdown, as it does in Jerry Schatzberg's *Puzzle of a Downfall Child* (1970), where Dunaway gives one of the all-time most memorable crazy lady performances as Lou Andreas Sand, a fashion model who spins such intricate webs of self-deception that finally she is one of those girls who calls you in the middle of the night to tell you about an Anna May Wong movie she's watching and how she hasn't slept, really, in a week. Dunaway's imagination is so fertile that she excels most in parts where there is no distinction between fantasy and reality, where there is no limit on desire or self-dramatization.

In Arthur Penn's *Little Big Man* (1970), Dunaway is a horny preacher's wife who finally leaves her faith to join a brothel, only to find that so much

Faye Dunaway as the mentally unstable fashion model Lou Andreas Sand in *Puzzle of a Downfall Child*.

sex is monotonous; she's very funny here because she makes dissatisfaction seem like a pandemic condition that crosses many lines and barriers.

She did some commercial films like *The Three Musketeers* (1973) and *The Towering Inferno* (1974), for she did care deeply about maintaining her star status. In credits like that, Dunaway was like Lou Andreas Sand coming up with a "look," as in her entrance in a monocle in *Voyage of the Damned* (1976), where she asks, "Somewhat overdressed, perhaps?" or the drippy/morbid hair for her photographer in *Three Days of the Condor* (1975). But she was raring to go when another classic part came her way.

As the haughty Evelyn Mulwray in *Chinatown* (1974), Dunaway chooses to speak like Grace Kelly enduring a perpetual anxiety attack (listen to the way she hesitates over the word "father") and presents a carefully made-up and lacquered surface (thick marcelled hair, penciled brows) that finally begins to scream this woman's vulnerability, her deeply violated inner life, her delicate, smashable victimhood.

Yet Evelyn doesn't go down without a fight. She is clearly trying her best to get away from her evil father (John Huston) and get her daughter by him away from his influence; she is a woman of mystery who has secrets so awful that they need to be kept, sometimes, even from herself. Dunaway charts the way Evelyn dissociates herself from social interactions and makes her own habitual unease into Evelyn's own heroic struggle with the simplest tasks of life. For someone this damaged, opening and shutting a door is a problem, and Dunaway clearly understands that kind of dysfunction. Her own mannered, pre-occupied, actressy quality is ideal for this woman who is always putting on an act to hide from others.

Dunaway's Evelyn in *Chinatown* is more than a lady in distress. She is a beautiful artificial flower hauntingly marked to be tossed in the mud and stepped on, the "flawed" iris of one of her eyes a portent of what a bullet will eventually do. Dunaway clashed on the set with director Roman Polanski, but he appreciated the genteel manner of her work and the core of her interpretation. At the end of one scene, Dunaway touched her throat in a helpless and conventionally feminine way, and Polanski told her that when she made that gesture she reminded him of his mother, a woman who had died in the Holocaust.

Dunaway reached the height of her career with her Diana Christensen in *Network*, winning the Oscar for best actress as this comically ruthless, lethal TV executive with demonic, avid, "gimme" eyes, a heartless woman who is nearly touchingly aware of her own heartlessness. Dunaway breathlessly builds Diana's arias of chilly, sociopathic, orgasmic excitement about ratings and shares and what's next in the line-up. She goes as far as possible with these speeches, so far that she finally begins to suggest a whole new breed of human without moral compass but addicted to sensation, riding waves into instant little gratification grooves.

Dunaway gets through the heightened Paddy Chayefsky dialogue fast in *Network*, nearly throwing it away as she walks through offices with ladylike daintiness, seemingly no bra or panties under her tight clothes, an advertisement for sex with no sex underneath, a trap. This was an unsettling, iconic, suggestive performance, all of a piece.

She played on TV with Bette Davis in *The Disappearance of Aimee* (1976), raising Davis's ire off screen when she was late to the set and not entirely focused on her role, but Dunaway's appetite was so large in this period that she could devour a juicy part like 1920s religious evangelist Aimee Semple McPherson as if it were nothing more than a tasty side dish. She did a nasty-sexy thriller called *Eyes of Laura Mars* (1978), playing a fashion photographer who sees visions of murder. And then Dunaway made the mistake of playing Joan Crawford in *Mommie Dearest* with a level of detail and empathetic involvement that the movie cannot control or deal with.

Director Frank Perry seems cowed and agog at how far she's going with her visually bold Crawford impersonation in *Mommie Dearest*, and so he leaves Dunaway stranded for long scenes that play out like dailies that need some serious editorial finessing and some retakes to tone down her overdone facial and vocal pyrotechnics. She goes big in the big scenes (far too big in the scene where Joan strangles her adopted daughter Christina), but the real problem here is that she goes big on campy flourishes in the small, ordinary, cuttable moments, too.

Always lost in her own world on screen, Dunaway allowed herself to get lost in Crawford-land, uninhibitedly riffing on the stiffness and grotesquerie of the middle and late Crawford image. It was probably inevitable that the cerebral Dunaway would get caught in that unthinking camp Crawford trap as she let herself be possessed by the demon of Joan's perfectionism and careerism. "Let's face it, Faye went bananas," said a producer of the film. "She *became* Joan Crawford."

On one level, Dunaway is doing diligent and psychologically probing work in *Mommie Dearest*, tirelessly searching out specific motivation for all of Crawford's bad behavior, but the detached and aimless quality of the film itself limits and fragments her efforts, and leaves her open to ridicule. There are several silent close-ups of Dunaway's Joan that are very loaded with some totally private psychic disturbance that does not communicate anything specific to the camera, and this is very Strasberg-like Method work where Dunaway's own process shuts us out. She is working in a void with the spirit of Crawford haunting and driving her on, and so she screeches into luridly staring, cross-eyed Halloween fright-ville in the infamous Kabuki night raid scenes where Joan is on a rampage that cannot be stopped, appeased or tidily explained.

In embracing the feral drag "look" of Crawford, with the shoulder pads and thick eyebrows and everything else, and also her artifice as an actress and as a person, Dunaway treads a dangerous line where she sometimes seems to be playing that artifice as an actress and sometimes seems to be buying into it herself and letting it taint her work. Audiences laughed at the film, and at Dunaway, who was not prepared for what she had wrought.

She sliced the ham thick on TV in 1981 as Evita Peron, emphatically singing her lines, and sliced it even thicker for *Supergirl* (1984) as a camp villainous. Dunaway then retreated to England for a few years and did some sub-par projects before returning to form with her down-and-out, sexily louche lady boozehound in *Barfly* (1987), where she nicely smoothes out her mannerisms. After *Arizona Dream* made an impact at Cannes but didn't get the attention it deserved when it was cut for limited release, she tried a TV sitcom and worked steadily and without much reward throughout the 1990s and afterward.

Dunaway was game for the slapstick humor of something like *Dunston Checks In* (1996), where she lands backwards into a large pink cake, and she was most encouraged when she could try an accent and a different way of behaving in credits like *The Twilight of the Golds* (1996), where she was a Jewish mother, or *Gia* (1998), where she supported Angelina Jolie in a maternal fashion, or when she played real people like Margaret Sanger on TV or an aged Mae West in *The Calling* (2002). She could seem unduly affected in this period, putting hammy quotation marks around her every line, yet she still cut a formidable figure as a matriarch in James Gray's *The Yards* (2000). After that her films and material deteriorated badly, and her addiction to plastic surgery, to a "new look," increased.

Dunaway never gave less than her best to even the most lackluster of her latter-day projects. She brings a knowing camp style to her role in *Anonymous Rex* (2004) and a "look" that suggests Mother Goddamn in *The Shanghai Gesture*. In the Gothic thriller *Jennifer's Shadow* (2004), Dunaway treats us to very old-fashioned glamour, with elaborate hair and black clothes and fire engine red lipstick, and she does get beautifully backlit in her last scene. She begins to seem heroic in something like *Ghosts Never Sleep* (2005), where she has a whole characterization worked out for a film that is so poorly made and edited that her performance keeps getting interrupted and cut on at the exact wrong moments.

Few people have subjected themselves to late Dunaway credits like the unspeakable *Cougar Club* (2007), and few will remember that Dunaway hosted a reality TV show called *The Starlet* where she was a talent judge. She wanted to stay in the game, and so she had to stoop down and hold her nose for experiences like these as she wandered the lower depths with players like Eric Roberts and Malcolm McDowell. Late-period Dunaway was maybe as self-deceiving and deluded as her Lou Andreas Sand in *Puzzle of a Downfall Child*, but even that level of self-deception has its limits.

For several years Dunaway shot footage for a film of Terrence McNally's play *Master Class*, where she would have played opera diva Maria Callas, but that project was abandoned, and her film career finally halted in 2010 around age 70 with a Daphne Zuniga TV movie, *A Family Thanksgiving*.

She was on Twitter for a bit, fielding questions and exposing her anxieties, and then it was reported that she was signed to write a book about making *Mommie Dearest* to go with her well written 1995 memoir *Looking for Gatsby*, where she judged her own films and work in an insightfully critical fashion. She returned after seven years away for a cameo in a horror film, *The Bye Bye Man* (2017), and then started racking up some more useless credits before getting drawn into another infamous moment: recklessly announcing the wrong best picture winner at the 2016 Oscars.

Many have told stories about Dunaway's high-handed, difficult behavior with crews, assistants, and film festival employees, and most of these stories end with her either throwing something or breaking something; maybe there were meds she should have been taking, but like Elaine Stalker in *Arizona Dream* she felt like being off the hook.

The diva-ish notoriety of her off-screen antics keeps her current while her best screen work remains among the litter of the rest of her many credits. For she was hungry enough to do *Bonnie and Clyde, Little Big Man, Puzzle of a Downfall Child, Chinatown, Network,* the basic core of *Mommie Dearest, Barfly, Arizona Dream,* and *The Yards,* and that's a legacy few actresses of her era can touch.

Ellen Burstyn
The Shadow Self

In 1964, Ellen Burstyn was 32 years old and was working on television under the name Ellen McRae. She appeared in her first two feature films that year, Vincente Minnelli's *Goodbye Charlie* and *For Those Who Think Young*, and in both of those movies she played her stock roles tensely, almost contemptuously, as if she were only following orders under duress. She radiates anxiety in those films, and this did not suit the early 1960s, but it would very much suit the 1970s. And so she had to wait, and wait.

In her third and last feature from the 1960s, *Pit Stop* (1969), her autoworker husband calls her "a good little welder" and says she did a good "ladylike job" on a car, and she looks like she's dying to get her consciousness raised. Burstyn fidgets uncomfortably here, and she's very present, and she can't hide how angry she is. Her anger is very out of place in a hot rod movie like *Pit Stop*.

She was born Edna Rae Gillooly in Detroit, Michigan, and it had taken her a lot of time and trouble to pull herself out of her rough milieu to become Ellen McRae, a pretty girl who looked good and smiled a lot. She knew what it was like to be desperate and one step away from being out on the street, and that showed in her wide, sensitive face.

If you look at her in some of her early TV appearances, she seems uncomfortable, discontented, but still trying hard to please. Her voice was very high, slightly frayed, plaintive. It was only when she attended her first acting class with Lee Strasberg in 1964 that she started to become her final self. Strasberg told her in his class that it was all right to make a mistake, and her people-pleasing ingénue mask cracked and fell away when she heard that. What was underneath it would take time and patience to excavate.

There are not many actors, let alone actresses, who fully come into their own at the age of 40, but that is what happened for Ellen McRae, who took her third husband's last name and began billing herself as Ellen Burstyn in 1970 after appearing full frontally nude (and un-credited) in *Tropic of Cancer*, a graceless film of the Henry Miller novel. It had not been a smooth road for her on any level up to this point, and Burstyn's own mother cruelly told her that she hadn't "done much" with her acting career.

But by 1971 she was ready, and the parts started to come for her (luckily Burstyn would always look and seem younger than her actual age throughout her life). Only years of study with the most demanding acting teacher can possibly account for the performance that first made her name: Lois Farrow in *The Last Picture Show* (1971). Lois is worldly, kind, bored, smart, limited, hopeful, funny, free, boxed-in. In every moment of her work in *The Last Picture Show*, Burstyn presents us with one facet of Lois and then its opposite, and she makes Lois's regret and competitiveness seem deeply attractive.

This was virtuoso acting that heralded the arrival of a major talent, and it was topped the following year by her Sally in *The King of Marvin Gardens* (1972), where Burstyn dove into the deepest end of the behavioral pool and came up with a nerve-scraping portrait of a middle-aged beauty, degraded by years of sexual selling and compromise, whose physical appearance has meant everything to her. When Sally chops off her own hair and burns her make-up products on a beach, it's like watching someone commit suicide right in front of you.

Self-destruction on screen had never been this close to the bone, this personal, this upsetting, or this implicitly feminist. No one around her really notices just how much the over-reaching, managing Sally is deteriorating mentally, and this will have fatal consequences. From Strasberg, Burstyn had learned all about how to be private in public, how to unearth all the demons that live in our psyches. Some noted Strasberg students were never able to fully control their effects, so that their personal demons blurred their work. The miracle of Burstyn's work, and the reason why she played a large part in changing the face of an art form, is that she mastered the technique of shaping the most seemingly uncontrollable emotions.

After the enormous success of *The Exorcist* (1973), which Burstyn holds together with the intensity of her belief in the material, she had a brief period where she could write her own ticket, and she used this opportunity to make two personal films, *Alice Doesn't Live Here Anymore* (1974) and *Resurrection* (1980).

In both of those Burstyn movies, she loses her husband in the opening reel and must learn to stand on her own. In both of them, Burstyn makes sure to include all kinds of realistic notes of impatience, frustration, anger, fear, and doubt, things that Ellen McRae was supposed to smile her way out of. She was nominated for an Oscar five times in this period and won for the gritty *Alice*, for which she chose a young Martin Scorsese as her director.

Burstyn's improvisational scenes with her son (Alfred Lutter) in *Alice* are vividly lived-in, always on the verge of outright bickering but very loving, too. There is an immediacy to everything Burstyn does on screen, a refusal to sand away hard edges, a willingness to let it all hang out in a constructive, tender way.

Her daughter to Art Carney in Paul Mazursky's *Harry and Tonto* (1974) is a bitter woman, a grudge-holder, and Burstyn lets us feel the full sour tang of grudge-holding, of letting feelings fester. In Alain Resnais's arty *Providence* (1977), Burstyn applies some much-needed curt common sense and warmth to her scenes and to the very heightened language by playwright David Mercer, but she could do nothing to prevent her stage hit *Same Time, Next Year* (1978) from seeming like a slick Broadway comedy.

In *Resurrection,* the movie that meant the most to Burstyn, she brought out her own interest in healing and spiritual love, which she sought to connect to sexual love. All during her star period of the 1970s, Burstyn was being stalked and tormented by her schizophrenic ex-husband Neil Burstyn. When he committed suicide in 1978, his family sent her a note that read, "Congratulations, you've won another Oscar, Neil killed himself." As always, she rose above low blows like that.

Burstyn made a feast of the title role in *People Vs. Jean Harris* (1981) for TV, which allowed her to build a multi-faceted character over the course of two-and-a-half hours of trial transcript testimony. A former headmistress accused of shooting her lover, Burstyn's Harris often looks snobbish and disdainful in her pearls and careful hairdo, and she keeps putting on and taking off dark glasses in a diva-ish way.

Though she attempts to play "the good girl" on the stand, Harris seems very insincere until she starts to psychologically unravel, and of course that kind of unraveling is Burstyn's specialty. When Harris is sentenced to prison, Burstyn reacts with incongruous irritation that displays this woman's sense of privilege and superiority, and she fleshes out all of Harris's contradictions.

She worked mainly on television again in the 1980s and '90s and seems to have accepted most parts she was offered in this period. In a rare worthy role, like the uptight British neighbor to spies who unravels in *Pack of Lies* (1987), Burstyn was miscast, quivering with nerves right from the start (repression was never her strong suit). In *When a Man Loves a Woman* (1994) Burstyn was reduced to a bit role, and the parts she was playing on TV steadily worsened.

In the 1990s she played mothers, mother in laws, and more mothers, often with special billing, but with no opportunities to exercise her talent. The lowest points in this period for her on television were probably her ludicrously villainous Nurse Cooder, a martinet who torments poor cute little Fred Savage in *When You Remember Me* (1990), and her therapist who helps Melissa Gilbert "recover" childhood trauma memories in *Shattered Trust: The Shari Karney Story* (1993).

But Burstyn re-emerged as Sara Goldfarb in Darren Aronofsky's *Requiem for a Dream* (2000), where she exposed the annihilating loneliness of so many older women who lived for their families and felt that they had nothing to live for once that duty was done. In this movie, Burstyn once again raised the stakes for what was possible in acting, and she did that by going to the basement of her being and bringing up everything we have been taught to hide: fear and loathing, hate and insecurity, the ruined hopes of a limited, good-natured woman who has been discarded and who lets her need for approval destroy her. Burstyn in *Requiem for a Dream* is a Brighton Beach Queen Lear, a stand-in for millions of wasted and disregarded elderly lives.

By feeling this much and daring to experience the worst, Burstyn worked a catharsis for us and purified us. In the now-famous scene where Sara tries to talk honestly to her son (Jared Leto) about her life and her feelings, Burstyn is so unprotected, so exposed, that we seem to be seeing something more than just a human, worried face. We seem to be seeing the visible core of a soul, and this was only possible because Burstyn had spent a lifetime honing her deepest feelings at the Actors Studio. The drugs that Sara is on allow Burstyn to reach for heightened behavior, so that she sings the word "old" almost like John Gielgud might have in the midst of this woman's great shuddering turmoil.

Because she studied with Lee Strasberg, this height of her art came from a personal place in Burstyn. "We rehearsed it just once, and I was surprised that when I said, 'I'm old,' I felt these tears rise," Burstyn said when I interviewed her in 2017. "And I went, 'Oh, what is that?' And so I decided that I didn't want to explore that except on camera. So I went to Darren and I said, 'I don't want to rehearse this, and I don't want to shoot a master shot and then shoot him {Leto},' which would be the natural way to do it because of the set that's behind him. I said, 'I want you to just shoot me.'"

"Ordinarily a director wouldn't do it because it would mean taking down a background and putting it up again," Burstyn said. "But I only asked him for that one thing in the shooting because I knew there was something there, and I didn't know how I was going to experience it. And so we did it, and it came out like that. And we only did one take, and then we did another because you always do one for protection. But I knew that was it and so did he, and I don't know if we even did one for protection, I don't remember that."

There was a near-miss with this take. "The next day, when I came in, Darren came to my dressing room, my so-called dressing room, and he said, 'We have a problem with that scene,'" Burstyn remembered. "And I said, 'What's the problem?' And he said, 'The focus puller was off, and your nose goes out of focus. I fired him, he's already gone, but I want to re-shoot it.' I said, 'How bad is it?' And he said, 'If we don't get it, it's not so bad that we can't use it.' And I said, 'OK, I'm going to do it, but you have to swear on your life that if we don't get what we got yesterday, that you will use what we did yesterday.' He said, 'I promise.' So we did it again, and it was flat. And he said, 'OK, we use yesterday's.' And that's what's in, and nobody has ever noticed that my nose goes out of focus."

Asked if she used any specific imagery for this scene, Burstyn said, "I don't remember that. I knew there was something alive in me that was right for that scene, and I didn't even know what it was. It had to.... I can't even talk about it! Because I feel it, and I know I can access it, and I don't question it, I let it rip, and that's what happened. I do use images from my own life. Is it ever not helpful to do that? I don't think I've had that experience. I have a lot to call on in my life. First of all, many years worth of experience, and also, I haven't had a quiescent life, so I've got a lot of material in there to work with. I don't think I remember having to go to some other realm than my own."

"Sometimes there are surprises," Burstyn said. "Like that whole scene you're talking about in *Requiem*, that was a surprise to me! I can't tell you where that came from. I had feelings about getting old that I didn't know about. It was a surprise to me. Feelings were coming up that I didn't know I had. And so I wanted to let those feelings out and I knew they were only going to be that real once, because after that it wasn't a surprise."

In *Requiem for a Dream*, Burstyn starts with a "character" voice and certain semi-fluttery mannerisms but then she transcends them in a nearly unaccountable way. Sara is the sort of character (and this is the sort of performance) that is usually relegated to a supporting role if she is seen at all. But this movie puts her at its center, and Burstyn saw her chance. This is maybe the key film performance in modern American cinema, a culmination of certain Method tendencies and also a way forward.

Ellen Burstyn gets a fateful call on the telephone in *Requiem for a Dream*.

Burstyn was excellent in James Gray's *The Yards* (2000), but in the years after that her inventiveness was often spread thin again through overwork. She began using the same ragged vulnerability that had characterized Sara Goldfarb in any number of trivial parts on TV and in an accelerating amount of plain independent films, giving her all to all of them when her considerable all was not necessary. Burstyn was never one to let any opportunity pass to show her soulfulness on screen, and so that constant showing of soul began to feel a bit promiscuous in minor features like *Main Street* (2010) or trash like *The Madam's Family: The Truth About the Canal Street Brothel* (2004) for TV.

As president of the Actors Studio and the most successful female proponent of Strasberg's controversial version of the Method, Burstyn was often a serious figure, but she also had a sense of humor about herself. When she was nominated for an Emmy for a 14-second bit in *Mrs. Harris* (2005), Burstyn responded to the controversy by saying, "I thought it was fabulous. My next ambition is to get nominated for seven seconds, and ultimately I want to be nominated for a picture in which I don't even appear."

In her frank 2006 autobiography *Lessons in Becoming Myself*, Burstyn related all of her early insecurities and embarrassing mistakes, letting it all hang out as she always did on screen. After a number of painful relationships, Burstyn wrote that she had gone 25 years without male companionship. Finally, at age 71, she felt she was ready for a relationship, and though she feared that it was too late for her, she defied the odds yet again by taking on a lover two decades her junior.

She had always been a late-bloomer. At 32, she was awkward, down on herself, an also-ran. At and past 80, Burstyn was a star, sure of herself, radiating control and openness both. She proved that age doesn't need to be a decline only but can also be an ascent.

Gena Rowlands
Love Streams

In her early work on television, and in movies like *The High Cost of Loving* (1958) and *Lonely Are the Brave* (1962), Gena Rowlands has a distinctive, nearly haughty presence, but there is something held back about her work, mainly because of the limited roles she was given to play, like the sexy deaf-mute wife of a cop on the TV show *87th Precinct* (1961–62). There were quirks and little disruptions already in her manner, and they came a bit to the fore in the first film she made with her husband John Cassavetes, *A Child Is Waiting* (1963), where she plays the mother of a handicapped child.

At 33 in *A Child Is Waiting*, Rowlands is young and pretty, a cool blonde, seemingly, but there is something unstable about her, and an animal-like look of questioning in her wide-set eyes. She has one strong scene with Judy Garland where her character explains her situation in life and the strength she needed to stay with her child, but the conventional writing holds her back from fully conveying what she's trying to do.

She is riveting and very beautiful in her recurring role on the nighttime soap opera *Peyton Place* in 1967, but the poor writing and convoluted plotting meant that she was treading water only and reduced to signaling what she might do. Through her twenties and most of her thirties, Rowlands was not allowed to express the fullness of her talent.

That would come at age 38 when she played in Cassavetes's *Faces* (1968) as Jeannie Rapp, a good-time girl entertaining some gentleman friends. Rowlands looks straight into the camera sometimes here, and her Jeannie is fierce and then amused and then impatient, coasting along these feelings as she drinks more and more alcohol. The unusual sideways quality of Rowlands's unmistakable voice comes out for the first time here, the bottom-of-the-glass, one-of-the-boys emphasis she has, with special relish on words like "terrific," which she stretches out, landing hard and joyfully on the second syllable.

Jeannie is 28 but pretends to be 23, and of course Rowlands herself is older than that and pushing 40. "I'm too old to be lovely," Jeannie tells Richard (John Marley). "And I haven't got a heart of gold." Jeannie is a real, faceted person, and always changing before our eyes. Rowlands is very precise with her transitions in *Faces*, and the film desperately needs her precision, for a Cassavetes movie is always threatening to collapse into formlessness. That's the lure of his cinema, and the excitement, and the tedium, sometimes, and the obscurity.

Rowlands's Jeannie lives on the edge: on the edge of boredom, on the edge of despair, on the edge of her own sanity even. So many of her reactions in *Faces* are unexpected, her face sometimes registering a private sort of amusement behind her Veronica Lake curtain of blonde hair.

"You learn how to be feminine," Rowlands says in her third film with Cassavetes, *Minnie and Moskowitz* (1971), where she plays prim Minnie Moore, a watcher of movies on the Late Late Show who complains that she never met a Humphrey Bogart or a Charles Boyer. Rowlands can be very masculine on screen, and Cassavetes allows her to be, watching her carefully and bringing out all her oddities and specialness, even the scary, unaccountable things inside of her.

It's clear in *Minnie and Moskowitz*, when Rowlands has passed 40, that she's a beautiful blonde with the soul of a Bowery bum. She's always pulling faces so that her nose wrinkles and her forehead wrinkles … *everything* about her wrinkles and grimaces, and she loves to mix emotions: toughness and vulnerability together, or anger and goofiness. Her eyes look so widely spaced here that in profile she often works with just one eye, and one eye is enough. A kind of agitated human carnival, low-down but high-handed, Rowlands has everything Cassavetes needs and everything that her earlier Hollywood parts had never needed or welcomed.

In 1974, Rowlands took on her signature role for Cassavetes, or at least her most demanding dare from him: Mabel Longhetti, a housewife and mother on the edge in *A Woman Under the Influence*. This is a film that pushes Rowlands to the limits of sanity, and some in the Cassavetes troupe worried that he was pushing her too far.

Mabel nervously loves too much, feels too much, and has no sense of proportion. A kind of thwarted mad genius adrift in domestic life, smoking Virginia Slims in her baby doll dresses and pink socks, she is an alien presence in her blue-collar milieu, all in pieces that no longer fit. "Tell me what you want me to be," she desperately says to her husband Nick (Peter Falk), a crass guy who loves her madly and maybe has a screw or two loose himself.

The unpredictability of Jeannie in *Faces* has given way in Mabel to a woman whose reactions make no logical sense. She wants people to "loosen up," but she's so loose and so unfettered that she's floating away. Mabel makes weird and embarrassing faces all the time and talks to herself, twitching and grimacing to her own musical score, and Rowlands plays the film out on a limb and then takes a plunge into behavioral chaos.

When Mabel is finally threatened with being committed to an insane asylum, Rowlands's eyes roll up into her head, as if she is erasing herself, or maybe looking up to God for help, Lillian Gish-style. (There is a cross on the wall of the Longhetti home, and Mabel makes a cross in front of her with her fingers when a doctor wants to sedate her.) This is the kind of acting that is so deeply imagined that it makes sense that the others on the set were worried about Rowlands's own sanity. When Mabel cries, "I don't want anything, just let me stay in my house, please!" to Nick, Rowlands hits a very deep level of abjection.

Nick's mother yells that Mabel, who used to be Mabel Mortensen before Nick got her pregnant and married her, is "empty inside," and that's one way of looking at it. It also might be said that Mabel is so exposed and so helplessly aware of things that most people have learned to ignore that her fear and insecurity has both a feminist and an existential validity. Mabel is incapable of social distancing or lying to herself, and she yearns for a utopia where she is a good or better mother to her three children, and also a kind of artist in her backyard, a dancer (she always wants to dance and to get people to dance). You could rightly say that Mabel is oppressed, yet being a wife and mother is one of the few things that grounds her in life at all.

When Mabel comes back from the asylum, she is mortified and painfully demoralized, but just as socially inappropriate as ever. Nick tries to hold her together, but it seems to be no use. "Dad, will you stand up for me?" Mabel asks her father, the line that James Dean made famous in *Rebel Without a Cause* (1955). Mabel is a borderline outcast like Dean is, but she has precious little of his glamour or authority.

Unable to handle the pressures of her life any longer, Mabel tries to cut her wrists, and this lowest possible moment acts as a mysterious catharsis in

In search of a self: Gena Rowlands in *A Woman Under the Influence*.

A Woman Under the Influence, at least momentarily. "You know, I'm really nuts," she tells Nick, wonderingly, after they have put their three children to bed. "I don't even know how this whole thing got started." The trauma of the innocent Mabel Longhetti is seen, miraculously, as a sort of show that has ended, for now.

Cassavetes and Rowlands mortgaged their house to finish *A Woman Under the Influence*, and when no distributor was interested they basically distributed it themselves, taking it to small theaters and college campuses and introducing it. This film won Rowlands an Oscar nomination for best actress, but Ellen Burstyn took that Oscar for *Alice Doesn't Live Here Anymore*, a film that is as explicitly feminist as *Woman* is implicitly so. "That's an Academy Award-winning part," Burstyn said of Rowlands's Mabel years later in a documentary. "Just not *my* award."

The sense of searching in her acting and pushing out into new frontiers is even more pronounced in Rowlands's fifth film with Cassavetes, *Opening Night* (1978). In that movie she is Myrtle Gordon, an alcoholic theater actress of a certain age struggling to find reality in a second-rate play about aging. Myrtle seems to be a Lee Strasberg Method–based mess, following any emotional whim but sometimes sneering at herself in a mirror.

Rowlands's Myrtle is childlike and ruthless and nearly comically self-absorbed. As a young actress her emotions were close to the surface, but now she struggles to find them, and she is willing to do anything to get to that level again. Like Mabel Longhetti, Myrtle Gordon is admirable on one level and a pain in the neck on another. And also like Mabel, Myrtle has lost touch with reality, yet she is aware on a deeper level of human futility in the face of impending death, and that is death for her as an actress. Nick deeply loves Mabel in *A Woman Under the Influence*, but no one loves Myrtle except her public, and she needs to hang on to that love. This is the main reason that Myrtle turns the sad play she is starring in, *The Second Woman*, into an audience-pandering comedy by improvising most of the last act.

Cassavetes isn't much interested in backstory or characterization but in the crisis he is filming in the lives of his people *right now*, so that we have to fill in a considerable number of blanks here. The Cassavetes-Rowlands movies are open-ended and amorphous works that can be interpreted any number of ways, and the sense of reality in them is always shifty. These are pictures that are dependent entirely on Rowlands's emotional intuitiveness, which Cassavetes makes radical demands on.

Upset by the death of a young fan outside the theater one night, Myrtle tries anything to re-engage with the play she's in: retreat from others, desperately people-pleasing improvisation, self-abuse. And somehow the worse she looks the more glamorous Rowlands seems here. This actress Myrtle has an outlet for all her nonsense whereas the housewife Mabel in *A*

Woman Under the Influence does not, and *Opening Night* makes that, at least, very clear.

Cassavetes seems to be on Myrtle's side, but he also details the hell she puts everyone around her through. Like Kim Stanley, the ultimate self-destructive Method actress, Rowlands's Myrtle will do anything to make her acting "real," and that reality finally comes to her, it would seem, through the consumption of an excessive amount of alcohol. This is an extreme view of what it can take to be a great actor, but *Opening Night* is also about what the tyranny of a star in the theater can do.

Rowlands was at her very best in this period in two movies for TV, *A Question of Love* (1978), where she played a lesbian mother fighting to keep custody of her children, and *Strangers: The Story of a Mother and Daughter* (1979), where she went inch-for-inch with the formidable Bette Davis. When her son denounces her in court in *A Question of Love*, Rowlands's animal-like pain is so deeply felt and expressed that it feels like we shouldn't be watching it.

Rowlands brought a new power and held-back simplicity to her scenes with Davis in *Strangers*, letting the older actress star shine more brightly by tactfully counterpunching until the final scene, where she lays out the whole of her character's life with such end-of-the-line grace that she is very moving, even more so than in the pyrotechnics of the Cassavetes films.

Cassavetes created an old-fashioned kind of vehicle for her in *Gloria* (1980), a more commercial film with all the gritty underpinnings of the New York of that period. It's a movie that works in spite of its clumsiness and not because of it, as in other Cassavetes films, and it runs on Rowlands's near-lunatic nerve. As an aging former gun moll who protects a little kid from the mob, Rowlands is so believably tough that we do not question all the tight squeezes she pulls the kid out of.

A kind of wacky blonde Clint Eastwood, Gloria is a little crazy, too, crying, "C'mon, c'mon, ah, I'd love it, c'mon, don't hang back!" when she has nearly gotten away from the men who have been pursuing her. "Sissies!" she taunts, holding a gun, her hair in her eyes. "Ya let a woman beat ya, huh? You little tiny nothing!" In a situation that would frighten and intimidate just about anyone else of either sex, Rowlands's slightly cracked Gloria mainly enjoys herself.

Four years later, there was a seventh and final film for Cassavetes called *Love Streams* where Rowlands played his sister, a woman who memorably brings home most of the animals from a petting zoo because she thought it was a good idea at the time. Rowlands's work for Cassavetes is always in the spirit of James Dean's Jim Stark in *Rebel Without a Cause*, and other Nicholas Ray romantics. Her films with Cassavetes are odes to misfits with new ideas and ways of doing things, women and men who are almost not crazy.

A few years later for Woody Allen, Rowlands was the repressed philosophy professor Marion Post in *Another Woman* (1988), a modest film where she gave a totally different kind of performance: disciplined, realistic, unshowy, full of tightly-reined-in feeling. Cassavetes died in 1989. After that, alas, it was back to the kinds of conventional parts in which Rowlands had labored in her twenties and thirties.

For her son Nick Cassavetes, Rowlands revived her haughty dame routine for *Unhook the Stars* (1996), and she tentatively sang in Terence Davies's *The Neon Bible* (1995). At age 84, Rowlands was still wrinkling her nose and acting snooty in *Six Dance Lessons in Six Weeks* (2014), where she plays a 75-year-old pretending to be 68 who says, "If you say your real age out loud, your face hears you." She was given an honorary Oscar in 2015.

In her later career, Rowlands generally played mothers and then grandmothers, and nearly all of them were alive with her vibrant there-ness, that thick blonde hair, her crooked grin, her sheer bonhomie. If she had never met Cassavetes, maybe we would never have known about what was underneath all that.

Maggie Smith
The Acid Queen

The persnickety yet lethal Maggie Smith was born in 1934 to a working class family, and her mother was a cold and penny-pinching stickler for propriety. Smith's brother Ian noted that there was antagonism between mother and daughter but it "never erupted into the open; it just sort of simmered."

Smith saw her first movie in 1946, *The Jolson Story*, and her father beat her after he found out she had gone to the cinema. She was a lonely child, but already tart and sarcastic from the sidelines. Because of her background, Smith intimately knows the kind of lower crust English striving for gentility that she explored, in both comic and dramatic ways, in some of her best movie work.

Her mother told her that she could never be an actress "with a face like that," but Smith was not deterred, and as a young girl she had an instinct for mockery. In high school a tutor named Mrs. van Beers gave Smith a speech of Helena's from *A Midsummer Night's Dream*. "She sent it up!" Mrs. van Beers recalled. "A child of 14 ... she had, even then, marvelous comedy timing, and she never made a mistake."

In her late teen years Smith started working in repertory English theater, and a young actor from this time, Patrick Dromgoole, remembered that Smith was one of the first girls he saw wearing blue jeans; he observed her sitting in them in bath water and "allowing them to dry to shape around her figure." The rebellious and sensual young Smith loved J.D. Salinger's novel *The Catcher in the Rye* so much that she wrote Salinger a fan letter. This was before Salinger withdrew from public life, and he actually wrote back to her, but Smith's mother destroyed Salinger's letter before her daughter could read it.

She scored in a revue called *Share My Lettuce*, where she met a man who would help shape her comic style, the camp comedian Kenneth Williams. Smith thrived among gay men like Williams, and she liked a good gossip, what she called "laying people out to filth." (She was noted for her sharp nicknames for others, too; she called Vanessa Redgrave "the red snapper.") Smith met her first husband, Robert Stephens, while they were acting together on stage. "She was very raunchy," Stephens remembered. "She swore like a trooper."

Smith started to work in TV and film, but her most notable acting in the 1960s was as a member of the National Theatre under the guidance of Laurence Olivier. She played Desdemona to his Othello on stage and stood up to him as best she could, but everyone seems to agree that their best work together was in Ibsen's *The Master Builder*. When a reviewer wrote that Smith acted Olivier off the stage in that play, this did not sit well with the great man, for he knew that Smith was the only member of the company who was serious competition for him.

Smith made an impression in the clichéd role of a lovelorn secretary in *The V.I.P.s* (1963) precisely because she is the only member of the cast who doesn't seem to be trying to make an impression, and she does soulful work with almost no material. Smith was funny, sexy, and scheming in the brief but memorable role of the home-wrecking Philpot in *The Pumpkin Eater* (1964), slyly taking charge of the domestic space around her as the anguished Jo (Anne Bancroft) finds herself supplanted by Philpot's blithe chatter.

She made for a merely dutiful Desdemona in a film of *Othello* (1965) with Olivier, but she was very touching and sensitive in the role of a shy book clerk in love with an Irish playwright (Rod Taylor) in *Young Cassidy* (1965), making her feeling for this man into a living and breathing thing until she has to tearfully give him up. And Smith overcame being miscast as a dense sexpot in the comedy *Hot Millions* (1968) through sheer talent.

She blossomed opposite Robert Stephens in a Franco Zeffirelli stage production of *Much Ado About Nothing*, and she got a huge laugh with the line, "This haddock is disgusting" in a revival of Noël Coward's *Hay Fever*. Smith also triumphed in difficult Restoration comedy plays like *The Way of the World* and *The Beaux' Stratagem*, and she did a noted *Hedda Gabler* for Ingmar Bergman in 1970, stressing the interior pressure on this thwarted character and shooting herself at the end in full view on stage. Almost all of Smith's finest work dramatizes the conflict between her puritan side and her hedonist longings, a very rich vein of opposition that flows directly, and sometimes indirectly, from her own private character.

Smith married Robert Stephens in 1967 and had two sons by him, but there was trouble in their marriage once she won the Oscar for *The Prime of Miss Jean Brodie* (1969), where she played a Scottish teacher who inspires her girls (or "gels" in her fancy pronunciation) to both good deeds and bad. Here was a performance that revealed Smith's full talent on camera, with all of her little trickeries of tone and emphasis, her heartfelt affectations, her mannerisms, which played out on the angular exterior of her face and body to hide rather harsh and mysterious depths of feeling underneath. Smith's Miss Brodie likes to hold her chin high and keep her eyes half-closed, and her hands and wrists seem to have a snake-charming life of their own. She can do just about anything with her voice, taking it up and down the scale and manipulating words until we are as dizzied by them as Miss Brodie's pupils are.

Maggie Smith works wonders with her wrists in *The Prime of Miss Jean Brodie.*

Every choice Smith makes in *The Prime of Miss Jean Brodie* is impeccable, both decisive and alive with Miss Brodie's furtive indecision, confident on the surface but deeply troubled and secretly weak within. The catch in this film is that though Miss Brodie is entertainingly colorful and amusing she actually is the corrupting influence on her students that the conservative headmistress Miss Mackay (Celia Johnson) takes her for, an admirer of the fascist Benito Mussolini and the Spanish dictator Francisco Franco, a lover of authority and brute force.

There is an emotional drive in Smith in her best screen roles that cannot be easily analyzed or explained. When she wants to, she can summon and focus an emotion in a way that feels like a wide brick wall coming down and then moving forward over both co-stars and camera. This might not be the most camera-friendly work, and there are times on screen as a young woman when Smith seems uncomfortable, as if she is remembering what her mother said to her about not being good-looking enough to be an actress. But as Jean Brodie she gives one of those performances that feels like a full-course meal, detailed, funny, moving, complete, especially in the last confrontation scene with the betraying Sandy (Pamela Franklin), in which we see Miss Brodie stripped of her illusions before she puts them right back on again.

The same year she won her Oscar for Jean Brodie, Smith contributed a hair-raising cameo to the film *Oh! What a Lovely War* where she played a hard-faced music hall singer recruiting men for the army with a sexual bait and switch. Smith revealed new depths of control here, and also deep knowledge of the worst human instincts. The song her character sings, where she offers to "make a man" of the men watching from the audience, is delivered with a perplexingly winking sort of snarliness that is cynically dropped once she has signed up all the men she needs to. The way that Smith drops the pose she has adopted during this song is fearsome, and it illuminates her own basically negative judgment of humanity.

Her husband Robert Stephens, who is in *Jean Brodie* himself, did not get the parts that would have made him a movie star at Smith's level, and his disappointment in that and his womanizing gradually destroyed their marriage. The early 1970s were not a good time for Smith either personally or professionally. Both on stage and on screen in this period she began to overdo her comic mannerisms, especially in *Travels with My Aunt* (1972), where she postured as an older woman.

This is the kind of failed performance that is particularly excruciating because it looks as if Smith is fully aware that the huge acting choices she is making are not working, and so she is caught rifling desperately through her bag of tricks to find something that might get her out of this jam, all to no avail. *Love and Pain and the Whole Damn Thing* (1973) was an attempt at romance for Smith, and she has guarded but sensitive moments here that are marred by ill-advised stabs at humor (Smith has always had a weakness for comic pratfalls).

After she divorced Stephens in 1975, Smith did four seasons at Stratford in Ontario where she took on most of the major Shakespeare roles and pared down her acting style for maximum effect. It was a time of renewal for her, and of marshaling her strength and her talent. At Stratford she played Cleopatra, Lady Macbeth, and Rosalind in *As You Like It* among many other parts, and those who saw her in them, from 1976 to 1980, still speak of the considerable things she accomplished on stage in this period.

Brian Bedford acted opposite Smith in many of these plays at Stratford, and he told her biographer Michael Coveney about stopping by Smith's dressing room at one point during the intermission for Noël Coward's *Private Lives*. Bedford asked her, "How are you, darling?" and she replied, "Oh darling, one is nothing, off!" Around this time Smith told a reporter, "I don't like myself very much. I'd much rather be someone else."

While "off," she was a somewhat strict mother, and a stickler for certain things just like her own mother. "She was very hot on articulation," said her son Chris Larkin. "We were not allowed to slur our words.... Above all, I remember this very piercing voice from my childhood: 'It's pardon, not what!' And she was fairly rigorous about table manners."

Smith won a second Oscar for supporting actress in the Neil Simon adaptation *California Suite* (1978), but this film was not a happy experience for her. "I thought you were supposed to be funny," director Herbert Ross told her, and he berated her so often on the set that she was reduced to tears.

The Simon material is far from Restoration comedy, but Smith and Michael Caine make something stylish and touching out of it anyway, working over and against their wisecracking one-liners. Smith speeds through her joke lines in a deadpan way that lets them land and also somehow transcends them, whereas Jane Fonda in the same movie is very heavy-handed with her own jokes.

In *California Suite*, Smith plays an actress named Diana Barrie who has done Shakespeare and Pinter at the National Theatre, but she has been nominated for an Oscar for a "nauseating little comedy" film called *No Left Turns*. Smith plays Diana's vanity and insecurity very well, and she has become a particular expert at drunk scenes. (Bill Murray is a vocal fan of the Smith-Caine scenes in *California Suite* and praises their faultless comedy timing.)

Smith did some of her best filmed work in the 1980s, particularly in two scripts by Alan Bennett, *A Private Function* (1984), where she played a genteel Lady Macbeth–type housewife and hit just the right note of delusional snobbiness, and the monologue *Bed Among the Lentils*, which was done for TV in 1988. If you want to see great acting with no fuss and deadly accuracy look no further than Smith doing this 50-minute Bennett script about the alcoholic wife of a vicar who finds sexual fulfillment with a much younger grocer.

Smith seethes with controlled rage and irony throughout *Bed Among the Lentils*, keeping such a tight hold on her effects that she barely seems to breathe. She discloses the passionately sexual nature under this woman's mouse exterior, and in *A Room with a View* (1985) she was a passive-aggressive mouse, an unwanted relation who makes a memorably embarrassing spectacle out of herself when she insists on paying for a cab but can't find or part with money. Her character's name is Charlotte, and she is the sort of person who is always referred to by others as "poor Charlotte," though she does comically insist that she is a "woman of the world" in her "small way."

Smith makes an enormous impact in *The Lonely Passion of Judith Hearne* (1987), a character study about an alcoholic piano teacher whose small hopes are getting smaller all the time. Smith's Judith Hearne is the artistic height of her screen work, a performance so concentrated and unsparing that it leaves nothing but scorched earth in its path, particularly in the scene where we first see Judith taking a secret drink after a bad disappointment, and in a follow-up scene where Smith cries, "You made me spill it!" in her most centered, annihilating, and forceful voice when the clumsy Bernie (Ian McNeice) accidentally knocks over her bottle of whiskey. Smith uses that same brick wall tone when a drunken Judith goes to church and kneels and screams, "I hate you!" at the altar, one of the most painful scenes in all cinema.

Michael Palin, her co-star in *A Private Function*, said that Smith is "formidable when crossed. There's an intensity of animosity sometimes, which comes out in her acting and can be quite chilling. Maggie in a bad mood is clearly a few degrees worse than most people in a bad mood." Her colleagues have been known to call her "the Acid Queen" because she is always ready with a well-timed barb, and that aspect of her personality has been emphasized in most of her latter-day film and theater work.

She scored on stage in the 1990s in verbose, rancorous Edward Albee plays like *Three Tall Women* and *A Delicate Balance*, and her bitchy matrons had become a specialty well before her Dowager Countess on *Downton Abbey* for TV. She gave some first-rate performances in challenging roles on film in the 1990s, like her poisonous, frightened, and ashamed Mrs. Violet Venable in a TV version of Tennessee Williams's *Suddenly, Last Summer* (1993) and her voyeuristic Aunt Lavinia in an adaptation of Henry James's *Washington Square* (1997), where her swift and unexpected vocal rhythms are made for James's hang-gliding dialogue.

Smith's steady gig in the *Harry Potter* movies was un-rewarding, but at least they gave her some security and a new audience. There have been some recent films, here and there, that have taken advantage of her full skill set, like the TV movie *My House in Umbria* (2003), where she played the frequently sloshed romance novelist Mrs. Delahunty and once again transcended sketchy material with her sad eyes and tart presence.

Smith played in Alan Bennett's *The Lady in the Van* on stage in 1999, and so she was working from a firm base for the 2015 movie version. As Miss Shepherd, an itinerant lady who actually took up residence in Bennett's driveway for 15 years, Smith lets us see that this woman lives in a world of her own; she is a totally powerless person who survives by believing herself to be busy and powerful.

When Bennett (Alex Jennings) at one point asks her for an apology, Smith's Miss Shepherd replies, "Sorry is for God." That's an archetypal Maggie Smith line, and *The Lady in the Van* is a welcome addition to her gallery of snobby, ruined eccentrics. With Vanessa Redgrave and Meryl Streep, Smith stands as one of the top female acting talents of her time, and at her best she outstrips nearly every actor of either sex.

Julie Christie
Darling

Sometimes extreme physical beauty grows more complex and more satisfying with age. It's rare, but it happens. Such is certainly the case with Julie Christie, a blonde British Helen of Troy with the most frankly carnal lower lip in film history. Her eyes and brows rival Garbo in their velveteen symmetry, and her nose is a poem, a genetic triumph of heart-shaped, concealed nostrils.

When she first made her lush visual impact in the 1960s with a brief part in John Schlesinger's *Billy Liar* (1963) and then an Oscar win for her empty model in Schlesinger's *Darling* (1965), Christie seemed slightly abashed by her resplendent looks, much as Paul Newman did as a young man. Her voice was chesty and strained, as if she were trying to be a good sport, and she moved awkwardly, as if she wasn't quite sure what was expected of her. In other words, there was a disconnect between Christie's appearance and who she seemed to be as a person. She looked made for mystery and renunciation, but when she talked it was clear she was ready to go out to the discotheque with her mates.

Christie had a run of good roles up to about 1975, and she gained in assurance and lusciousness as each went by. She tried to do the Twist in her second film *The Fast Lady* (1962), where she's very tense and awkward, like Vivien Leigh in some of her own early English films. The drab *Darling* sets Christie off with two coldly un-giving leading men (Laurence Harvey and Dirk Bogarde), and scrutinizes her for signs of "the decay of our times." There's another movie lurking here, too, which Schlesinger finds in the long section where Diana spends a holiday with her gay photographer friend, but this film would probably be a bisexual sex comedy, and it couldn't have been made in 1965.

Christie was indelibly and nearly unbelievably sexy when seen briefly in her white underwear in *Young Cassidy* (1965), but she could do little to enliven romantic epics like David Lean's *Doctor Zhivago* (1965) and Schlesinger's *Far from the Madding Crowd* (1967). Lean uses her only as a ripe beauty in *Doctor Zhivago,* which is mainly about the many different ways of concealing and highlighting parts of her face: covering her lips, putting a light right on her eyes. (At one point in this movie Rod Steiger runs his finger along her lower lip.) All Christie has to do is present herself to the camera and look pensive and vaguely concerned.

She was conventionally kooky, modestly touching, and never more beautiful than in Richard Lester's anguished, jagged *Petulia* (1968), but Shirley Knight brings such tension and subtext to her own scenes with George C. Scott in *Petulia* that Christie's limitations are made more obvious by comparison.

Christie had been given one of the most beautiful faces imaginable, yet she doesn't know how to work her extreme close-ups in *Petulia*. All she would need to do to slay us would be to stay still for a moment, but she is always quickly and nervously moving away, as if she doesn't want the camera to really see her. It could be said that this style suits the abused woman she is playing, but it often feels like Christie is nervous and armored rather than her character.

Christie's work improved dramatically in the 1970s. Her highborn beauty in Joseph Losey's *The Go-Between* (1971) stands as an archetypal boy's crush and ruiner of hopes. In that adaptation of L.P. Hartley's novel, Christie has to represent a dream girl, as she does in *Billy Liar*, but the difference is that this dream girl has a cruel, teasing side that is brought out by the limitations set upon her by her own class and position in society.

Julie Christie tries to evade the scrutiny of the camera in *Petulia*.

Co-starring with her lover Warren Beatty, Christie shed her Mod image completely for her finest film, Robert Altman's *McCabe & Mrs. Miller* (1971), where her real scrappiness was finally utilized. Something releases in Christie here because she gets to do a Cockney accent and play a complex, well-rounded character, a hardheaded businesswoman and whorehouse madam who needs to smoke some opium sometimes as a counterbalance to her managing toughness.

Altman sets Christie within the world and the ensemble of his film, and she rewards him with a deeply imaginative, un-self-conscious performance with a political undertone, for a case could be made that Mrs. Miller represents capitalism at its best and its worst. Christie presents many sides of Mrs. Miller in her usually brief scenes, and she finally reaches an end point where there is nothing left but the human mystery of this character, her eyes all pleasantly detached by the dope she smokes in the last shot of the picture. It was clear here that Christie was at last unconcerned about being either likable or approachable or conventionally attractive as an actress, and this was what set her free.

Christie did an explicit love scene with Donald Sutherland in the thriller *Don't Look Now* (1973) that looked very real, and it was as if she were pushing herself to be more and more exposed on screen. She did a very tough comedy character study of a kept woman with Beatty in *Shampoo* (1975), where once again Christie seems to have no qualms about looking selfish and hard and un-likably pragmatic, just as her Mrs. Miller was. In both *McCabe & Mrs. Miller* and *Shampoo*, Christie winds up being touching because she refuses all easy roads to that response from her audience.

Christie left Hollywood after Beatty's mild *Heaven Can Wait* (1978), and she worked sparingly throughout the 1980s, usually in obscure films with some left-wing political content, like Sally Potter's preachy, experimental *The Gold Diggers* (1983) and the Argentinian drama *Miss Mary* (1986). The special glamour of her name and looks was close to being forgotten when she was reclaimed by Alan Rudolph for *Afterglow* (1997), a sexy, crazy movie where she commanded the camera with long speeches in lengthy takes.

All her skittish self-consciousness had melted away in *Afterglow*, and in its place was the moving spectacle of a still gorgeous, once-inhibited woman who has decided to relax and toy with our affections. With her beauty truly ripened, she lets it all hang out in that Rudolph movie, and she nearly arrogantly holds the other characters, and the camera, in her thrall.

Christie re-emerged again, piercingly lovely at 66, in Sarah Polley's debut feature as a director, *Away from Her* (2006). She is beautifully dressed in her first scenes: there's one coat here that might almost have been used in *Darling*. But the pretty coats and sweaters are used in this film to make a point. As Christie's character Fiona gradually succumbs to Alzheimer's disease, her clothes get lost and mixed up with other resident's clothes at her nursing home, and this signals the helpless gravity and stripped-down simplicity that the passage of time has given to Christie.

In the first scenes of *Away from Her*, Polley creates a portrait of what seems a blissfully contented marriage between Fiona and Grant (Gordon Pinsent). While in bed with his wife, Grant strokes those iconically ripe lips, as any older man lucky enough to be married to Julie Christie would do. It's a big point in this film that Fiona was always a little vague, so that the start of her disease doesn't seem too different from her natural behavior at first.

Christie stands very still in her close-ups in *Away from Her* and opens her face up for us, allowing the camera to see Fiona's confusion, her humor, and the mystery that begins to cloak her eyes as her mind goes. The uneasy darling of the 1960s is gone. In her place is a woman who has held onto her beauty by letting go of her fears, and an accomplished actress who steers well clear of "Disease of the Week" television and puts together a deeply imaginative portrait of a self-aware woman lyrically falling into unawareness.

Away from Her sometimes stresses that there might be something pleasurable about forgetfulness. Faced with oblivion, Christie's Fiona chooses to treat it as an adventure, and we really feel her pain and panic only because she rarely shows it to us. Towards the end of the film, when Fiona has begun to fade, Christie does not take the easy way out into pathos. As she lies in her bed, Fiona's face seems ravaged by time and grievance, her white hair framing a look of disappointment. When Fiona is wheeled to the second floor of a hospital where the hopeless cases are housed, Christie lies collapsed in her wheelchair, her head to the side, her face completely walled up in ecstatic contemplation.

This image is both disturbing (Fiona is simply not there anymore) and exciting (what could she be looking at, feeling?). It's moments like this that justify Al Pacino's comment that Christie is the most "poetic" of actresses. Her beauty will always be remembered, but Christie's improvement as a performer over time is her own achievement.

Glenda Jackson
Tension Clenching

Glenda Jackson retired from acting in 1992, when she entered into British politics and was voted Labour MP for Hampstead and Highgate in the London borough of Camden. She seemed hands-on and hardworking as MP and was not afraid to be one of the first of her party to criticize Tony Blair over his participation in the Iraq war. Jackson won some attention in 2013 when she denounced the creed of personal selfishness preached by Margaret Thatcher shortly after Thatcher's death, and when congratulated on this performance she coolly said, "It was only the truth."

Jackson had achieved a great deal in her first profession. Her film career took off after her initial best actress Oscar for Ken Russell's *Women in Love* (1970), and Jackson's competition that year actually included Ali MacGraw in *Love Story*, so this first win is understandable. Her second best actress win, for a joyless sex comedy called *A Touch of Class* (1973), is much less explicable.

Then again, Jackson's stardom in the early 1970s has its inexplicable side. Has any other actress made such an impact on screen by purveying nearly nothing but abrasive bad temper? In film after film, Jackson carped, sniped, bitched, moaned, barked, and howled at her leading men and her audience, but there would be moments when she let us see glimpses of a wounded adolescent defensiveness in her moody, pockmarked face, with its mistrustful eyes and disagreeably pouting mouth, and at moments like these she could be touching, if the role required it.

Jackson caused a stir in the 1970s as a kind of British S&M sex symbol, always taking her clothes off and rolling around on the floor for Russell, and she was often quite limited, really, but so particular in looks and manner that she carved out her own cinematic world where she is forever telling off men and disparaging their sexual technique, not to mention putting down America (a few lines of English chauvinism must have been written in as a requirement in her contracts).

If Jackson hadn't retired, Judi Dench and Helen Mirren most likely wouldn't have made such stellar film careers for themselves as older women.

Surely Jackson would have scooped up most of Dench's roles and maybe even won a third Oscar for a cameo Elizabeth I in *Shakespeare in Love* (1998). Surely, too, Jackson would have put Cate Blanchett through an even worse ordeal in *Notes on a Scandal* (2006) and provided a much more critical portrait of the second Elizabeth in *The Queen* (2006).

On the indispensable *Datalounge* site, one commenter on a Jackson thread wrote that she had "only a few tricks, but they were impressive when you first saw them," and these "tricks" can be quickly itemized. For general frustration or melancholy, Jackson always squeezes her eyes shut as hard as she possibly can. Her mouth seems to have a life of its own; it stretches and purses and habitually crinkles up in disgust, and her tongue would sometimes emerge from this drawbridge mouth when she was trying to be sexy/snake-like.

Every now and then, her face would get an apprehensive, self-deprecating look, most clearly seen when she first meets Tchaikovsky (Richard Chamberlain) in Russell's demented and very vulgar *The Music Lovers* (1971). When she has no idea what to do, Jackson falls into a mode of withdrawn perversity, as in the end of her marathon performance as Nina Leeds in *Strange Interlude* (1988), where she starts to parody Eugene O'Neill's Freudian material. Sometimes she spoke in a hushed, purring monotone, trying to fake out George Segal or Walter Matthau in her sour 1970s comedies before unleashing a mercilessly enunciated verbal attack on them.

She's very hard to take in some films, especially her tantrum-throwing Sarah Bernhardt in *The Incredible Sarah* (1976). "I'm lousy in that," Jackson later admitted to the *Guardian* in 2016. "Because I couldn't believe in it, or because I couldn't convince myself of its reality in some way." And then there's her very miscalculated queen in Russell's *Salome's Last Dance* (1988). But Jackson certainly wasn't remotely like anyone else. Perhaps she made the right decision to retire from acting when she did. At her worst on screen, she tensely bulldozes her way through reams of dialogue with no nuances or modulation of tone. During her extended absence from performing, Jackson still had many fervent fans who insisted that she was one of our finest actresses, but that's open to debate.

After a working-class childhood, Jackson spent nearly ten years of dues paying in repertory theater and odd jobs before finding her métier by joining Peter Brook's experimental Theater of Cruelty, which had its roots in the teachings of Antonin Artaud. The Brook company made a sensation, in London and then in New York, with *Marat/Sade*, a Peter Weiss play about a madhouse performance directed by the Marquis de Sade.

This was in-your-face 1960s theater, with the actors, or "inmates," terrorizing the audience from the stage nightly, just as they attempt to terrorize the camera in the 1967 film version. Jackson is clearly a star in the making in the middle of the ensemble, playing a semi-catatonic girl playing Charlotte Corday, the assassin of Jean-Paul Marat. She constructs a whole performance that's emotionally disconnected from every word she says, and it could get tiresome very easily if she wasn't so immersed in madness, plotting the pitiful rise and fall of this girl's confused mind with rigorous discipline and imagination.

Ken Russell's blunt sensibility does a disservice to D.H. Lawrence's finest novel *Women in Love*, but his film adaptation is often diverting and colorful on its own terms, and Jackson's Gudrun, uncharitably modeled by Lawrence on writer Katherine Mansfield, is still an impressive creation. She's stylishly modern here in her blue cloque hat and green stockings, and her incisive voice is good-humored for once, with a touch of likable bitchery. Jackson is at her most physically expansive in *Women in Love*, and her Peter Brook training shows in the sequence where she scares off a herd of bulls with an angular, aggressive dance in the open air.

She is pretty funny when she first takes her top off for Oliver Reed towards the end of the film. At first, Jackson has a "why not?" look on her face, but after she bares her breasts for him, it quickly changes to a frank "what am I doing?" expression. She makes an agonized grimace when Reed humps her, like an aged dowager having a stroke, and her ball-busting persona comes to the fore in the last scenes, hatefully but strikingly. Russell cannot shape or use what she is doing, but her Gudrun remains a three-dimensional bohemian in a hairy, clammy film that smells of sweat and unsatisfactory sex.

In *Sunday Bloody Sunday* (1971), a John Schlesinger movie about a bisexual

Glenda Jackson commands a herd of bulls in *Women in Love*.

love triangle, Jackson does a real star turn as Alex Greville, a woman encased in turtleneck sweaters against the English cold, sipping bad coffee, smoking cigarettes to their bitter end. This is the rare Jackson film where words are not paramount; in fact, most of her performance has to be given in silent close-ups where she is asked to look with rueful longing at her unfaithful lover (Murray Head).

Unlike practically everything else she did, *Sunday Bloody Sunday* requires Jackson to drop her take-charge theatrical manner and settle down into film acting with the camera close in, so that her every thought can be read. She clearly has misgivings about this way of working, but she lets these misgivings feed the emotion of her work. At the end, trying to free herself from her miserable situation, her Alex says, "There are times when nothing has to be better than anything," and Jackson has personalized this woman's need for solitude to such an extent that it feels like a glimpse of her soul that has nothing to do with technique, which she too often used as armor for battle to keep herself hidden or safe.

Jackson is at her sharp-clawed best in *Mary, Queen of Scots* (1971), a fast-moving Hal Wallis production on the rivalry between her Elizabeth I and Vanessa Redgrave's foolish Mary Stuart. It came out in the same year as Jackson's famed and nearly ten-hour Elizabeth I television series for the BBC, *Elizabeth R*, but her sly vaudeville turn as the Virgin Queen in *Mary, Queen of Scots* is preferable to her rather plain performance in the series, which goes on and on but produces little in the way of drama or even character development beyond the intrigue of the first two episodes and the physical deterioration that Jackson fully commits to in the last episode.

Elizabeth R highlights Jackson's tendency to push or force emotion strenuously, which impressed many but left many others cold. *Mary, Queen of Scots* lets her mix tones, and she never overstays her welcome. When Jackson cries, "I am but barren stock!" in this movie, she manages to be campy and tragic at once, and her explosion of "Jesus!" at Redgrave's exasperating Mary could be our own. We don't get a chance to get tired of Jackson's "few tricks" in this film, and they are impressive enough to make us see why she was such a distinctive actress in this period.

Jackson was appealingly restrained in *The Triple Echo* (1972), and she was at her best as a vulgar, drunken, and thoroughly un-lady-like Emma Hamilton in *A Bequest to the Nation* (1973), but she was at her most graspingly and suffocatingly theatrical in *The Maids* (1975), an adaptation of Jean Genet's play. A theatrical creature, she did another straightforward play adaptation called *Hedda* (1975), where her portrayal of Ibsen's Hedda Gabler is tightly controlled, mannered yet somewhat nuanced, and fairly enigmatic, especially in the key moment when Hedda burns the manuscript of Ejlert Løvborg (Patrick Stewart), which Jackson plays in a puzzlingly low-key fashion.

Jackson is well cast in some ways as Hedda Gabler and can play her strength and perversity, but she is not convincing when trying to play this woman's fatal weaknesses. This Hedda got Jackson a fourth Oscar nomination for best actress, even though it was barely seen. There were so few rewarding roles for women in English-speaking 1970s films that anything Jackson did for a time was deemed worthy of acclaim.

The articulate Jackson was critical of her own material in interviews, often scathingly so, but she seems to have enjoyed playing the poet Stevie Smith, both on stage and in the film translation *Stevie* (1978). When I interviewed Jackson in 2013, she said, "Stevie was a very special person, wasn't she? I met her once, you know."

"I was still with the RSC and they used to do kind of poetry evenings on a Sunday and I was roped in to do one, and I was standing at the side of stage, and this funny little woman came up to me," Jackson said. "And she'd got a fringe, you know, and straight hair and a white blouse and a dark cardigan and a terrible dirndl skirt and she wore sandals and very thick tights and ankle socks, but the brooch at the neck of her white shirt was this very beautiful Victorian cameo."

"She stood absolutely straight," Jackson said. "I don't mean like a guardsman, but there wasn't a kind of protective curve on her anywhere. I'd never heard of her. Then she romped onto the stage and did 'Not Waving But Drowning.' And I thought, 'Who the *hell* are you, lady?' And I rushed out and bought everything that was still in print. Having the opportunity to do that play where virtually every word was hers was just wonderful."

"I liked Stevie Smith," Jackson said, high praise for her. "She stood four square and looked the big things straight in the eye." These "big things" include Smith's morbid yet tonically cheerful obsession with death, expressed to the full as she scrawled her poems at her office job and at home in the suburbs with her aunt (Mona Washbourne).

Though Jackson has some help from Washbourne and Trevor Howard, who plays a convenient male friend, *Stevie* is basically a one-woman show where she delightedly unwraps bits of Smith's novels and poems for us, sometimes directly to the camera, sometimes with her slanted eyes cast sadly or humorously askance. Jackson replaces her own hollow, unpleasant laugh with a likable kind of hooting giggle drawn up directly from her nose, and she keeps her mouth under control for once, unless she allows it a childish little moue, for Stevie Smith was childish, in a severe, magical way, and she made her own tiredness and boredom seem like adventures.

Jackson is problematic in almost everything she did, but not in *Stevie*, where she uses cheerfully insistent upwards inflections and places unerring emphasis on the right words in each bit of Smith's verse, so that every line reading feels like a treasurable fetish object. Jackson's negative temperament matches up with Smith's macabre viewpoint so ideally that her own blockages and tensions are lightened and dissolved. Her performance in *Stevie* is a perfect melding of acting technique and deep feeling, and the best argument that something was lost when Jackson went into politics.

She worked steadily throughout the 1980s, but her films were obscure and usually very modest and socially conscious. Jackson did two very poor pictures with Robert Altman, and she was oddly cast as Patricia Neal in a TV movie about Neal's stroke, though she got through that all right. Jackson was rather touchingly repressed in *The Return of the Soldier* (1982) and in *Turtle Diary* (1985), which was based on a Harold Pinter screenplay. Towards the end of this period, Jackson did three more films for Russell, unrewardingly, and by the early 1990s she had had enough.

After retiring from politics at the age of 80, Jackson returned to the stage at the Old Vic as King Lear in a stripped-down production directed by Deborah Warner. Against all reasonable odds, she received rave reviews for this very ambitious comeback, with critics calling her "tremendous" and "shattering" and the *Telegraph* saying that her performance would be "talked about for years to come."

Even after nearly 25 years away from acting, the power of her voice was said to be undiminished. Jackson always had been androgynous, and it seems that age had made her even more so. In the 1960s, Penelope Gilliatt had written that Jackson's Ophelia in a production of *Hamlet* was so dominating that she was ready to play Hamlet himself, and so Jackson's late triumph on stage as King Lear had a sense, perhaps, of historical and feminist inevitability.

Jackson won a Tony for playing the very unpleasant central figure in Edward Albee's *Three Tall Women* on Broadway in 2018. She forced emotions as she always had, but with such ferocity and such undiminished ill temper that her old mannerisms impressed a lot of people, perhaps because it had been so long since they had seen them in action.

Diane Keaton
In the Moment

On the one hand, Diane Keaton does a lot of things you're not supposed to do as an actor. She is one of the most mannered performers of all time, with a collection of highly idiosyncratic tics, stammers, and grimaces that she carries with her from part to part, from comedy to drama, and seemingly in life, too, if we are to judge by her talk show appearances.

Every one of these mannerisms is meant to broadcast her elaborate insecurity and seeming bashfulness, but there is a well of fathoms-deep anger running underneath them as a kind of motor, along with rich veins of tenderness, pure kindness, and childlike vulnerability. A real creature of the 1970s, she speaks always with hesitations, with repeated words, with "oh's" and "um's," even in period pieces.

Physically she can be very awkward, a stomping walker and a bumper into things, especially if she is interacting with another actor in the same frame. Just watch the way Meryl Streep dusts the floor with her in their confrontation scenes in *Marvin's Room* (1996), and the "high school play" way she uses her hands in her scenes with Leonardo DiCaprio in that movie, where she extends them with palms out just to give them something to do.

If you observe Keaton closely, you can see her fall into amateur habits like that, and her insecurity, which is no doubt based in some kind of reality, leads her to mug and show us what she's supposed to be feeling, often in a comically elaborate way. These are all serious faults, but here's the catch: beneath Keaton's habitual facial indicating and her other mannerisms there is an access to emotions so pure that they qualify as major, sometimes otherworldly events on screen.

There is an immediacy to her work when she is at her best, and a very distinctive forcefulness, because she flings herself so totally into the moment, and there's a special excitement when she does that because we can feel how fragile her ego is, both performing and otherwise. Acting is dangerous for Keaton, but she needs to risk what she is risking in order to work a sort of catharsis for herself, and wring herself out. Does being in the moment in such an extreme way inevitably lead into the jags and grooves of set and recognizable mannerisms? With Keaton, it does seem that way, especially as her career continued past age 40, but in her best early work she transcended this.

Keaton studied acting in the 1960s with Sanford Meisner, and he is best known for a repetition exercise where you stare deeply into the eyes of your scene partner and repeat things you notice about them: "You're wearing blue," one actor will say, and the other actor will repeat, "I'm wearing blue," and so forth. That training shows in Keaton's work because she is often able to burrow deep down into a scene when she feels comfortable with another actor (though this was clearly not the case with Streep or DiCaprio).

She was born Diane Hall in Los Angeles in 1946, and she gained notice as the one member of the cast of the hippie musical *Hair* who would not disrobe for the nude scene. (She changed her last name to Keaton, her mother's maiden name, because there was already a Diane Hall in Actors' Equity). She then played on stage with Woody Allen in *Play It Again, Sam* and briefly became his girlfriend, and this association would turn out to be key for her. When he saw her in that play, Jack Benny reportedly said, "That girl is going to be gigantic."

Keaton played the ever-thankless part of Kay in both *The Godfather* (1972) and *The Godfather: Part II* (1974), and she suffers in those movies from the inattention of the writers, the director Francis Ford Coppola, and even from the costume designers and wig makers, who outfit her awkwardly. You can see her talent struggling to make an impact, particularly in the second film, but her role is always such an afterthought that her gaucheries and inexperience are exposed in certain close-ups, while in others she has her full mature emotional fire.

Keaton then worked with Allen on screen in the movie of *Play It Again, Sam* (1972), and already she was dressing in her own eccentric but beautifully stylish way, covering up as much of her body as possible with long skirts, high-necked shirts, hats, and large belts (Edith Head dressed Barbara Stanwyck in the 1940s in a similar way). "You're such a knock-out, why are you such a mass of symptoms?" Allen asks her in that movie, where they are two neurotics talking themselves through anxiety attacks and therapeutic overkill.

She spread her wings a bit more as the high-style, futuristic bad poet Luna in *Sleeper* (1973), exclaiming that a painting is "Keen ... no, it's not just keen ... it's cugat!" Keaton finds her own blithe, wacky comedy timing in these early Allen movies, delivering her lines in a breathless rush and knowing just when to fall into a droll sort of deadpan tone within that rush.

She was creating her own comic character on screen: hedonistic, maybe a little dim, spoiled, and lovably zany. Keaton rides her own emotions very high and then surfs on them, so that there is a curious extra intensity about her. Her impression of Brando's Stanley Kowalski to Allen's Blanche DuBois in *Sleeper* is funny precisely because it's such an inexact sketch of his performance, with a mannered little head tilt.

Somehow Keaton turns what might be seen as performing deficiencies into comic assets because she seems so game for anything, and so non-professional, somehow. Watching her is like watching someone bluff their way through something difficult on sheer nerve, or like seeing a familiar family member in a hilariously unfamiliar situation. That was her considerable charm in her early Allen movies, and luckily the last scenes of both *Sleeper* and *Love and Death* (1975) involve Keaton and Allen trying to bluff their way through a situation and fool people, so this plays right into her strengths as a comic.

Love and Death is probably Allen's funniest movie, and Keaton makes a key contribution to it, finding exactly the right tone of straight-faced silliness. When she is complimented on her skin by an admirer, she says, "Yes, it covers my whole body," firing off this odd little one-liner so fast that it barely has time to land.

She rings lots of changes on loopy selfishness in *Love and Death*, and her composure is formidable: not only does she manage to keep it when being offered the mustache of her beloved Ivan (Henry Czarniak) at his funeral, but she even manages to shed a tear before being offered Ivan's "letters," which turn out to be a bunch of paper alphabet letters. This doesn't sound very funny in description, but anyone who has seen *Love and Death* many times knows that it kills as a routine, just as many others do. (If you look closely, you can see that Keaton is just dying to laugh here, and that makes it even funnier.)

Also in *Love and Death* there's the classic "fields of wheat" bit where Keaton stares right into the camera while Allen stares slightly off and she worries about suffocation in a relationship with him and cries, "Open a window ... no, not that one, the one in the *bathroom*." The slightest wavering or lack of conviction in facial expression or intonation would kill the bit, which is sending up pretentious art films while also harkening way back to Groucho Marx's send-up of Eugene O'Neill's play *Strange Interlude* in *Animal Crackers* (1930), but Keaton stays just focused enough without ever pressing too hard.

And then there's a wonderful sort of blooper scene here where a prop doesn't quite work and Allen cuts the sound and keeps hitting Keaton over the head with a bottle, which she takes gamely and apologetically, as if to say, "Of course!" until she finally falls back down a wall and pretends to be knocked out, like a kid playing outside with friends and clearly having a ball.

Keaton then took her signature part for Allen, *Annie Hall* (1977), a film-length valentine to her quirks and hesitations for which she won the best actress Oscar. Annie is a would-be actress, photographer and then singer from Chippewa Falls, Wisconsin. She puts all of her insecurities right on the surface of her behavior, editorializing on her own self-consciousness with real charm. Dressed in baggy male pants, a vest, and a tie, Annie pursues

Allen's Alvy at the start rather than the other way around, and they have real opposites-attract chemistry (watch the way the normally dour and eye-rolling Allen really laughs in response to Keaton in the famous scene where they try to cook lobsters).

Alvy says that Annie is great sexually because she's "polymorphously perverse," alive to pleasure, but she's a pot smoker who needs to smoke up before going to bed with him. Alvy pushes her to take college courses to get her up to speed for the intellectual Upper West Side of Manhattan, and under his influence she grows more poised and reflective, singing "Seems Like Old Times" in a nightclub in a high, small, sweet voice, so that the sincerity of her delivery stops the movie cold.

That same year, sporting the same long, flippable hair, she took a risk and played the sexually hungry teacher of deaf children Theresa Dunn in the rambling, disco-set *Looking for Mr. Goodbar*. Her insecurity was explained here by scoliosis of the spine and a scar on her back from it, and the character's sexual promiscuity seems to grow out of her lapsed Catholicism, her reaction to her obnoxious father, and her day-dreamy nature. Keaton got naked for this role, a decade after her refusal to do the group nude scene for *Hair*, which signaled her new will to explore. (In a piece of deft casting, the similarly mannered and cerebral Tuesday Weld plays her flaky sex bomb sister.)

She doubled down on her "uh huh's" and her elaborately flinching delivery of words in *Goodbar*, and she retreats sometimes into a kind of blank-faced fugue state from which she reacts with exaggerated alarm when someone breaks through it. Keaton seems to be jolted by emotion when something hits her or strikes her fancy, and she falls into strange routines of mockery and inward-turned dialogue, as if she were constantly in a state of eccentric behavioral flux, often catching up late with what someone else says or does like Jean Arthur used to in her 1930s-40s movies.

Keaton is in her own world and style in the 1970s, but she is very far from a dithering Lee Strasberg actress like Sandy Dennis because everything she does is ultra-legible in a distinct way that helped to make her a truly popular star. She will sometimes press down unexpectedly hard on a word or a reaction because she wants to keep us off balance, and always there is a sense of spontaneity, so that she seems to be living and working out her part in the moment, right then, which makes her capable of surprising both us and herself.

Keaton lets herself get overcome by things, opening herself up to feel anything she can as deeply as she possibly can, especially her girlish delight with her most dangerous sexual partner in *Goodbar*, Richard Gere's Tony. At her best, no one is more responsive and more alive on screen than Keaton, which is why Theresa's brutal murder at the end of *Goodbar* carries such a special, unfair sting.

Keaton played the poet Renata in Allen's first drama, *Interiors* (1978), where her poems are supposed to be better than Luna's efforts in *Sleeper*. Renata is a smoker, a gloomy woman who says to her therapist that the "intimacy" of death embarrasses her, and Keaton's gestures of anguish are just as self-conscious as the chilly art film style of the visuals.

She worked for a sixth time on screen with Allen as the pseudo-intellectual Mary Wilke in *Manhattan* (1979), who at first seems the opposite of Annie Hall, a hyper-critical, privileged Radcliffe woman. "I'm beautiful, and I'm bright, and I deserve better!" Mary whines to her married lover Yale (Michael Murphy), but Allen's Isaac eventually quips that her self-esteem is "a notch below Kafka's." Keaton plays the scene where Yale breaks up with Mary at an outdoor cafe very well: barely able to look at him, stuck deep in some trough of despond that makes her look puffy and bilious.

Keaton had gone as far as she could with Allen, and she entered the 1980s with a new male collaborator, Warren Beatty, with whom she had a romance and worked on the epic *Reds* (1981) for quite some time. Beatty demanded interminable takes of each scene, and he pressed on Keaton so much that she reveals new depths of rage and impatience in the arguments that occur between her failed writer Louise Bryant and Beatty's more assured John Reed. She also reaches a new depth of feeling in her scenes with Jack Nicholson's Eugene O'Neill that form a memorable little playlet about a bitter love affair amidst the sprawl and reach of *Reds*.

Louise Bryant in *Reds* is a dentist's wife from Portland who wants to be an emancipated woman circa 1915, and she can be very defensive, petulant, and passive aggressive when she isn't being aggressive aggressive. Keaton's early heroines for Woody Allen had been so likable as to be adorable, but her Mary Wilke and Louise Bryant are unlikable women, jagged and hostile.

A production source on the set of *Reds* calls Keaton "a real rage rat" in Peter Biskind's biography of Beatty, and clearly this affair with him, and her working with him on *Reds*, was not a particularly happy time for her. There are certain close-ups in *Reds* where Keaton seems touched to the core by fear and anger, so that she radiates the pain of that exposure, and there are also times when her wide-set eyes hold the clarity and the detail that Lillian Gish used to display in her silent film close-ups.

The relationship with Beatty ended, which pained Keaton, and she used this pain creatively in what is certainly her most out-there, limitless dramatic performance in *Shoot the Moon* (1982), where she played Faith Dunlap, a wife with four young daughters who finds herself in the middle of a tough divorce from her writer husband George (Albert Finney).

Performances are sometimes called "raw," and this is certainly a case in point, for this is a Strasberg-style performance from Keaton (she had been introduced to the Strasberg version of the Method by Al Pacino) where

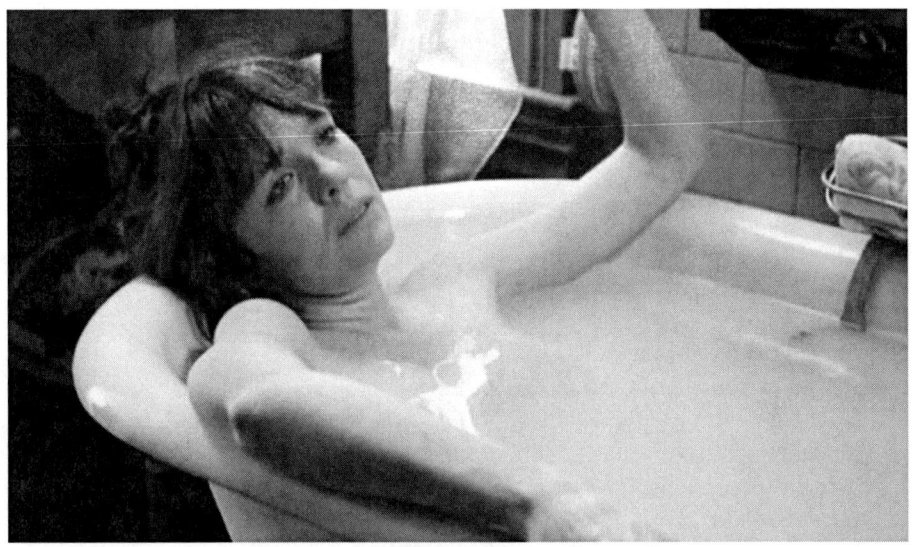

Diane Keaton emotionally disintegrates in *Shoot the Moon*.

she actually inhabits ruined psychic states instead of acting and shaping them, and the result is touching, of course, but touching in a way we might feel if we saw someone crying in the street. Keaton allows herself to be seen disintegrating on screen, dissolving into a puddle in the scenes where Faith is alone. When she smokes grass while taking a bath and sings the Beatles' "If I Fell," Keaton reaches such an intimate place of emotional exposure that she looks transparent, and this is really something to see, an event, even.

And in the fight scenes with Finney, a great actor who is also digging very deep into himself in this movie, Keaton achieves a bruising domestic battery realism. The decisive scene where Faith calls George on his seeing another woman and they start smashing plates in their kitchen is one of the most believable couple fights ever put on screen: look particularly at the expressively awkward way Keaton drapes herself against a window when the fight dies down.

When she makes a gesture of anger here, whether it's flipping her hair behind her ear or taking a Bette Davis–like puff on a cigarette and sitting decisively on the stairs of her house, Keaton can fill her whole body with emotion and blast it out to us. The scene where Finney and Keaton argue in a restaurant marks a strange shift in tone in *Shoot the Moon*, accompanied by a much speedier, surface delivery by Keaton that's more like Luna in *Sleeper* and Sonja in *Love and Death* than Faith, but she is back on firm ground in the uncompromisingly rough closing scenes.

Keaton was only able to scratch the surface of the pro–Palestinian actress in *The Little Drummer Girl* (1984), and it didn't help that the puffy circa-1984 clothes in that film seemed to swallow her up. But then she excelled in *Mrs. Soffel* (1984), a period piece in which she was the repressed wife of a prison warden in 1901 Pittsburgh who opens up to Mel Gibson's prisoner Ed Biddle.

She plays the first scenes in a haze of illness and cloudy unrest, but as she falls in love with Gibson's Ed, Keaton slowly breaks out her most star-like smile, and she even leers at him, in a pretty modern sort of way, as he takes a saw from under her skirt (this anachronistic performing risk really pays off as a relevant shock amidst the film's moody languor).

"Put your hands on me, Ed…. I'm so cold," she tells him, when they're on the lam and they're finally about to make love. The morning after, when he confesses to her that he killed a man, Keaton's Kate is so far-gone with love for him that this new information registers awfully sadly on her ghostly, out-on-a-limb face. In this momentous romance, evocatively shot in snowy landscapes by Gillian Armstrong, Keaton was at her very best, even managing to sneak in a few notes of screwball comedy when Kate is feeling most liberated.

She worked herself into neurotic tizzies as the self-defeating sister in *Crimes of the Heart* (1986), and she did a star turn in the yuppie comedy *Baby Boom* (1987), which was a big hit for her, and then she was at her most mannered in *The Good Mother* (1988), where she was punished once again for following sexual urges. Nothing was ever quite the same for Keaton after that.

She did Kay one more time for *The Godfather: Part III* (1990) and clearly used her own feelings about her real-life failed romance with Al Pacino in the one scene that gave her leeway to do so. She stepped into Allen's *Manhattan Murder Mystery* (1993) and tried to work up her old chemistry with him, and she had another hit in *The First Wives Club* (1996), still doing her self-deprecation act but in a more cartoonish key.

Keaton had one good scene talking about a boy she once knew as the dying sister in *Marvin's Room*, a monologue that was watched over indulgently by Meryl Streep. And she confirmed her limits as an actress when she failed in Christopher Durang's *Sister Mary Explains It All* (2001), strong, funny material that she lazily did not grapple with, substituting inexact, re-heated old mannerisms instead.

Keaton had a large personal success in the romantic comedy *Something's Gotta Give* (2003) with Jack Nicholson, and in that movie she "did" Diane Keaton, but in the best scenes she allowed herself to be sexy and vulnerable, and hedonistic. Beyond that hit, unfortunately, there was a succession of ramshackle commercial vehicles where she teamed up with any older male actor she could and really tested the patience of fans.

Probably her funniest appearances as an older woman were on Ellen DeGeneres's talk show, where she did her frazzled, semi-edgy thing while throwing back red wine on ice. She had coasted for a long time, but her films for Woody Allen and her three major dramatic performances from the 1980s secure her reputation as one of the most distinctive screen stars of her era, a one-of-a-kind romantic, always so ready to throw herself recklessly into anything life or the movies had to offer.

Sissy Spacek
Down Home

In her modest 2012 autobiography, *My Extraordinary Ordinary Life*, Sissy Spacek says that she prefers to play "ordinary" people like herself rather than the more "glamorous" type of role. Her Texas childhood, as described in her book, was happy and idyllic until she lost one of her brothers to illness (she was born Mary Elizabeth Spacek but her brothers always called her Sissy, and it stuck).

Small, strawberry blonde, and freckled, with a nose that looked like somebody squeezed it up into a point, Spacek went to New York in order to try to be a singer-songwriter, staying at first with her cousin Rip Torn and his Method actress wife Geraldine Page, both of whom were encouraging.

She lugged her guitar around, appeared as an extra in *Trash* (1970) for Andy Warhol (she was cut), and energetically recorded a novelty song about John Lennon and Yoko Ono called "John, You've Gone Too Far This Time" under the stage name Rainbo. She studied briefly at the Actors Studio with Lee Strasberg, long enough to learn about sense memory and substitutions, memories from her own life that she could use for a part.

Spacek got her first movie role in *Prime Cut* (1972), where Lee Marvin saved her from sex slavery, not the most auspicious debut. She had been advised to lose her Texas accent by various agents and casting directors, but Terrence Malick wanted her voice and her unassuming, plaintive face for his first film *Badlands* (1973), on which she met her husband and soul mate, production designer Jack Fisk, a man of talent who was best friends with David Lynch.

Spacek was called on to narrate *Badlands* in clichés ("Little did I realize..."), and she does so in a flat, affectless voice, for her character Holly, who is 15 years old, mostly feels "just kind of blah," a sociopathy that she shares with her killer boyfriend Kit (Martin Sheen in tight blue jeans). Spacek offers a nearly deadpan, naturalistic performance in *Badlands*, dreamy and oblivious, that exactly suits the style of the film. It's very Strasberg-Method work in that she gives almost nothing away of Holly's inner life, and of course this mystery is what makes this character so continuously fascinating, because she's so hard to read.

On the one hand, she's a traumatized girl who just goes along for the ride after Kit kills her father (Warren Oates). On the other hand, she's a passive but troublingly pragmatic person, enigmatic but looking out for herself, both very different from Kit and very similar. At the end, when Kit wonders if his unusual character will be taken into consideration when the law judges him, Holly nearly smiles, but not quite; she thinks better of it. And that moment is the key to Spacek's Holly. She does what she needs to do to survive, without any noticeable moral qualms.

Spacek played a flaky hippie in *Ginger in the Morning* (1974), singing some songs she wrote herself like "Sweet Cheeks." ("I got a bad case of sweet cheeks … it's showin' all over me.") But then she got her second oddball part that fitted her to a T: Carrie White in Brian De Palma's nasty *Carrie* (1976). Spacek goes big in this role, deliberately, spookily, and touchingly, playing in an Expressionist style hardly seen since Lillian Gish in *Broken Blossoms* (1919).

"Jack had a book of Gustave Doré's Bible illustrations that I pored over every day," Spacek wrote in her memoir, "studying the body language of people being stoned to death by their persecutors or tortured for their sins. I tried to start or end every major scene in one of those melodramatic positions." She had been voted homecoming queen herself at her high school, but Spacek totally inhabits her total outcast role with her long hair often in front of her face for protection. Her Carrie is picked on and humiliated, but storing up anger for telekinetic vengeance.

At the prom, Spacek's Carrie looks pale and fragile and lovely in her pink slip dress and thin wrap (Carrie made the outfit herself), a pre-Raphaelite figure stuck in a scuzzy 1970s milieu. She is sweetly nervous and suspicious about why she has been asked to the prom by jock Tommy Ross (William Katt), but he gradually wins her over and out of her shell.

Carrie is a movie that pushes a lot of primal buttons all at once. It needs the humanity that Spacek brings to it and also the silent movie extravagance that she brings to Carrie's staring look as she decimates her high school after getting pig's blood dumped on her head, a sequence where Spacek seamlessly moves from Gish to Lon Chaney in *The Phantom of the Opera* (1925). Her dedication to the part was proved when she insisted on being buried in the earth so that her own hand could come out to grab lone survivor Sue Snell (Amy Irving) at the end.

Spacek took what she was doing as Carrie to the next level in Robert Altman's dreamlike *3 Women* (1977), where she was expected to improvise and create her character from the ground up. As Pinky Rose, an empty vessel of a girl who gradually steals the identity of the nearly empty Millie Lammoreaux (Shelley Duvall), Spacek is impulsive, flirtatious, and stalker-ish. Both Pinky and Millie come from Texas, and if the chatterbox Millie is pitiful, Pinky is at some larval level below that.

When Millie yells at her, Pinky slinks away and jumps from a height into a swimming pool and lands herself in a coma. When she wakes up, Pinky refuses to recognize her parents, and she has made some sort of transformation. Pinky turns into a bratty teenager, and Spacek is particularly disturbing and possessed when she imitates the low laugh of "Dirty Gertie," a wooden figure at their favorite bar, Dodge City, where Millie and Pinky eventually seem to wind up as mother and daughter.

She was miscast as the worldly Carolyn Cassady in *Heart Beat* (1980), but that same year Spacek won a best actress Oscar for her Loretta Lynn in *Coal Miner's Daughter* (1980), where she aged from a backwoods bride of 14 to a country music star with large hair and a larger entourage. Spacek is so good in the first parts of this movie precisely because she's so un-actressy, so natural, wide-eyed but strong-willed.

She did her own singing here, charting how Lynn's singing voice solidified over the years and matching her smoky tones, and the movie takes its time so that this is a very believable progression. (Spacek stayed in character for most of the filming.) Director Michael Apted doesn't shy away from the roughness of Loretta's life with her much older husband Doolittle (Tommy Lee Jones), or the embarrassment of the scene where the overworked Loretta breaks down on stage in the middle of a concert. Spacek has a little trouble with the star flamboyance when Lynn first makes it big, but she and Jones make sure that the difficult and sad marriage they are portraying is true to life and unresolved.

Her husband Jack Fisk directed her next in *Raggedy Man* (1981), where she played a dissatisfied, divorced rural telephone operator with two young boys to raise during World War II. In this movie, Spacek moved away from the eccentrics she had been playing and seemed an adult finally, coming into full flower, and working up a gentle romantic chemistry with Eric Roberts, who plays a sailor coming to court her.

In the scene where she dances with a broom in *Raggedy Man*, Spacek is truly private, as if no one is watching her, so that she is communing with herself (all very Strasberg, but striking). Unfortunately, this small character study turns to violence for its conclusion, with villains intruding arbitrarily, and so the strength of Spacek's work as a star and lead gets overwhelmed.

Spacek was miscast as a free spirit and firebrand in *Missing* (1982), coming across instead like a petulant teenager, and she was one of a number of actresses who were trying to save their farms in 1984 in *The River*. She was nominated for an Oscar for both films, and then racked up another nomination for her impulsive sister Babe in *Crimes of the Heart* (1986). Spacek does one of her eccentrics from a more comic angle in this movie, widening her eyes and making them blank whenever Babe is caught up in one of her least conventional patterns of behavior.

Spacek retired for a few years after that picture, and when she returned it was often in thankless wife and mother roles, like her Mrs. Garrison in *JFK* (1991). But she was at her most extreme and imaginative as the mentally handicapped daughter Rose in David Lynch's *The Straight Story* (1999), and she made a comeback in the distanced, nearly morbid *In the Bedroom* (2001), playing a woman who loses her son to murder. Spacek reveals her character's pettiness and rigidity in the scene where she awkwardly slaps her son's girlfriend (Marisa Tomei), whom she blames for the murder.

Once again in this movie, Spacek's very smallness and seeming ordinariness is a cover for something finally monstrous yet everyday. The calm with which Spacek delivers the line, "Do you want some coffee?" to her husband at the end, after vengeance has been taken, is as chilly as the film itself. She stole scenes in *The Help* (2011) with a cartoonish performing style, and this showed just how flexible Spacek could be.

Debra Winger
Feathers in a Tornado

There was a time when *Terms of Endearment* (1983) was constantly on television. Flipping through channels, most people would stop to watch it again because it went down so easy; that's why they played it so often. Jack Nicholson was always a riot doing his star turn, and Shirley MacLaine got her laughs. Their section of the movie was like a well-oiled sitcom.

But when Debra Winger came on, you were not watching a sitcom anymore. When Winger is on screen in that movie, it feels like eavesdropping on a real person, and this sensation is compelling but slightly uncomfortable. We've all known somebody like Winger's Emma Horton. She laughs louder than anyone else, she follows her instincts wherever they take her and, in general, she raises the stakes of any situation she finds herself in.

When Emma doesn't have enough money for groceries, this mundane situation becomes epic as Winger takes items away from her children and then defiantly puts them back on the register. Critic Pauline Kael, a key supporter of Winger, wrote that she was "incredibly vivid" in *Terms of Endearment*, and it's true. That's why it's so hard to watch Emma die of cancer.

Winger never compromises during the death scenes, never lets us off the hook with noble self-pity. Dying in movies is usually a swift, even glamorous process, so it comes as a shock when we see Winger seething with rage and disgust instead of expressing wistful, ladylike regret, like Margaret Sullavan would have in her 1930s movies. Even when Winger's Emma says goodbye to her small children, she refuses to sanitize or sentimentalize the situation. Nothing Winger ever does on screen is pretty or ingratiating. When Emma feels sorry for herself at the end, she's closed-off to us, sullen, as most of us would be in life.

Winger doesn't care if you like her or not. Even when she tries to be charming, she can't quite go through with it. Her instincts tell her to scorn charm, and so she does, clinging to resentment and hurt feelings. She can turn us on, but she delights in turning us off. That quality is what makes her such an unusual actress, and it is that same quality that alienated many people and earned her important enemies in Hollywood. A reputation for being difficult began to limit her choices and, as time went on, self-consciousness began to affect her performances.

In 2001, I met Winger to talk about her return to films after a long hiatus, *Big Bad Love*, which was directed by her husband Arliss Howard, and she instantly magnetized me somewhere between "come hither" and "back off, buddy!" Some actors are rather ordinary in person, as if a light switch has been turned off, but Winger carries her own sort of charismatic turbulence into a room.

"So, are you going to ask some good questions?" she said to me challengingly. "These other guys! Man! Will you please promise not to ask me about stuff that happened years ago? It's probably my fault for not doing press then. They didn't get the answer they've been waiting for for 20 fucking years! 'So, what was it like to kiss Richard Gere?' I don't remember!" she croaked merrily.

Gere can be a cold acting partner, but in *An Officer and a Gentleman* (1982), which also used to get a lot of play on television, Winger got the most out of him in the love scenes, actually waking Gere up and transcending her "girlfriend" part. I began asking her about her breakthrough film *Urban Cowboy* (1980), where her face is soft, unformed, open to adventure. That movie made her a star, mostly because of a few scenes where she writhed on top of a mechanical bull.

"Yeah, *Cowboy* did it for me," she said. "You know, when Pauline Kael wrote about it, I was shocked when she made a big thing out of the stuff with the mechanical bull. Now, when I played that scene, I honestly wasn't aware of … what it looked like, you know? Sometimes critics confuse you with the characters you're playing, which I guess is a compliment. But that review taught me that if you want to be sexy, you can't think about it. It's like when someone you love does something adorable and you tell them about it … you destroy it, because then they become self-conscious about it. Most people, who haven't done it, think actors are extroverts, but it's very intimate while you're doing it, and you don't quite realize how it's going to be perceived when it's on the screen."

Her early credits in the late 1970s couldn't have been less auspicious. At age 21, she made her debut in a humiliatingly bad girlie exploitation movie called *Slumber Party '57* (1976), where she was expected to get topless a lot (when the other girls swim in a pool in their underwear, Winger keeps having to pull their bras off). "You guys," she says, "I have a super-neat idea … how about we tell about the first time we ever *did* it?"

Winger laughs and just exudes a lot here and is very much in the Diane Keaton mode where she feels she always needs to be doing something or reacting BIG, all the time, to anything and everything. Playing Wonder Woman's sister on TV was a step up after *Slumber Party '57*, but only by comparison.

She does some clumsy lady physical comedy in the disco dud *Thank God It's Friday* (1978), but she is lost in a crowd of low-level sitcom actors.

After *Urban Cowboy*, which director James Bridges fought to cast her in, the one-two punch of *An Officer and a Gentleman* and *Terms of Endearment* cemented her reputation, but trouble lay ahead. The blazing certainty of her acting in those three films deteriorated into hit-or-miss instinctual playing in *Cannery Row* (1982), an adaptation of a John Steinbeck novel co-starring Nick Nolte that didn't work out well. Winger seems constrained in that movie, and a humid discontent began to show in her eyes, as if she were anxious about something.

There was a gap in her career due to difficulties with *Mike's Murder* (1984), a star vehicle directed by her mentor James Bridges. Panned by most critics, *Mike's Murder* disappeared soon after its release, and that's unfortunate, for it is a tantalizing sun-struck film noir. It begins with a languid tennis game that dissolves into a slow-motion love scene between Winger and the questionable Mike (Mark Keyloun). Winger's Betty is having a non-committal, on-off affair with tennis instructor Mike, who deals some drugs on the side.

Winger reaches for half-articulated, amorphous feelings as Betty deals with Keyloun's cuddly Mike and with her pleasantly boring job at a bank. Gone is the volatility of her Emma Horton, for Winger is trying for something

A search for meaning: Debra Winger in *Mike's Murder*.

more exploratory and intuitive here. She is cast against type as a somewhat prudish, repressed woman who has been drawn out of her shell by revelatory sex, and this great sex she has with Mike opens her up but blurs her, preoccupies her, haunts her even as she is having it.

When Betty learns that Mike has been killed, the film ventures into very disquieting territory, down into the depths of the LA drug scene. Winger fleshes out Betty's pain at having lost Mike and how her love for him only grows to its full height after his death. She has a kind of brave loneliness here, and it lingers in the memory. "Well, in life, and in acting, the things that are unspoken are sometimes the stronger message," Winger said, reflecting on her work in *Mike's Murder*. "I mean, I always compare it to the relationship with your mother, because it feels strongest to me. Did she say everything? Or are the biggest lessons you learned from your mother the things she *didn't* say?"

"When acting is working right, it can be very invigorating," she said. "If you're a junkie for being awake, that feeling of being very awake and alert, well, that's the kind of alertness I find when film is running through a camera. I can say those same lines during a rehearsal, but something happens to me when the camera is running. When I stopped acting a few years ago, I taught a fellowship at Harvard, a literature class. I had read some of those books before, but reading them with the knowledge that I would be teaching something like Tolstoy's *The Death of Ivan Ilych*.... I read these books with that *awareness*. That's what I'm a junkie for, that awareness."

After *Mike's Murder*, she seemed to be a junkie looking for a new fix. By the time she made *Black Widow* (1987), Winger could no longer hide her furious restlessness. As a lawyer on the hunt for serial killer Theresa Russell, Winger seemed like someone in a perpetually bad mood, unfailingly spontaneous and interesting, but a turn-off, too. Her hard edges began to feel abrasive.

But watch the scene in *Black Widow* where she goes into a fake sob story about her abusive father and then laughs at her boss's gullibility, a moment that echoed Jeanne Moreau's gulling of Stanley Baker in *Eva* (1962) with a similar story. This is a perfect demonstration of how threatening Winger is to conventional notions of femininity and easy sentiment.

Winger had caused a controversy by publicly criticizing *Legal Eagles* (1986), a weak film packaged by agent Mike Ovitz. The director Ivan Reitman lashed back at his star, which added to her reputation for being difficult. She made a disturbing androgynous cameo in Alan Rudolph's *Made in Heaven* (1987) as Emmett, a punkish, male-ish emissary from the beyond, playing it with pink hair, lines under the eyes, and a steady twitch.

After that, Winger turned in multi-faceted performances in three impossible parts. In *Everybody Wins* (1990), a noir penned by Arthur Miller that keeps risking absurdity, Winger does a high-wire act as Angela, a schizo femme fatale and hooker. When Winger's Angela feels threatened, she moves into a snooty sort of Englishwoman persona (or a version of the stilted elocution that Miller's wife Marilyn Monroe used to fall into), and she comes across as a purely speculative person with no center at all. At one point Nick Nolte's private investigator calls her by her name and she says, "Ugh, Angela," as if she is tired of playing the role of herself.

Winger pitches her voice higher here and wears lighter hair and flings herself into a kind of void, and sometimes she even does work in *Everybody Wins* that could easily be mistaken for bad acting, or "bad acting," because Angela herself feels the need to be a bad actress sometimes. Talk about not playing it safe! At one point, trying to describe dealing with Angela, Nick Nolte's bewildered private eye proclaims, "It's like trying to chase feathers in a tornado!" and that nails Winger's very strange behavior here.

Winger somehow pulls off her Monroe-like character in *Everybody Wins* through sheer chutzpah, using a camp performing style and then sometimes dropping it very quickly to reveal immense hurt and sexual disturbance underneath (the editing helps her in some of her key scenes here, cutting on just the right disturbed facial expressions). And Winger held fast to her conception of the difficult Jane Bowles–like woman she played in Bernardo Bertolucci's adaptation of the Paul Bowles novel *The Sheltering Sky* (1990), where there are moments when she is clearly personalizing the dissatisfaction and frustration of her character and mingling it with her own.

Amid the general ineptitude of *A Dangerous Woman* (1993), Winger created a poetically awkward, slow-minded, alien character, widening her eyes like a child when things go wrong, unable to understand the people around her but trying to pretend like she can. Winger seemed to intensely identify with the social pariah she was playing here, and she kept her prickly and isolated. Both *Everybody Wins* and *A Dangerous Woman* showed just how imaginative Winger could be, and they also displayed an acting talent operating on the highest possible level. These performances are sometimes very close to what Robert De Niro was doing in his best 1970s work, thematically if not technically.

Before her self-imposed exile, Winger had a last hit with *Shadowlands* (1993), a sentimental love story in which she looked truly lost. Again, her character died of cancer. It seemed as if the public was only comfortable with Winger on screen when she was killed off. "At my age, actresses have this whole facial surgery thing to deal with," she said candidly in 2001. "You can't tell what age a woman is anymore! I was passin' them on the way up, and now I'm passin' them on the way down, and they look younger than I do!" She laughed, that harsh, strangled, beautiful laugh of hers. "One day, I'll want to do it all at once, and I'll get confused and Botox my breasts!"

"But, you know, I love faces, I like them to tell a story," she said. "I like to point and say, 'This line is from when my Mom passed away,' and 'This one is my son's first concussion.' I've smiled a lot in my life, so these lines show up. I live on the earth, and there's gravity, you know. I will not say that it's easy to wake up in the morning and feel a certain way and then see your face in the mirror and go, 'What the fuck is that!' One little line suddenly becomes a peace symbol! But I've had enough bad things happen to me in my life that I couldn't control, so why would I voluntarily go under the knife? I don't want to look like I tie my ponytail too tight."

Robert De Niro, Al Pacino, and Dustin Hoffman all brought a kind of nervy, specifically ethnic vitality to the screen in the 1970s and '80s, and they thrived, whereas Winger, who is roughly their female equivalent, was castigated as a scourge and troublemaker and finally shunted aside.

"She doesn't like *anyone*," said her former *Wonder Woman* co-star Lynda Carter in an interview with Larry King, and that does about sum it up, for Winger famously feuded with practically all of her fellow actors and directors and badmouthed them. Some of them deserved it, no doubt, but that level of unrest must finally indicate something amiss within Winger herself.

There was not much of note for Winger after 2001 aside from her cold mother in *Rachel Getting Married* (2008). In the same year as that movie, Winger published a cryptic, fragmented memoir called *Undiscovered* that revealed little except her restlessness and anxiety. Playing Greta Gerwig's mother in *Lola Versus* (2012), Winger clearly looked bemused to still be acting, and in such a small, thankless part. In 2016, she was reduced to a very poor sitcom with laugh track called *The Ranch* for Netflix, where it was painful to see her trying to deliver bottom-of-the-barrel situation comedy dialogue.

But in 2017 Winger appeared in an exquisite romantic comedy called *The Lovers* where she looked her age and gave herself over to falling in love again with a long-time husband (Tracy Letts) after years of having an affair with another man, and it was clear that her worried face could still open up to a challenge and to deep emotions. And Winger's trail of great and near-great performances from the 1980s and early '90s are still there, still vibrant.

Sigourney Weaver
Above It All

Amazon-tall, clearly smart and erudite yet always game for nonsense and tomfoolery, Sigourney Weaver attended Yale at the same time as Meryl Streep and the playwright Christopher Durang. She has been a droll muse for Durang in the theater all her life, her calm voice steadying his absurdities and parodies, and her face always carrying a winning charge of slight panic and surprise for him.

Born Susan Weaver in Manhattan in 1949, she was the daughter of an NBC television executive and the niece of the comedian Doodles Weaver, whose specialty was the mixing up of words. She began using the unusual name "Sigourney" in 1963, after a minor character in F. Scott Fitzgerald's *The Great Gatsby* named Sigourney Howard.

She attended Sarah Lawrence and Stanford and earned her masters at Yale, so that by the time she took the role of Ripley in *Alien* (1979) she was educated and finished to an advanced degree. Always with Weaver there is a tinge of woodenness in her delivery of dialogue, a very slight stiltedness that is part of her brainy quality, but this is balanced by her access to many extreme and uncommon emotions.

Weaver played on stage in Albert Innaurato's *Gemini* in 1976 and John Guare's absurdist *Marco Polo Sings a Solo* in 1977 at the Public Theatre. And then she was Ripley in the first *Alien* movie, a sci-fi grunge thriller classic in which she emerged from the ensemble cast to be the last surviving member of the spaceship Nostromo.

Weaver is impressively commanding yet vulnerable in that first picture already, even if it does ask her to play part of the climax in a tight t-shirt and skimpy panties (and surely playing all the fear in the last part of this movie must have been a very draining experience). Weaver's screen image, both in the *Alien* movies and some of her other pictures, is wondrously butch and warrior-like, and sexy in a distinctively Sapphic way, even if Weaver herself is publicly heterosexual.

Weaver appeared Off-Broadway in Durang's *Beyond Therapy* in 1981, and she was excited by the young Mel Gibson in *The Year of Living Danger-*

ously (1982), working up so much chemistry with him on screen that her rather poor English accent in that picture could be overlooked. She was then a reasonable goddess pursued by a nerdy accountant (Rick Moranis) and a sarcastic (Bill Murray) in the dispiriting hit *Ghostbusters* (1984), where she became possessed by a demon and subject to 1984-era special effects.

At the same time she received a Tony nomination for her role on stage in David Rabe's *Hurlyburly* and married the theater director Jim Simpson, who eventually founded the dynamic Flea Theater in downtown Manhattan. Fluent in French, Weaver made a comedy with Gérard Depardieu called *One Woman or Two* (1985), and she appeared nude in the sleazy and absurd *Half Moon Street* (1986), where she played a doctor-turned-escort.

In the theater, she played Stella in a Williamstown production of *A Streetcar Named Desire* with Blythe Danner as Blanche and Christopher Walken as Stanley, and Portia in a production of *The Merchant of Venice* at Classic Stage in Manhattan. Her level face and voice seemed ready for anything, either trash or the classics.

Weaver returned to Ripley as the central starring figure in James Cameron's *Aliens* (1986), which has all the hallmarks of its time. The first *Alien* movie directed by Ridley Scott is about how a crew of blue-collar space workers are deemed expendable by their employers, and it is filled with cigarette smoke and distrust of authority. This new *Aliens* knows that the government and bureaucrats exploit the military as "expendable," but it is a far sleeker and more streamlined entertainment. Weaver is allowed to show many different sides of Ripley as she suffers from post-traumatic stress and gradually comes into her own as a warrior fighting for an orphan girl she adopts. (Weaver has an indelible audience applause moment here when she cries, "Get away from her, you bitch!" to the alien before doing battle.)

Weaver got an Oscar nomination for *Aliens*, but she was several degrees fiercer than even Ripley as Dian Fossey in *Gorillas in the Mist* (1988), for which she received another best actress Oscar nomination. Her Dian is an obsessional and self-absorbed anthropologist and lover of gorillas, and she is not to be trifled with. As Dian starts to act more like the gorillas to befriend them, she is told, "They think you're a witch," to which Weaver replies, "They wouldn't be the first" with a very butch sort of swagger. As a younger woman especially, Weaver likes to introduce camp elements into serious roles, and this might explain her kinship with Durang.

Gorillas in the Mist seems somehow afraid of her (it feels like key scenes have been cut), and we never quite understand Dian's need or madness as she hardens into a woman beyond all reach, but Weaver bites hard into this part and takes it as far as she can. She received her best actress nomination for *Gorillas* the same year she got one for best supporting actress for her wickedly self-assured boss to Melanie Griffith in *Working Girl*, where she memorably and off-handedly says, "and I am, after all, *me*." This was a peak in her film career.

Yet Weaver did some very adventurous work throughout the 1990s in risky and ambitious material like *Death and the Maiden* (1994), a Roman Polanski adaptation of a play about torture and revenge in which she was alternately fearsomely strong and touchingly vulnerable. She was a victimized Ripley with a shaved head in David Fincher's *Alien 3* (1992), weeping as the monster came after her again and finally sacrificing herself.

Weaver was surprisingly damaged and conscience-stricken in the little-seen *A Map of the World* (1999) as a woman consumed by guilt after her negligence causes the death of a child. This is one of her very best and most unexpected performances, a rather alarming confession of shame and inadequacy that somehow still manages to hinge on Weaver's jock-like physical presence as a kind of contrast to the very unattractive emotions on display.

She was elegantly sexy in *The Ice Storm* (1997) and excelled as a blonde TV actress in the clever comedy *Galaxy Quest* (1999) and as a gold-digger in *Heartbreakers* (2001), further proof that the tony Weaver was often most relaxed and inventive in rather lowbrow commercial contexts. In *Alien: Resurrection* (1997) Weaver was a clone of Ripley who blithely announces, "I'm the monster's mother" while striding around Winona Ryder (who is wearing a baby lesbian sort of haircut) in her most commanding fashion.

Weaver was more marginalized after that, often working in obscure films and small roles before returning to James Cameron for *Avatar* (2009), where a little of the enormous budget certainly could have been allotted to get her some hair dye that looked less like Lady Clairol from the local drugstore.

She flooded the small screen with tears in the earnest gay rights TV movie *Prayers for Bobby* (2009) and did her best to bring emotional insight and flavor to the TV series *Political Animals* (2012) while taking more small roles and leads in obscure features.

Weaver returned to Durang material at Lincoln Center in 2012 and on Broadway in 2013 in *Vanya and Sonia and Masha and Spike*, where she gave a desperately busy performance as a vain actress. But of course unpredictability in everything had always been her watchword.

Glenn Close
Command Performances

It was only later in life that Glenn Close disclosed how she had spent her childhood and adolescence in a cult called the Moral Re-Armament (MRA) and managed to break away from them, in a painful fashion, when she was 22 years old. Her father was a doctor who worked in the Congo, and her mother was a socialite, and both of them had joined MRA when she was seven.

After she got away from this cult, Close studied theater intensively at school and began a stage career, mainly Off-Broadway in New York in the 1970s. She made her movie debut at the age of 35 as the mother in *The World According to Garp* (1982), which won her an Oscar nomination for best supporting actress. Close played an eccentric nurse in that movie with a direct attitude about sex, and she seemed patrician and authoritative in the manner of Katharine Hepburn.

Close got another supporting nomination for a scene where she cries in a shower in the ensemble movie *The Big Chill* (1983), which was the first film to show just how voluptuously and strikingly she gave herself up to weeping (only Julianne Moore can compete with her when it comes to photogenic crying). She got a third supporting nomination in a row for her girlfriend in *The Natural* (1984), an idealized woman who benefits from lots of backlighting.

It was only at the age of 40 that Close really broke through to lead actress status in the huge hit and cultural touchstone *Fatal Attraction* (1987), a coldly effective melodrama in which she played Alex Forrest, a book editor with tendril-like blonde hair and a childishly clinging attitude who sleeps with the married Dan (Michael Douglas) and then develops an obsession with him, stalking him, tormenting his family, and insisting that she is not going to be ignored. Close knows that Alex is her big chance, and so she pulls out all the stops in a way that surprised people who only knew her work in supporting roles. She is very present, focused, and commanding here, with a low, sexy, powerfully resonant voice, and she makes Alex into a great villain but also a ruined little girl.

Fatal Attraction doesn't give too many clues about what might be wrong with Alex, psychiatrically speaking, or what might have happened to her to make her what she is. In retrospect, Close seems to be hinting that Alex might have been molested by her father (she reverts to a little-girl beseeching look periodically, and she kills her father off in conversation with Dan before admitting he is still alive). Is she manic-depressive? That might be, because her sexual high with Dan (making crazy love to him and then wanting to go out dancing right after and then wanting to have sex again in an elevator) would suggest someone who is in a manic state.

Alex sinks low very quickly, attempting suicide when Dan tries to leave and then pretending that she is pregnant with his child. But Alex is a desperately unhappy person, and her unhappiness makes her behave in a desperate and finally despicable way. Close holds on to her larger conception of this woman when the movie wants to just turn her into a shrew; look at the sad semi-smile she gives Dan after he has attacked her and she has come at him with a knife, as if she is saying, "Why has it come to this?"

The original ending had Alex committing suicide by slitting her throat with a knife as she listens to *Madame Butterfly*, her favorite opera, and this was Close's preferred ending. (She has said in interviews that she knows people like Alex usually do more harm to themselves than they do to others.) But she came back and shot the more commercially viable conclusion where Alex has had a psychotic break and has to be strangled and then shot before her crazed passion can finally be put to rest. To her credit, Close put up a very staunch fight for her character before being forced to capitulate to this.

She got a lead Oscar nomination for her Alex, and then another one for her Marquise de Merteuil in *Dangerous Liaisons* (1988), which is most memorable for the penultimate scene where Close has an enormous breakdown after hearing that her former lover and partner in manipulation Valmont (John Malkovich) has been killed.

It all happens very fast: she is howling with grief as she opens the door to her room, and then the Marquise smashes some candles off a table and smashes a mirror. She hurls another small candelabra against a wall and starts tearing at the top of her dress like a wild animal as her ladies in waiting come to see what's wrong.

"Get out! Get out!" the Marquise howls at them as she starts to sink to her knees, heaving and gasping as her grief looks to be ripping her apart physically. This scene lasts just 25 seconds, but it makes a startling impact, particularly because Close's performance up to this point has been all about how the Marquise hides her own very turbulent emotions behind an icy and calculating façade.

This is a woman who brags about being able to smile at table when she has to jab a fork into her hand to contain her fury and boredom, and so this letting go emotionally has the impact of a natural disaster, and Close plays the full size of it. In her finest scenes in *Fatal Attraction* and *Dangerous Liaisons*, Close has the kind of virile emotional push of Bette Davis.

She was again at her demanding best as the unloved socialite Sunny von Bülow in *Reversal of Fortune* (1990), narrating the movie with a knowing voice from her hospital bed, where she is in a coma that might have been caused by her husband Claus (Jeremy Irons). Close was then an energetic Gertrude to Mel Gibson's extremely energetic *Hamlet* (1990), where they both tear passions to tatters.

She worked regularly throughout the 1990s in a curious mixture of plain parts that indulged her talent for tears and fancier villains that allowed her to go over the top, and her most notable credit in this time was on Broadway in the musical version of *Sunset Boulevard*. Close labored with the Andrew Lloyd Webber score, acting it when her singing didn't quite make it, and she also labored to replicate the long-vanished acting style of silent pictures where eyes were everything, and she had at least a personal success. (She was very hammy, but of course no one expected a subtle Norma Desmond.) Close won a Tony for Tom Stoppard's *The Real Thing* in 1983, and she got another for *Death and the Maiden* in 1992, and then another for her Norma in 1994.

When she was well into her fifties, Close made an ill-advised attempt to play Nellie Forbush in a 2001 TV movie of the musical *South Pacific*, and then she returned to Hepburn territory with a TV remake of *The Lion in Winter* in 2003, and she was at least exuberantly game in both. In *Evening* (2007), which featured every actress in SAG and her daughter, Close did her big breakdown set piece from *Dangerous Liaisons* again to call attention to herself.

She returned to TV as a high-powered lawyer in the series *Damages*, for which she won several Emmy awards, and then she starred in, produced, co-wrote, and probably whipped up some food for craft service for *Albert Nobbs* (2011), a role she had played Off-Broadway in the early 1980s. As a victimized woman who dresses as a man in nineteenth century Ireland, Close was "meek" in a hopelessly studied and hammy way, and she really let her own worst habit of self-pity get the better of her. But she got a sixth Oscar nomination for it, losing to Meryl Streep, who grabbed her third Oscar for *The Iron Lady*.

Close appeared on Broadway in Edward Albee's *A Delicate Balance* in 2014, and she played Norma Desmond again in London in 2016 and then on Broadway. In spite of some later missteps, this is clearly a substantial career made by an actress very comfortable with the spotlight and with the most demanding roles, to which she always brings her full and sometimes gaudy talent to bear. Surely a competitive or honorary Oscar is in her near future.

Kathleen Turner
Lust for Life

One of the most vivid of 1980s female movie stars, Kathleen Turner was very unusual in looks and manner, as if she were high on her own charisma. Her father was a diplomat who had to go where he was posted, and so she had grown up in various countries, including Cuba, Venezuela, and England. This affected her smoky voice, which seemed to take on different unaccountable flavors and bits of accents in a nearly eccentric way.

Like Faye Dunaway, she is incapable on screen of being either calm or straightforward; she is always in some kind of tumult or upheaval. Turner was a sultry blonde, and she had an odd habit of narrowing her eyes and then opening them to punctuate statements, as she does in her first starring role, *Body Heat* (1981), when her femme fatale Matty Walker speaks derisively of her role as a sexpot.

Matty is a devious person, capable of setting in motion the most complicated noir-style plot to get what she wants. *Body Heat* does not explore her motives or psychology, presenting only the surface of her sexual appeal and her flair for revving up her engine for lying and for sex. We learn in the last scene that her name is actually Mary Ann Simpson, and in her high school yearbook she was known as "The Vamp." (It also says that her ambition was to "To be rich and live in an exotic land.") Maybe Ned Racine (William Hurt) feels in the end that all his sex bouts with Matty were worth a life in prison for murder. After all, she had introduced herself with the line, "You're not too smart.... I like that in a man."

Turner smartly decided to send up her new image in the broad Steve Martin comedy *The Man with Two Brains* (1983), where she played a shameless tease energized by what seemed like sexual desire but was actually murderous anger. And then she really consolidated her stardom by playing the slobby romance novelist Joan Wilder in the hit comedy adventure *Romancing the Stone* (1984), where her heroine changes from cosseted single cat lady to a fully blossomed woman of action and appetite. It was in letting us see her gain the confidence that she already so evidently had that Turner really made an impression on everyone as a shy woman who finds it in her to become a

Kathleen Turner is comic and tragic at once in *Crimes of Passion*.

kind of female Indiana Jones, and she met her ideal screen partner in the sharkish Michael Douglas.

Turner took chances, like the designer by day and hooker by night in Ken Russell's *Crimes of Passion* (1984), a deliriously blunt and vulgar movie in which Turner did the nasty comedy scenes full out, like a child at play, rolling her eyes at men and hurling herself into extreme role play scenarios.

She walks the streets with a camp physical swagger here that might have impressed Mae West. ("Disgusting is my middle name, honey!" she tells manic preacher Anthony Perkins.) Yet all the while Turner is also doing a subtle, touching, and original exploration of sexual control issues. Very few actors are as skilled as Turner is when it comes to playing a role with a double edge, with doing two opposed actions and tones at once.

In *Crimes of Passion*, Turner was able to go from the X-rated comedy burlesque of her scenes with Perkins to a graphically sexual scene where she dominates a cop with a nightstick and then confronts her own psychic damage in a mirror afterward. It's hard to imagine anyone else giving this role such strength, such humor, and such sexual insight, all while dealing with a screenwriter she found unpleasant, Russell's heavy drinking, and Perkins's constant sniffing of benzyl nitrate both on and off camera, which made her afraid for her safety sometimes. (She deserves particular kudos for keeping a straight yet slightly perplexed face when Perkins ties her up and then suddenly starts belting out "Get Happy" on her piano.)

Turner had had no formal training, and so she wasn't an Actors Studio person. "If I play a fifty-dollar whore on Hollywood Boulevard, I'm not going to go out and walk the street to see what it's like being a cheap whore in Hollywood—thank you, no," she wrote in her 2008 memoir. "I will use my imagination, and what knowledge I've been given in the script." With Turner, we can see a return to a more heightened style that is less concerned with psychological bric-a-brac. She could have easily been a star in the 1930s or '40s, even if she became an emblem of the greedy and sleek 1980s.

William Hurt, very much a Method actor who wanted to stay in character all the time, hated how Turner would laugh and joke around right up until they started shooting a scene for *Body Heat*. "Well, I don't want to be in that character until I start to act her," Turner said. "Staying in character when I am not on camera or on stage feels very fake to me. I really don't think about acting until I do it, and then when I do it, I do it completely."

In the strange dark comedy *Prizzi's Honor* (1985), Turner was at her most vibrantly starry as a hit woman with a lie for every occasion, effortlessly catching Jack Nicholson's sexual interest and then his anger at her inevitable betrayal. She got an Oscar nomination for the high-concept *Peggy Sue Got Married* (1986), where she played a sad divorcee who travels back in time to her youth. Turner is alive with feeling here, as ever, but the movie neglects her, as if director Francis Ford Coppola were more interested in arranging colors for the screen rather than people.

Her sultry voicing of Jessica Rabbit in *Who Framed Roger Rabbit* (1988) was the height of her vogue, but she gave maybe her finest or most exploratory film performance in *The War of the Roses* (1989), a sharp satire on 1980s materialism in which she and Michael Douglas were a warring couple splitting apart and unable to split their possessions. Turner reaches a high peak of fed-up female rage here when Douglas sputters, "You weren't even multi-orgasmic before you met me, were you?" and she responds, "Do you really expect me to keep *on* reassuring you sexually even now when we disgust each other?"

The part of Barbara Rose in *The War of the Roses* is her best on film because the jagged, insightful writing allows her to bring forth and brandish all of her own sharpest edges, and even discover a few she hadn't even known were lurking in her. *The War of the Roses*, like *Crimes of Passion*, is a movie that isn't afraid of the brazen strength and contradiction Turner can bring to a role. In the late scenes, Turner becomes such a scourge, such a powerhouse of resentment, and so Medea-like in her focus that she sometimes stuns the camera with just her level gaze, just the husky timbre of her unforgiving voice.

She played Maggie the Cat in *Cat on a Hot Tin Roof* on Broadway in 1990, and there were movies that didn't really work after that, but there was also one final lead that made the most of her drive and comic skill: John Waters's *Serial Mom* (1994). In that picture, Turner at 40 toed a line between camp good cheer and frighteningly murderous rage (she is like something from a nightmare when chasing a neighbor down a street at top speed with a knife), and again it was tough to think of another actress who could have done both the camp and the rage full out yet keep them both in balance.

At this point, Turner became ill with rheumatoid arthritis, so that she was in constant pain on Broadway in *Indiscretions* in 1995. Turner was told she would probably never walk again as the illness progressed, and the medicine she took for it, coupled with increased alcohol intake to dull the pain, made for a noticeable change in her appearance.

She had broken her nose on the set of *V.I. Warshawski* (1991), and with a weight gain she began to look very different. Turner's performing style had always been based in her confidence and sometimes even her over-confidence in herself, and part of this confidence came from her physical appearance. And so there was a poignant disconnect now between her broadened face and body and the discomfort she was obviously feeling—both physical and emotional—and her plummy starriness of manner. This made her tough to cast in the late 1990s.

Sofia Coppola used her as the stern and puritanical mother in *The Virgin Suicides* (1999), a good but small role in which she was nearly unrecognizable as her former self, and she played Chandler's drag queen father on *Friends* on TV in 2001, and her low voice had gone even lower. She did a nude scene in *The Graduate* on stage in London in 2000 and then in New York in 2002, and she made clear that she could still be "Kathleen Turner" in the theater if not on film.

Turner played Martha in a revival of Edward Albee's *Who's Afraid of Virginia Woolf?* on Broadway in 2005. This was a role Turner had worked hard to secure and had always wanted to do, and she had a success in it both in New York and in London. Though she was a little too busy and reactive in the first act, by the end of that play Turner had reached down into herself and brought up the stripped-bare essence of her damaged character, and this had the feeling of a hard-won battle.

There were lesser stage vehicles after that, though she did do *Mother Courage* at Arena Stage in 2014 and seemed hearty and well cast. The best she could do in film the same year she did her Mother Courage was the role of Fraida Felcher in *Dumb and Dumber To* (2014), in which Jim Carrey refers to her "blowfish jowls." The whole joke of Turner's role in the first scenes of *Dumb and Dumber To* is that she looks different, but after this change in her looks has been acknowledged the second half of the movie lets Turner be sexy and wacky and full of energy as she used to be, and dressed-up and looking well.

Turner showed some of her old verve and pluck here, selling her laugh lines with gusto, and she also showed an ability to roll with the punches and laugh at herself. After all her physical and career setbacks, Turner was still throwing her whole body into her work with that sense of childlike play she always had, that same hyper-active abandon, and this was wholly admirable.

Alfre Woodard
Wait and See

Alfre Woodard steals Steve McQueen's *12 Years a Slave* (2013) in her four minutes on screen, just as she stole Robert Altman's *Health* (1980) away from a large group of flashy and established stars, though maybe "steals" is not quite the word. She brings *12 Years a Slave* to a new level, something a lot more unconventionally human than what we have so far seen.

As Mistress Shaw, a slave who has attained a higher status as the lover of her enslaver, Woodard has a lot to accomplish in those four minutes McQueen has allotted her. She has to offer a peculiar oasis to Solomon (Chiwetel Ejiofor), the free man who has been brutally captured and held on a nearby plantation, and she also has to make a crucial judgment on the life around her and make it seem like more than wishful thinking. Her scene is a hinge in the film.

Sitting on her porch with Solomon and the continually violated Patsey (Lupita Nyong'o), Mistress Shaw smiles at them and presides over a kind of mad tea party. Mistress Shaw, as Woodard plays her, is maybe a little mad, but her madness could also be seen as will power. There's something deliberately absurd, or absurdist, about her, and she can afford this luxury because she has come to some conclusions about her place in the world and her debased milieu.

McQueen has given Woodard what seems like the key line of his film, and she pronounces it with such airy authority that it has haunted my consciousness ever since I heard her say it. "The plague of the Pharaohs is but a poor sample of what awaits the plantation class," she says to Solomon, in a way that makes it seem like an open-and-shut case that barely touches the hem of her own private, locked-away consciousness. This line augurs earthly punishment for the American South, but Woodard suggests much more than that. Will there really be a judgment for human evildoing after death? I'm assuming you've given this idea some thought at one time or another. I've never been sure. But I'm slightly surer that there might be because of the smilingly certain way that Woodard says that line.

Woodard made her film debut in Alan Rudolph's highly eccentric *Remember My Name* (1978). She has racked up over 100 credits since then, and a lot of her best work has been done for television. In the 1980s, she won

Emmys for her performances on the TV series *Hill Street Blues* and for the pilot of *LA Law*, where she played a rape victim who is dying of leukemia, a heavy load for any actress to carry, but one that Woodard lightens with the shy, particular details of her playing.

Woodard's large eyes are so intensely direct when she focuses her attention on something or someone that they might be intimidating if the base of her talent wasn't so unabashedly warm and tender. Look at the way her eyes hone in on her scene partner Ving Rhames in her scenes from the TV movie *Holiday Heart* (2000), as if they could actually reach out to touch him. Watch the way she listens to him, disengaging sometimes and seeming to stare into her own resentment and then gradually starting to soften for him.

A generation of African American actresses have done the "Somebody Almost Walked Off With All My Stuff" monologue from Ntozake Shange's *For Colored Girls Who Have Considered Suicide When the Rainbow Is Enuf*, and it is nearly always played on a note of rambunctious, self-actualized defiance, yet Woodard chooses to play it in a muted, almost furtive way in the 1982 PBS film of the play.

She doesn't like to hit us with committed defiance or anger. Woodard is drawn to emotions that actors usually skip or leave out, feelings of inadequacy, self-doubt, lack of center, worry. She can be very internal, but when her searchlight eyes really turn back on themselves, you can see all of the things that most of us hide. Watching her here is a little like seeing someone's messy room with clothes on the floor and an unmade bed. Woodard's character wants to be loved for herself, unmade bed and all, and she is scared that she won't be.

When Woodard turns her attention to sex, she is never overt about it. As with everything else, she comes at it sideways. "My entire career has been a matter of slipping it in when they don't know it's coming," Woodard said in an interview. "I'm here because I didn't try to come through a door. I came in through the window. Because they weren't going to let me in through the door. Ever!"

In a TV adaptation of James Baldwin's *Go Tell It on the Mountain* (1984), a fully-clothed Woodard exudes sex in her first scene with absolutely no obvious sexual signifiers, just the buzzing tone of her smoky voice and the way she moves as if she is ill and only sex can possibly cure what ails her.

For two of her best-known roles, *Cross Creek* (1983), which earned her an Oscar nomination for best supporting actress, and *Passion Fish* (1992), Woodard was asked to play helpmates to white women, and she did her self-effacing, detailed best in both of those parts, but she is far more memorable as a weird dork moved by surprising impulses of unconscious sexual energy in *Miss Firecracker* (1989) and as a vibrantly hedonistic woman in *Down in the Delta* (1998), where her responses to life are always very extreme.

The real root of Woodard's talent is the depth of her responsiveness to

Alfre Woodard stealthily commands the camera in August Wilson's *The Piano Lesson*.

outside stimuli, and her formidable craft shows in the way she is able to make smooth transitions between such extreme feelings without ever tripping over any of them. Her movie career is studded with small placeholder roles, cops and judges and school principals, but on television she has been able to do August Wilson's *The Piano Lesson* (1995) and Carson McCullers's *The Member of the Wedding* (1997), where she reinvented the role of Berenice and turned it inside out.

Ethel Waters, the original Berenice, gave a major performance in that part both on stage and in Fred Zinnemann's 1952 film. The way Waters played her, Berenice was wearily finished with a lot of things in life, but Woodard's Berenice, by contrast, is a woman who still seems to have some options, and so her gradual loss of those options as the play goes on seems even more tragic than it did with Waters.

As a black woman in show business, Woodard has had to deal with many of the limits that others seek to place on her, but the remarkable thing about her career is what a haul she has managed to make in terms of varied but usually non-ostentatious roles across a wide range of moods. She can be both restrained and bold at once, both sexy and withholding, commanding yet as cautious as a cat intensely watching for any sudden movement.

Her achievement as an actress is singular because Woodard will never pretend that she is more confident or in charge than she actually is. She wants to show us the sidelong feelings of people who have little power but still harbor a few small hopes, and that's why her performance in *12 Years a Slave* feels so crucial to the narrative of that film and so emblematic of the creative character of one of our best American actresses.

Judy Davis
High Anxiety

Judy Davis is visually unmistakable. Her chalk-white skin tone fights for precedence over her dark red lips, and her frizzy, unmanageable hair frames burned, sensitive eyes. She wears a mask, in a way, a face that is drawn on, and she is very much a creature of artifice.

Davis does not believe, really, that people have consistent or plausible characters, and so her work is made up of bold little stylized fragments of behaving where she signals her own discomfort and her own anger and weakness and many other unattractive things but makes them into a colorful mosaic. This is a jagged style that might cut you.

Even if some people might not recognize her name, on screen Davis is emotionally unmistakable, refusing any kind of sentimentality so obsessively that she often runs the risk of making herself into a shrew. (People who know her work invariably say, "She overdoes it sometimes, doesn't she?") Davis is a virtuoso in her way, but she is always being pushed underground to supporting roles and lots of obscure television.

Critic Pauline Kael called Davis "a genius at moods," and at her best (meaning when she's at her most relaxed), this is an actress who can take a silent close-up and give us the illusion that we are seeing pure, sneaky, unguarded behavior. Yet she always underlines the fact that we are watching an illusion, an act, before she moves on to something else, breathlessly, as if she were being hunted. Watching Judy Davis jerkily shake her head to punctuate a wry point, which is her most consistent physical mannerism, is one of the real joys of watching movies and television.

Davis was born in Australia, and she was brought up by strict Catholics who wouldn't allow her to see movies. She ran away from a convent education to sing and study theater, and she played Juliet to Mel Gibson's Romeo at drama school. She appeared briefly in the trashy *High Rolling in a Hot Corvette* (1977), where she is a coltish, skeptical, small-waisted young beauty.

Davis made her official debut in Gillian Armstrong's *My Brilliant Career* (1979), a film that she later dismissed (her cranky outspokenness on sets and in interviews has surely cost her work). In that big chance, the young Davis is a pale, freckled, disquieting presence with problem hair, and the camera flinches from her impatience with her role.

Most actors aren't critical at all about their own performances or the films they appear in, whereas Davis is probably too critical, but that critical spirit is also the essence of some of her best work. "I just didn't like the character I was playing," she said of *My Brilliant Career* in 1993. "I didn't like the woman it was based on. She wrote these silly books about her early childhood in the bush that nobody was interested in."

Davis is a showboater in *My Brilliant Career*, and intimidatingly discriminating, "plain, useless, and Godless," as her mother calls her. Her Sybylla is sometimes a lovable freak, and sometimes distinctly unlovable, harsh, demanding, unappeasable. "I'm so ugly," she says at one point, crying. "And nobody loves me." But she is also playful, a play-actor, rough and fearless and intense. She is unconventional, and she will not be denied, and this conception of the character in the script was too simplistic for Davis, whose bullshit detector wanted to sniff out the tiresome loser in this girl.

That slightly perverse instinct of hers would keep Davis away from too much mainstream success, even though she clearly possessed the spirit of the young Katharine Hepburn, a similar freak who couldn't have done more to please mainstream tastes past 1940. Davis had the talent and the character to be another Hepburn or Bette Davis, but she did not have the drive or ambition that they had, the warrior spirit, and so she did her best work in small films and TV movies and became a cult figure.

She stayed in Australia for several obscure pictures like *Winter of Our Dreams* (1981), where she played a junkie prostitute with urine-yellow, cropped hair who is continually putting off advances from Baz Luhrmann (her work in this film needs a firmer structure supporting it). In *Hoodwink* (1981) Davis was sensitive and open and naughty, with very direct and piercing yet emotionally exposed eyes, as a religious woman opening herself up to a love affair with an ex-con named Martin (John Hargreaves).

"I want you to know me," she tells Martin in *Hoodwink* as they stand in the sun, the wind riffling her hair as she unbuttons her blouse. Davis is so touching and sexy here because it obviously means a lot for her to let her guard down like this, and she is offering herself up to the camera in the way her character is offering herself up to the man she is in love with.

She played a terrorist in *The Final Option* (1982), and she got an Oscar nomination for best actress for her sexually repressed Miss Quested in David Lean's *A Passage to India* (1984), a cautious version of a major book, and another film where Davis let her unhappiness with the final product be known, in print. Her hair is straightened here, and her cornflower blue eyes are bleary with discontent and blocked desire.

Davis does all she can with Miss Quested, but she makes a few careless small mistakes here and there (a little bit of mugging in response to others, a sulky lack of engagement in some scenes), and seems as impatient with the conception of her part as she did with *My Brilliant Career*, albeit in a far more low-key fashion.

So much of her best work is hard to find, or out of the way, but she merits the fullest sort of search. Davis played both Cordelia and the Fool in a 1984 stage production of *King Lear* in Australia, and she also played Strindberg's Miss Julie. She did Hedda Gabler on stage in Australia in 1986, an ideal role for her. That same year, she did *Rocket to the Moon*, an HBO recording of a half bad/half inspired Clifford Odets play that is buoyed by Davis's portrayal of Cleo, a skinny, pretty, nervous flirt and pathological liar who dreams of being a dancer.

Cleo is an impossible role that calls for old-fashioned personality playing and theatrical technique. Everyone in the play has to fall in love with Cleo, and so if Davis isn't fascinating every moment she's on then the story won't even make sense. She runs with the part at a galloping pace, as if she were stimulated by the challenge of making it live, and she fills every moment (watch the way her hands fly to her face when John Malkovich calls her out on her flighty bullshit). Paradoxically, Davis is at her most believable when

Judy Davis at her most open and vulnerable in *High Tide*.

she's lying here, which adds dimension to the film. This is the kind of acting that calls attention to itself constantly, but the artifice is extremely exciting.

High Tide (1987) contains what is probably Davis's career-best work, or at least her most emotional and her most personal. This is a delicate film in which she plays Lilli, a lofty gadabout and loser who is backing a third-rate Elvis impersonator. Lilli can't help teasing her self-important boss, and she gets herself fired, takes to the bottle, and finds comfort with a sweet teenaged girl who turns out to be her abandoned daughter.

Armstrong allowed Davis an unusual amount of freedom on *High Tide*. She let her improvise, and Davis even did some writing of her own for this movie, contributing a speech that explains why Lilli left her daughter after her lover died. This poetic license seems to have lowered Davis's defenses, so that her gifts emerge from their carapace and she moves from far-out emotion to far-out emotion with woozy fluidity.

To speak in musical terms, most of Davis's work is staccato, sometimes ruinously so, but her performance in *High Tide* is one smooth legato line. Look at the bewildered way she cries when she's upset, picking the tears off her face as if they were wiggling bugs. Look at the complex, wondering way she watches her daughter shave her legs in a shower stall. Surely Armstrong deserves some credit for a scene as affecting as this, but Davis is the clear creator here, putting together a portrait of a selfish woman who runs away from motherly feeling and then finds herself romantically drawn to it.

Her performance in *High Tide* is especially moving in the context of Davis's embattled career; followers of that career know how much on-screen vulnerability costs her. Partly it helped that she was very taken with the girl playing her daughter. "Claudia Karvan, the girl who plays the daughter in there, was so beautiful," Davis said in 2016 to the *Village Voice*. "I was so madly in love with her. We were filming way out of Sydney, but one day her mother came down to visit her, and during lunch I saw them walking up this hill, hand in hand, and I got these terrible pangs of jealousy, 'cause I had become very emotionally connected to her."

Davis is known for liking to play real women, mainly for TV. She played Edith Piaf on stage in Australia in 1980, and she made for an entirely believable, earthy young Golda Meir in *A Woman Called Golda* (1982), speaking in a much lower, rougher voice and steamrolling over her gentle husband (Leonard Nimoy).

She gives one of the great modern comic performances as George Sand in *Impromptu* (1991), a small film that is galvanized by her haughty, daring, androgynous physical and vocal presence. Like *High Tide*, this is a movie that takes its cues from Davis. She rules every frame of it, flamboyantly, eccentrically.

In an outstanding 2003 article about Davis in this movie for *Senses of*

Cinema, Lesley Chow wrote, "From the moment she arrives on screen, her flexible free walk contrasting with the small 'period' steps of the other characters, we are aware of the postmodern aspect of Davis's presence; the exact, enforced rhythm of her stride indicates an identity which is superimposed onto experience rather than a naturalized part of it."

Chow analyzes how much fun the non-naturalistic Davis has with conscious acting effects, which is sometimes why, in her worst work, she can be very bad. If she doesn't feel a connection with a role, if the role doesn't stimulate her performing sense, then Davis disconnects and mugs like any amateur would, but when she does connect, as she does with George Sand, she makes acting, or performing, into a great stylized, self-presentational pleasure.

"Davis's compressed, tense line readings and angular movements draw us into an aesthetic of imposed formalism and control," wrote Chow. "The element of artificiality is foregrounded, so that we have a sense of the constant effort of projecting the self outward; Davis's 'excessively' formal gesturing draws attention to the amount of work it takes to produce the effect of consistent character and individuality."

A Method actress like Julie Harris strove to make each line sound as if she had just thought of it, whereas Davis delights in highlighting the artificiality of her dialogue in *Impromptu*. "Davis has a habit of reading her lines as 'given'—drawing attention to the fact that they *are* lines, and that she has been waiting to say them for some time," wrote Chow. "'You're a menace to the future of art' is spoken very rapidly, in reference to the kind of impossible, ahistorical statement it is—but Davis throws away any conventional meaning the phrase might have by speaking it in a matter-of-fact way, stressing only the hardness in her utterance of the word 'art.'"

The excitement in *Impromptu* comes not from wondering *what* her George Sand will say but *how* Davis will choose to read her obviously given lines in the moment, and this is as far away from the traditional Method acting of the mid-twentieth century as you can get. It is close, in a way, to Bette Davis's tastiest 1940s work, which of course is not modern at all, but Judy Davis, maybe, is post-modern, as Chow suggests, because she seems to be conscious on some level of making the choice to work in this style, whereas Bette Davis had no naturalistic Method tradition to work against.

Her George Sand in *Impromptu* is always acting the part of herself, and we watch Davis act Sand acting, so that it becomes a double experience, watching the pleasure Sand gets from her act and watching the pleasure Davis gets from the pleasure Sand gets from it. She inhabits Sand's brusque masculine virility in a highly suggestive way, so that when Sand has to express real or "real" romantic emotion for the conventionally feminine Chopin (Hugh Grant), Davis highlights how uncomfortable she is with it, as any man's man would be. Her expression of this "genuine" emotion is slightly forced and strained, like an actress trying out different readings and not quite getting the one she wants.

"Take my strength," she tells Chopin. "I have too much of it." She physically swaggers here in a way that a man could never do without looking a little silly, so that her Sand is able to enjoy masculine prerogatives and mannerisms to the very limit. She says she "wants too much," and when Davis says that she sounds a note of sublime dissatisfaction.

Davis herself had trouble with the love scenes on the set of *Impromptu*, according to director James Lapine, and so this is partly her own problem, which she dramatizes as Sand's problem. "God knows, she gave us a lot of grief about certain scenes, like the big scene at the end of the movie when she and Chopin actually make love," said Lapine. "Judy has a hard time saying things like, 'I love you.' I said to her, 'Judy, do you tell your husband you love him?' She said, half-joking, 'No, only my child and my dog.' She's a twisted human being. She's not easy."

In Antonio Tibaldi's unsettling *On My Own* (1991), Davis explored the dark male inverse of *High Tide* by playing a schizophrenic mother to a teenaged boy named Simon (Matthew Ferguson). In her first scene, Davis's Mother smiles warmly at Simon from her hospital bed. Her curly hair here makes her look like a sea nymph, and her unnamed Mother character is a romantic figure that Davis seems to love and believe in.

"You're all wet, you look like a porcupine," Davis's Mother says to her son. "*My* porcupine," she says tenderly. This is a woman who lives in an old house and has been thinking of turning off the electricity. "I think it's important to learn to live outside systems based on money," she tells her son in a restaurant. She wants very badly to be a good parent or set a good example in the time she has with him. But her eyes look familiar with other realities.

Davis's Mother in *On My Own* speaks directly of her mental illness, but sometimes it controls her rather than the other way around. Late at night in a hotel room, Simon reads her poetry and she gets into bed fully nude. He gets in with her and she cradles him, but then she covers herself with the blankets and says, "I don't think that you should visit me," in a voice choking back tears. She recovers so instantly from this extreme emotion that it becomes clear that her mind is unbalanced, but her son rails against her as any abandoned teenaged boy would.

"I'm not good with people, that's why I live the way I do," she says by way of explanation, but this makes Simon even angrier. He locks himself in the bathroom until he hears glass breaking, and he emerges to see that Davis's Mother has broken a window with her head. She tries to get herself back on track: "Now she's done it, now she's really done it," she says contritely, speaking of herself in the third person. But then she gets inappropriate again and like a desperate lover when she cries, "Just hold me for a while, just hold me," to her son.

Davis's ill Mother in *On My Own* is a seductive person in ways that she cannot help, but her son eventually loves and forgives that. Standing on a train platform the morning after their fight, she winningly tells him, "Life is better than school, you know.... I mean, it gets better once you get out." She boards her train and mouths "I love you" to Simon through a window. Later we hear that she has died in an accident on a train platform, but Tibaldi has her re-emerge at the end of the film in a sort of dream.

We see the top of her head raise itself up in a barn until she is staring lovingly at Simon with her curls backlit. "Nobody knows I'm here, I'm not really dead," she tells her son. "I just had to disappear.... I have to go now, don't tell anyone you saw me." Davis is on screen for maybe a half hour in *On My Own*, which has been hard to see in recent years. But in that half hour she is a very stirring figure of emotional upheaval and grace under mental pressure.

Davis excelled again as an actressy French resistance fighter in *One Against the Wind* (1991) for TV. She has the hauteur of an opera diva here, with excessively grand physical mannerisms, and her very stiff-upper-lip British speaking voice is plummy and heightened, as if routing the Nazis were nothing but campy fun at a very high level of difficulty. Underneath these mannerisms, she is often as magnetically tough and stubborn as John Wayne.

In a confrontation with her daughter (Kate Beckinsale), who is seeing a Nazi officer, Davis plays anger and outrage cut at strategic moments with "this isn't happening" regret and childlike misgivings in her eyes. Again, she is at her best in precisely the moments when her character is uncertain of the attitude she is taking, because Davis is uncertain, uncomfortable, with all attitudes. There is always a tension between her projection of extreme confidence and the equally extreme insecurity underneath.

Davis sees living as an enormous problem, a problem of such enormity that she would really much rather not be acting at all on this particular stage ... but she has no choice. And she signals that lack of choice with existential, Beckett-like despair underneath her heroic yet parodic behavioral flourishes. When she puts off a besotted officer (Sam Neill) who has kissed her and puts a hand to her mouth, and then says that a romance isn't a good idea, Davis is staying true to her deepest instincts: she is essentially a radically anti-romantic, solitary figure.

On screen, Davis doesn't believe in love, though in life she has stood by her actor husband Colin Friels through the difficulties of a serious illness in the late 1990s. Friels, who has occasionally acted with her on screen, is one of the few people to survive pancreatic cancer and see it go into remission, and surely Davis was a powerful ally to him in this toughest of struggles.

This is a proud woman who's always up for a dare, a strange project, an untouchable emotion. Starting in 1990, Davis made a splash with her steady work for Woody Allen, sometimes in small roles, but especially for the psychodrama of *Husbands and Wives* (1992). In that film Davis plays Sally, a hypercritical bitch and scourge who knows just how Mahler might have improved one of his symphonies.

Davis was only 37 in *Husbands and Wives* but seems much older. In the first hand-held camera scene, when Sally announces with a flourish of her hand that she is going to try a separation from her husband (Sydney Pollack), Davis strikes that familiar note of theatrical confidence with enormous insecurity in back of it. She makes Sally more disturbing and more indelible the further she goes into self-protective aggressiveness; she is always pouncing on words and killing them. Davis is furiously awkward physically here, bumping into things, dropping her purse and all its contents in the street at the worst possible moment.

Sally has her first date after her separation with a man who is taking her to Mozart's *Don Giovanni*. "A Don Juan story? They should have cut his fucking dick off!" she says gruffly, thrillingly. The mainly African American audience I first saw this film with got out of their seats to cheer Davis on and applaud her flamboyant and extreme anger when she went into a notably profane anti-male aria in this "bad date" scene.

Davis really savors her purring American accent in *Husbands and Wives* and uses it for rough effects, like when she cries to her date, "Don't defend your sex! You're great until you start to show your age ... and then they want a newer model," after which she takes a staccato Bette Davis puff on her cigarette. Sally thinks she wants a new life and man while she still has "some allure left," but she actually just wants the security of her old unhappiness with her husband.

When Judy (Mia Farrow) tries to interest Sally in Michael (Liam Neeson) by saying that he cried at a party, Davis's Sally scathingly asks, "He weeps?" Michael tries to kiss Sally after a date, but she stops him, pats underneath her chin, and then says, "I can't go so fast ... metabolically it's not my rhythm." (And this is 1992-era Liam Neeson we're talking about here, a tall poetic hunk who would be a dream man for many women.) Sally is so "mentally hyperactive" that she cannot even enjoy making love with Michael, and she mentally leaves what he's doing to her physically so that she can categorize the people she knows into hedgehogs and foxes.

The pessimistic Allen tends to view the pessimistic Davis as an eccentric, which fits her into the scheme of his films, whereas Davis's best films (particularly *Impromptu*) allow her to dramatize the distance between repeatedly making a physical gesture and the emotion that gesture is supposed to signify. But of course she is just like Sally in her own hypercritical standards.

"I think it's a great film. Except for the bits I'm in," Davis said of *Husbands and Wives* in 2013 to the *Guardian*. "I was slightly over the top.... There's that golden rule that you don't want to see the acting. And I thought I could." You can always, of course, see the acting with Davis, except maybe in *High Tide*, which seems to be the only performance that satisfied her somewhat.

Sometimes Davis fails and her theatricality is indeed as empty as she fears it might be, as in *Where Angels Fear to Tread* (1991), where she is at her twitchy worst, unsupported by role or film. Davis is also at her worst in Allen's *Deconstructing Harry* (1997), where she cartoonishly and emptily chews the scenery in her first scene for a long take that feels like forever.

But she doubtfully opens herself up to River Phoenix in *Dark Blood* (partially filmed and abandoned after Phoenix's death in 1993 but put together in 2012 by director George Sluizer). Davis is not exactly natural casting as a former *Playboy* playmate named Buffy, but she is at her considerable best in the mid-section of *Dark Blood*, a guarded woman letting her guard down, quieting her mannerisms and settling into many distinctive moods of shy yearning with her husband (Jonathan Pryce) and treating Phoenix with tough-love tenderness.

She was ideally cast and had a roaring good time in *Children of the Revolution* (1996) as Joan Fraser, a self-absorbed Communist femme fatale who sleeps with Stalin and has his child. This outsized, monomaniacal character is a bold and fully realized comic creation that allows Davis to reach an Anna Magnani level of vital, peppery invention. Joan Fraser is a role that stimulates Davis's zesty anti-social side, which she sends up mercilessly. As her character gets older, Davis zeroes in on the narrowed, ugly aspects of paranoid old age, and especially its increasing focus on bodily functions and failures.

Davis is a termagant in *Children of the Revolution*, a demonic socialist workhorse, a whirlwind of activity, and a blustery crank: "Gorbachev wouldn't know his proletariat from his asshole!" she howls at her TV set in the 1980s. "Ronald McDonald's the devil!" In elaborately verbal conniption fits like this, a specialty act in many of her films, Davis is getting her jollies, obviously, but she is also both glorifying and condemning the ecstasies of detailed rage. She's drawn to cold misanthropes like Joan, and she reaches a revealing bad-tempered height with these archetypal Judy Davis lines: "Nice people have never done much for me. To tell you the truth they *irritate* me. I'd rather spend an hour with an interesting shit than a minute with a bloody nice person."

Dash and Lilly (1999), a cable biopic of Lillian Hellman and Dashiell Hammett, is sparked by one of Davis's most inventive performances. Her drunk scenes here are superlative: listen for how the Australian Davis manages to do an American accent with sly hints of the Southern accent Hellman is trying to hide and smooth over. As her predatory Lilly keeps drinking, her twang keeps creeping in, and Davis makes the fight to keep this regionalism in its place a dynamic, even awe-inspiring battle. Watch her blissful relaxation after her first night of sex with Sam Shepard's manly Hammett, and the look of unconditional love she gives him at his worst moments.

Davis's TV master classes continued into the next century. She won lots of acclaim and an Emmy for a bold and vulnerable portrait of Judy Garland in *Life with Judy Garland: Me and My Shadows* (2001). Outfitted with brown contact lenses, Davis exactly caught Garland's tentative speech patterns, her morbid, campy humor, her sexual hunger, her specialness, her neediness, her dark side, and her pain. When she lip synched to "Over the Rainbow" in a recreation of a 1950s concert, Davis did Garland's talent full justice while also making clear, with extremely subtle facial expressions, her own grieved position on Garland's tragic self-indulgence. Davis said she fell in love with Garland, but it was her own brand of tough love.

"Bob [Ackerman, the director] said, 'You have to sing along with it, because if you're just miming it, it won't be believable,'" Davis said to the *Village Voice* in 2016. "I said, 'Fine, fine, great.' *You* try singing along with Judy Garland more than once, maybe twenty times. It's hard! I am a bit of a singer, but she was a *phenomenal* singer. I was generally hoarse for the morning after. But interestingly, 'cause I've never challenged myself vocally that way, by the end of the filming, my voice had grown tremendously stronger."

The way Davis flings herself into mimicking Garland's manic later concert behavior might be more than a little absurd if taken out of context, but of course there's no reason or way to do a subtle Garland. At the 2004 Emmy awards, an impressed Meryl Streep said, "No one has put a better performance on film than Judy Davis in *The Judy Garland Story*."

Davis took small roles after that, but she had another major performance up her sleeve, perhaps her most disturbing of all. A Lifetime movie in name only, *A Little Thing Called Murder* (2006) is a sometimes very offensive black comedy that features Davis's riskiest work. As Sante Kimes, a trashy sociopath who wants to live the high life, Davis starts out in the sort of high camp/Kabuki mode that has marked some of her worst performances. She's far beyond over-the-top as she cheats, lies, steals, and grubs her way through life and takes her son along with her (she crosses her eyes Jerry Lewis–style as she faints in court, a comic high point).

Davis is depicting behavioral and moral chaos very directly here, and she is unafraid to look very foolish at first. Her eyes are heavily made-up and animal-like, and the voice she uses has an unaccountably harsh flavor, low and rough, always with a sort of smothered twang underneath, until Sante pushes it up into a high and pitiful register when she needs to manipulate someone into sympathy for her schemes. If you watch this performance closely, details begin to pile up, criminal, furtive subtleties beneath Sante's manically exuberant, clown/charismatic surface, until finally Davis is ready to play her aces.

When we see Sante murder a man, all the laughs we've enjoyed in the first half of the film catch up with us, and the fun freezes as we see her sadistic killer instinct emerge. In the backseat of a car, holding a hammer, we watch Sante revving herself up for the murder with the kind of disturbing, aggressively peppy sexuality that marked her uneasy singing of "Santa Baby" with a feather boa earlier in the film.

More disturbing than this is Sante's murder of a nice old lady towards the end of the movie, which she justifies with the flimsiest of excuses. In this eye-opening movie on a coddling cable network, Davis confronts and lays bare the most troubling problem of them all: people who murder others without a twinge of conscience. And she does it by staying true to her own outré, tense, yet ultimately tender and moral spirit.

Davis played an unhappy, center-less daughter to Charlotte Rampling in Fred Schepisi's *The Eye of the Storm* (2011), and in 2012 she did a series of short films for her old scene partner Baz Luhrmann where she played Italian fashion designer Elsa Schiaparelli with all the considerable verve at her disposal.

At age 60 she showed up as a cranky and comic self-described "hag" mother named "Mad Molly" in *The Dressmaker* (2015), a wayward Australian film that allowed Davis to show once again that she didn't care about naturalism at all. She played gossip columnist Hedda Hopper on the 2017 TV series *Feud*, where Davis shared the screen with Jessica Lange and eyed Lange's emotional abandon with both skepticism and respect.

She rarely leaves her native Australia, and her work and name are obscure to many. But of all the people in this book, Judy Davis is the one who sets new standards for modern-day acting by most frankly admitting that there is no such thing as the self … until there is, and until there isn't again. It is actors who understand this more intimately than any other kind of artist.

The Australian Davis wrestles with the idea of the self, whereas Robert De Niro built on Brando's example to be free of all self-consciousness. For De Niro and the many American actors he in turn influenced, there is no self or character, only behavior and imagination, and the beckoning void, which nearly consumes Gena Rowlands's Mabel Longhetti. Michael Corleone chooses his destiny in *The Godfather*, just as Sara Goldfarb in essence chooses her own destruction by trying to fulfill unrealistic dreams.

Yet English actors like Anthony Hopkins and Maggie Smith know or feel that there is indeed a self that cannot be ignored or transcended. Hopkins's Mr. Stevens cannot escape being Mr. Stevens in *The Remains of the Day*, nor can Smith's Judith Hearne stop being Judith Hearne, much as she would like to. This is perhaps the essential difference between American and English acting, and Davis is the player who most dynamically and colorfully straddles the line between these two viewpoints and disciplines.

Emma Thompson
A Star Danced

There was a golden period from 1989 to 1995 when Emma Thompson seemed to be everywhere, winning plum roles and being very witty in interviews. Meryl Streep was rather in eclipse in this period, living in Hollywood and trying to be commercial in a series of comedies, and perhaps this partly explains Thompson's ascendance. It is known that Streep fired her longtime agent Sam Cohn after she read for and lost the role of Miss Kenton to Thompson in *The Remains of the Day* (1993).

Thompson won the best actress Oscar for *Howards End* (1992), and she was nominated twice in 1993, for best actress for her Miss Kenton and for best supporting actress as the lawyer in *In the Name of the Father*. And she could easily have picked up a third nomination for her tanned and sharp-witted Beatrice in *Much Ado About Nothing*, in which she played with her impresario-like husband Kenneth Branagh.

The time of her best work was also the time of her marriage to Branagh, with whom she worked in thankless roles, too: in the uneventful series *Fortunes of War* (1987), as the wife in *Look Back in Anger* (1989) for TV, the female lead in his genre mystery *Dead Again* (1991), and a pathetic character in the comedy *Peter's Friends* (1992).

But on stage she had won acclaim as the Fool in his staging of *King Lear* and had been the French princess in his popular movie of *Henry V* (1989). This was the time of "Ken and Em," when they were a famous couple. After their painful divorce in 1995, somehow nothing was ever the same for either of them. They still worked in films, but as if their confidence and their interest had gone when the marriage went.

Thompson was the daughter of actors, and she was educated at Cambridge, where she did lots of sketch comedy and was part of the bright young thing smart set. She worked for 15 months on the London stage in a musical called *Me and My Girl*. ("I thought if I did the fucking Lambeth Walk one more time I was going to fucking throw up," she said later.)

Thompson did her own sketch comedy series for the BBC, and then she broke away from Branagh to be the leading lady for Jeff Goldblum in *The*

Tall Guy (1989), and it was in that modest, oddball picture that she really caught the eye. Thompson's Kate Lemmon is a nurse with short hair, clear blue eyes, and a serene expression that masks her wit and her sense of fun. Thompson has a Judy Davis–like way of delivering lines here that is highly conscious, as if shaping them is part of the joy of acting for her, and for us.

She isn't a particularly versatile actress. Most of the roles in her golden period are filtered through her own sensibility: brainy, droll, inclined to be naughty if encouraged, but in a winningly playful, faux-mild, teasing way. Her mad love bout with Goldblum where they nakedly roll around Kate's apartment and get all messy (she breaks a bit of crockery on his head in the heat of the moment) is one of the funniest and most inventive of all sex scenes, filled with pleasure and laughs and "why not?" abandon.

Thompson was very funny as the dippy Duchess D'Antan in *Impromptu* (1991), a lady with a ludicrous hairdo who is bored in the country and hungry for the genius and sexual bohemianism of the artists she invites to her home. This is high farce acting, and yet Thompson also manages to make the Duchess's hurt feelings touching when George Sand (Judy Davis) insults her.

Her role in *Howards End* was not an especially showy one, but Thompson makes the intellect of her heroine Margaret Schlegel exciting, letting us see how Margaret is seduced by Mrs. Wilcox (Vanessa Redgrave) and then led into compromise after this woman's death when she marries Mr. Wilcox (Anthony Hopkins). This was a role ideally suited to Thompson's sensibility: witty, kind, sensible, but capable of Maggie Smith–like industrial strength emotion underneath. It was maybe this revelation of emotion, which she shows at the end of the film, that won her that Oscar and a new plateau in her career.

Her Miss Kenton in *The Remains of the Day* was essentially supporting Anthony Hopkins, who was giving one of the performances of his life as the repressed butler Mr. Stevens, but Thompson disclosed an enormous amount of emotion in that role, particularly anger and regret, and it was all the more impressive because the lady she was playing had to always be reining it in.

Her Beatrice in *Much Ado About Nothing* is surely definitive, if only because the TV recording of Maggie Smith's performance in that role doesn't circulate much. This was a real star turn, confident, juicy, sexy, funny, full of wit and mischief, and sadness too, and then very surprising and full-bodied anger when Beatrice defends the good name of her cousin Hero (Kate Beckinsale) and demands that Branagh's Benedick kill Claudio (Robert Sean Leonard), the swain who has sullied the girl's reputation. This is maybe the best or at least most various and multi-faceted performance Thompson ever gave, in a classic theater role that will forever bear her stamp.

She played a Scottish woman cheated on by her husband in *The Blue Boy* (1994), an hour-long film for the BBC. And then she did perhaps her most demanding, dramatic, and unappreciated performance as *Carrington* (1995), a painter caught up in the Bloomsbury set who is madly and unrequitedly in love with the gay writer Lytton Strachey (Jonathan Pryce).

Thompson's Carrington falls in love with Strachey instantly, but in an unusual way, looking intensely uncomfortable and uncertain and reluctant about what is happening to her (he mistook her for a boy when he first saw her and is disappointed himself yet also somewhat stirred). When Strachey whimsically kisses her, she is very angry, breaking away and crying, "Would you mind not?" She goes into his room to cut his beard off to punish him, but somehow she finds she can't. Love for Lytton has struck her, and she stays struck.

Thompson fleshes out Carrington's unconventional and bohemian living arrangement with Strachey with unerring imaginative sympathy, and this is all set to Michael Nyman's lush, richly melancholy, insistent score. She hits unusual moods here of distant frustration, longing, willing self-abasement, wantonness, fear, mockery, jealousy, and many other in-between feelings.

Thompson's Carrington is a screen heroine we too seldom see, a girl and then a woman who never settles for easy answers about what she should need or want. "I don't think you have any idea how happy you've made me," she tells Strachey near the end of their lives together, and her idea of happiness is a strange but genuine one.

On his deathbed, when Strachey tells Carrington he has always loved her and wanted to marry her, Thompson hits a very dark comic note when she desperately asks the attending nurse if he will live. When Carrington stands with a shotgun at her stomach and wearily bows her head before shooting herself, Thompson is extremely moving.

Thompson won another Oscar for her screenplay for the Jane Austen adaptation *Sense and Sensibility* (1995), and her award show speeches, particularly the elaborate Austen pastiche she reeled off at the Golden Globes, were far more entertaining than the mild movie itself. At this point Branagh sought a divorce to be with Helena Bonham Carter, and Thompson sank into a severe depression.

In Alan Rickman's *The Winter Guest* (1997), in which she acted with her mother Phyllida Law, Thompson inhabited a state of grief in a way that felt uncomfortably personal. It was still rare to see a British actor work in this Strasberg Method mode, to see Thompson in a wrecked place and putting that wreckage directly on screen.

She played the Hillary Clinton figure in *Primary Colors* (1998) for Mike Nichols, and then she worked for Nichols again in the HBO film of *Wit* (2001), but she never approached the intensity that Kathleen Chalfant had brought to that tough play on stage in New York. Once again she was a cheated on wife in *Love Actually* (2003), where she breaks down and cries, and she skillfully played several roles for Nichols in his adaptation of *Angels in America* (2003).

Thompson was badly miscast as the religious femme fatale Lady Marchmain in *Brideshead Revisited* (2008), and she was reduced to a cameo in *An Education* (2009). Her main effort in this time was writing and acting in two modest films for children, *Nanny McPhee* (2005) and *Nanny McPhee Returns* (2010), and she was also the author P. L. Travers in the obnoxious Walt Disney commercial *Saving Mr. Banks* (2013), where she ended up in floods of tears.

After a long absence from the stage, Thompson returned as Mrs. Lovett in a concert staging of Stephen Sondheim's *Sweeney Todd* in 2014, where she seemed like a good sport who no longer took acting seriously enough to play a great role in a great work of musical theater (and she had major trouble negotiating the break between her chest and head voice as she sang).

But then she did a strong, angry, yet fearful Goneril in a BBC *King Lear* with Anthony Hopkins in 2018, and her performance was so original, grounded, and nuanced that she made it seem like a play about Goneril rather than the king. It was as if only Shakespeare could summon Thompson's full attention and talent as an older woman, but the talent was very much still there.

Jennifer Jason Leigh
Hard Knocks

After nearly 40 years in show business, Jennifer Jason Leigh finally got her first Oscar nomination for the Quentin Tarantino movie *The Hateful Eight* (2015). As a "diabolical bitch" and leader of a criminal gang being brought to justice, Leigh took many punches to the face, and she stared out sullenly from behind black eyes as she made coarse and racist remarks. Her Daisy Domergue has exactly one moment of human connection, when she looks lovingly at her brother (Channing Tatum). This is a very brief moment, but Leigh seizes it.

The Hateful Eight doesn't give her much room to maneuver or explore her character, but Leigh was used to such constraints. Her hard, pretty little face was generally unsmiling as she played victim after victim in the 1980s and 1990s, prostitutes and strippers, none too bright, who were often beat up or raped.

Leigh made a specialty out of playing the losers of life in the lower depths: junkies, stalkers, alcoholics, the mentally ill, the mentally deficient, the ill favored, the untalented, the abused. Tarantino was fully cognizant of that image and he toys with it, making her take lots of physical and verbal abuse stoically and then dish out as much as she can in return. Surveying the career of Jennifer Jason Leigh means that you have to endure some very unsavory films and situations.

Leigh, who was the daughter of Method actor Vic Morrow and actress and screenwriter Barbara Turner, had an intensity of focus and a deadpan look of expecting the worst from the very beginning of her career, from her first teenaged TV appearances. In the TV movie *The Best Little Girl in the World* (1981), which deals with anorexia, Leigh's inwardness and stubbornness is very disturbing, and very opaque in the Actors Studio style of her father. She makes this TV movie much more upsetting than you expect it to be, and she was most poignant when she tried to smile; smiling to Leigh is such an effort, such a signal of hope that she always seems afraid it will be struck down by some really bad news or punch to the jaw.

Leigh had a break out part in the comedy *Fast Times at Ridgemont High*

(1982), but her roles of this time were very limited. She was raped in a long and nasty sequence in Paul Verhoeven's *Flesh + Blood* (1985), she got torn in half in *The Hitcher* (1986), and she played the town beauty Madge in a Showtime version of William Inge's *Picnic* (1986), even though she would have been better cast as the younger tomboy sister Millie. She tried very hard to give a sensitive performance as a troubled girl in *Heart of Midnight* (1988) but was finally defeated by the exploitation material.

Leigh played the mean-minded hooker Tralala, a platinum blonde with a Brooklyn accent, in an adaptation of Hubert Selby's *Last Exit to Brooklyn* (1989) where she was gang-raped, and she played a comically and finally creepily dumb prostitute in *Miami Blues* (1990), a cuddly little gamine named Susie who can be seen calculating her next moves at a rock-bottom level of intellect. Leigh's Susie is an innocent in some ways, but corrupted in other ways. "He had some good qualities," Susie says of her difficult criminal boyfriend Frederick (Alec Baldwin). "He always ate everything I ever cooked for him ... and he never hit me."

Playing a cop made to become a junkie in *Rush* (1991), Leigh is rewarding to watch but finally not enjoyable to watch, her low-key style too tied to small details (and once again she was raped on screen, this time by her junkie boyfriend played by Jason Patric). And then she used this larval quality she had as the mousy roommate who gloms on to Bridget Fonda in the thriller *Single White Female* (1992).

Leigh was a sullen phone sex operator, rattling off the most graphic sexual talk as she attended to her young children in Robert Altman's *Short Cuts* (1993), and then she did her most searching work for two films that announced both her full talent and her creative interests. She gave a controversial performance as a depressed and mumbling Dorothy Parker in *Mrs. Parker and the Vicious Circle* (1994), a radical attempt at naturalism in a nonstandard biopic where she tried for what Parker might really have looked and sounded like, even if this was bound to alienate some audiences.

Leigh came under attack in some quarters because she based the mumbling, slurring way she spoke in that movie on a recording Parker made when she was an older woman; probably the performance would have been better received if she had used this voice in the scenes where Parker is older and addressing the camera with her verse and then lightened her voice and brought it up slightly for the scenes where Parker is younger.

But Leigh was set on strict verisimilitude, and she carefully lets us see how Parker's witticisms arose from a nearly willfully depressive personality. Once you get past the voice she is determined to use, her performance is beguilingly original and imaginative. Leigh fully inhabits Parker's drunken glumness and gives it both full weight (she just sits at the Algonquin round table like a bump on a log) and twisted glamor.

Her Dorothy is so disappointed and serious-minded that she has retreated into being detached and taking nothing too seriously, not love or work, only her platonic love for Robert Benchley (Campbell Scott). In a scene where Parker is older that plays under the credits, she is asked by a reporter what she'd like on her tombstone. "What a morbid thing to ask a person … you've just stolen my heart," she says, very sweetly.

She played Kathy Bates's damaged daughter in *Dolores Claiborne* (1995), and then she did the role of her life, the punk mess would-be singer Sadie Flood in *Georgia* (1995), a film written by her mother Barbara Turner. There are no easy answers in *Georgia*, only very complex questions.

At the center of this movie is Sadie's relationship to her sister Georgia (Mare Winningham), an icily controlled woman who has become a famous singer. Sadie watches her sister sing with pure love and appreciation on her face, yet she cannot admit to herself that she also hates Georgia for her success in the face of her own evident failure. Georgia plays arenas, singing in a pretty soprano, and she is beloved by all, while Sadie plays only bar gigs when she can get them and hurls out songs in a roughly intense voice that often doesn't stay on pitch. Sadie both needs her sister's help, financial and emotional, and she resents it.

Leigh gives a very mannered performance in *Georgia*, which was food for her detractors. She makes Sadie into a girl who is always cringing—as if she knows full well what a loser she is—yet there is a tiny bit of hope still there that she might at last be loved and appreciated, and it is this tiny bit of hope that makes her such an excruciating figure.

Like her sister Georgia, Sadie usually doesn't appear to be listening closely to others, maybe because there are so many aspects of reality that do not conform to her vision of herself. Her ambition and her needs have led her nowhere, and this is most apparent in the nine-minute sequence where Sadie tries to sing a Van Morrison song at one of Georgia's concerts, screeching "Take me back, take me *way* back!" over and over again until she has totally alienated the audience, who barely applaud at all when she is done.

On one level, what Sadie does here during this nine-minute song is amateurish and drunkenly unfocused, and it seems like she is having a personal meltdown rather than trying to really communicate with the people watching her. Sadie appreciates other singers, and she seems to be copying them in her head, but she just doesn't have that quality that makes an audience respond to a performer, and Georgia knows this.

"You don't sing, Sadie," Georgia finally tells her. "You can't sing." Sadie takes this in and knows the truth of it, but she childishly (and maybe rightly) says, "You wish." The film ends with Georgia doing one of her best-known songs for a huge audience while Sadie does the same song for a sparse audience at a bar. *Georgia* is such a troubling movie because it just presents a conundrum without ever telling us how to interpret it, and Leigh is both a trial in it (as Sadie is) and admirably brave, as Sadie is, too.

Leigh worked for Altman again as a tough-talking kidnapper in *Kansas City* (1996), and she was asked to react to a particularly horrific child rape scene, shown in far too much detail by director Anjelica Huston, as the mother in *Bastard Out of Carolina* (1996). She took her last really solid role of this time in *Washington Square* (1997), an adaptation of Henry James in which Leigh put a more modern spin on the last scene, where her emotionally abused Catherine Sloper seems to be at some peace with herself.

Leigh married writer-director Noah Baumbach in 2005, and so she appeared, in a thankless way, in some of his pictures until he left her for the younger Greta Gerwig. Her roles were smaller and more obscure until she took on Daisy Domergue for Tarantino. No matter what she does in future, her Dorothy Parker and her Sadie Flood will linger, if only as experiments.

Julianne Moore
Lying in Wait

The intriguing thing about Julianne Moore is that she is known for histrionics and emotional upheaval on screen (there has never been a more luxuriously abandoned and pleasing weeper in movies), yet her characters are almost always passive, furtive, repressed.

She got a late start in pictures, working on TV soap operas for most of the 1980s, and first came to attention at age 33 in Robert Altman's *Short Cuts* (1993), where she played a long argument scene nude from the waist down after her character spills wine on her skirt and needs to get the stain out. Moore has to share this opportunity with Matthew Modine, who makes a poor scene partner, yelling at her and then just yelling louder, but she keeps focus and brings her special brand of aggressive vulnerability to this first chance.

There's a febrile quality to Moore that seems to suggest illness or neuroticism that cannot be divided between the mental and the physical, and this would be the main theme of her signature film and performance: Todd Haynes's *Safe* (1995), which was voted the best movie of the 1990s in a *Village Voice* poll of critics. Haynes films Moore mostly in extreme long shot through most of that film, and so this limits the control she has as an actress, but this is apt because her character, Carol White, is a woman who is utterly without agency.

Repressed and self-hating but unable to admit how unhappy she is as a trophy wife in the San Fernando Valley, Carol starts to suffer from environmental illness, which does seem to be a real physical thing that is happening to her but is also wrapped up in her psychological state. She finally retreats to Wrenwood, a New Age healing center where for the first time she feels wanted and loved. The great sadness of *Safe* lies in showing us that the people who run this center don't understand or love Carol any more than her husband or former social acquaintances, but because her life has been so arid and loveless the wrongheaded preaching of self-love practiced at Wrenwood feels like a positive development to her.

Moore's Carol speaks in a high, disembodied voice that makes it sound like she is always asking a question and that she has no right to feel or think anything. She is a person that many of us would simply overlook, but Haynes and Moore make us care about her and her loneliness at the end, when she has retreated into a chemically safe bubble from which she is unlikely to emerge.

At this point Moore began appearing as a leading lady in commercial comedies and adventure movies that she mixed in with meatier independent assignments for balance, like her porn star Amber Waves in Paul Thomas Anderson's *Boogie Nights* (1997). Moore's Amber is a twisted maternal figure in the world of the film, her eyes glazed by drugs, sadness, and great sweetness.

Moore eerily catches the mannerisms of stilted, disconnected bad porn acting when Amber makes a movie with Dirk Diggler (Mark Wahlberg), and she gives her all to two big set pieces, one where Amber does cocaine with the younger Rollergirl (Heather Graham), who asks to call her Mom, and then the sequence where Amber—whose real name is Maggie—definitely loses any visitation rights to her young son.

Moore cries her heart out after this scene, and the last time we see Amber is when the porn patriarch Jack Horner (Burt Reynolds) extols her sexiness as she stares into a mirror. Moore is the picture of "hot chick" desolation here as Amber feels all she has lost and all she is to the world, which is very little. She was nominated for best supporting actress for her Amber, but the award went to Kim Basinger for *L.A. Confidential,* one of the most patently absurd Oscar decisions of all time.

Moore then excelled as the haughty, brittle trophy wife being pushed to hysterical breakdown as she waits at a drugstore in a furiously cross cut sequence in Anderson's *Magnolia* (1999). Her big meltdown speech where she yells at the druggists is unusual because Moore does it in a very high voice and with a very un-protected face. Most actors faced with this scene would have used a firmer voice and a more definite and lethal facial expression, but Moore tells them off in a disconcertingly fluid and open-ended way that's related to the fact that this woman is on a lot of drugs a lot of the time. She goes way over the top here, stimulated by the excess of the movie itself, but her work has drive, color, and originality.

Suddenly Moore seemed to be everywhere in a greedy range of parts. She was a watchful snake in the grass in Altman's *Cookie's Fortune* (1999) and she did one of her best crying scenes as a grieving mother in *A Map of the World* (1999). She got a best actress Oscar nomination as the Catholic British adulteress in *The End of the Affair* (1999), a movie that did not capture the pain of the Graham Greene novel it was based on.

She got two Oscar nominations in 2002, one for leading actress for *Far from Heaven,* a Douglas Sirk homage directed by Todd Haynes in which she was ever-so-slightly camp in just the right way but with strategic modern touches, and supporting actress for *The Hours*. Both of these films suggested that she needed to move beyond playing repressed housewives, however exquisitely wrought her performances were.

She worked in modest films for her husband, director Bart Freundlich, and then she took on a real challenge: the incestuous rich woman in Tom Kalin's very iffy *Savage Grace* (2007), where she returned to the kind of strange, brittle emotions that had animated her character in *Magnolia*.

Moore's work rate accelerated after that movie, and she seemed to specialize in doing well what shouldn't have been done at all. She laughed hysterically several times in *A Single Man* (2009) and was another very passive character who doesn't feel good about herself in *The Kids Are All Right* (2010).

At this point Moore seemed fed up with losing awards, as her fine work nearly always did. And so she chose some roles that might be more award-friendly, like the creepily limited politician Sarah Palin in *Game Change* (2012) for TV, which got her an Emmy, and *Still Alice* (2014), a real dud of a movie where she played a professor suffering from Alzheimer's disease, which got her a lead actress Oscar that should have been handed to her for any number of earlier performances.

She committed herself to the foul-mouthed actress Havana Segrand in David Cronenberg's *Map to the Stars* (2014), and she played the mother in a remake of *Carrie* (2013), where she would have been far more comfortable as Carrie herself if she had been young enough to cast in that role.

In 2015 Moore appeared in a very revealing sketch with comedian Billy Eichner for his YouTube show *Billy on the Street*. With Eichner at her side to encourage her, Moore acts monologues from her movies to passers-by in Times Square. "Do you want me to cry on cue?" she asks a man who doesn't recognize her, and then she immediately starts to break down.

When Moore does her speeches from *The Kids Are All Right* and the drugstore breakdown from *Magnolia* for this show, she instantly reaches the exact same emotion that she did in these films—in broad daylight out on the street and by request for a comedy sketch. Amusing as this is, it also says something about Moore, who is clearly an actor who doesn't need to "get into the mood" like Method actors of the 1950s, '60s and '70s.

Samantha Morton
Chaos/Control

There is a very uncomfortable feeling of disarray in some of the work of Samantha Morton, and this might be explained by her tough childhood. Her father was an alcoholic and her mother was in an abusive relationship with her second husband, and so Morton was placed in foster care from the time she was eight years old. She has spoken of being abused while in care, and she directed a tough TV film based on her experience called *The Unloved*, which played in 2009.

At the age of 16 she applied to RADA and got turned down, but Morton began working in television, and at 20 she was in adaptations of Jane Austen's *Emma* and then *Jane Eyre*, where she played the lead. Morton was already an intriguing presence on those shows, alternating between watchfulness and extreme vulnerability, but it was in the film *Under the Skin* (1997) that she made her first real impact as Iris, a girl fighting off depression over the death of her mother (Rita Tushingham) with masturbation and uninhibited sexual come-ons to men.

Morton was sexually in-your-face and uncensored from the start in this movie, full frontally nude next to the title card in the credits, open, lovely, and radically un-self-conscious. In *Under the Skin* it feels as if she will explore any emotion or situation, no matter how unpleasant or disturbing, without any fear. Morton doesn't seem to be acting at all here, or shaping anything, so that it feels like we could just be watching a narrative documentary about this girl Iris, and the film and performance is finally exhausting because it is played all at the same level of intensity, with no variation.

Woody Allen took note of Morton in this little-seen picture, and he cast her as the mute girlfriend to Sean Penn in *Sweet and Lowdown* (1999), which got her an Oscar nomination for best supporting actress. That part could have been sentimental, but Morton finds the tough core of her character and the stubbornness in scenes with Penn, so that her Hattie is a symbol of love and charity but also a real, prickly human being. She has to do everything with her face in that movie, and she enters into the near silent-screen clown-ishness of the style Allen calls for here with abandon.

She was very raw again in *Jesus' Son* (1999) opposite the beautiful Billy Crudup, who is extremely self-conscious as a performer, and this made for a romantic contrast in the film. In *Morvern Callar* (2002), Morton was asked to sustain many formless scenes of pure behavior as a girl who finds a novel by her dead boyfriend and passes it off as her own. Morton was really working in a kind of chaos in this movie, without any shaping or any through-line for her character, and the result was unsettling but also finally too undisciplined.

She was experimenting with acting in *Morvern Callar* and pushing herself to see just how far she could go without handholds or structure, and this impressed some people but left others alienated. That same year, with cropped hair, Morton got a rather surprising lead actress Oscar nomination for the far more conventional *In America*, where she was a wife and mother living in Hell's Kitchen in Manhattan and dealing with grief over the death of one of her children.

But in Michael Winterbottom's sci-fi film *Code 46* (2003), with cropped hair again, Morton gave an extremely erotic performance with not much help from either the film or her co-star Tim Robbins, with whom she has little chemistry. Somehow in that movie Morton managed to put herself in a sexual and yielding and hungry state of mind and she expressed these feelings with real power on screen.

The emphasis on sex gives her a kind of focus in *Code 46*, and when she beckons to the camera she is as sexy and commanding as any man or woman ever photographed. Like Barbara Stanwyck, who also endured a rough and abusive childhood, Morton can turn on her sexuality yet also keep herself somewhat distant from it, and that's why *Code 46* remains one of her most controlled and memorable performances.

For TV, Morton played the child murderer Myra Hindley in *Longford* (2006), which can stand side by side with Brian Cox's Hannibal Lecter in *Manhunter* (1986) as one of the most insightful and disturbing portraits of a sociopathic murderer ever done for film. We hear a lot about Myra and her crimes before we see her in this movie (though we do see Morton in a re-creation of Hindley's infamous mug shot, where she stares out with subtly deranged eyes under a pile of blonde hair). And so we expect a sort of monster, but when she makes her entrance Morton plays her cards very close to the vest for quite a while. Her Myra has dark hair in prison, and she looks dank and anonymous.

This is a very difficult role, because in the first scenes Morton has to be entirely convincing as a woman who is self-aware and rather meek, but then gradually we have to come to see that this is an act she is putting on. Morton is so disturbing here because she makes no obvious distinction whatever between this "meek" act and between what Hindley is actually like inside.

She doesn't perform the levels in Hindley at all, as a more conventional actress would; she imagines being this evil woman with immaculate, deadly

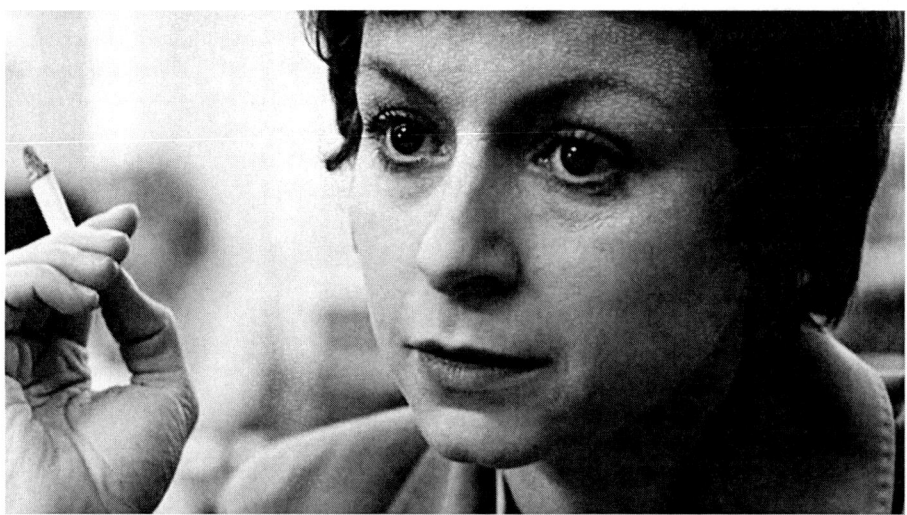

Samantha Morton incarnates pure evil in *Longford*.

simplicity. Morton conjures not histrionic or surface evil but actual evil of brute-like strength and cunning, and she has help here because Andy Serkis, who plays Myra's lover and fellow murderer Ian Brady, plays his part in a way that concentrates the evil nearly all on the surface of his lurid, direct, boastful face.

Morton has the confidence in *Longford* to "do" nearly nothing, in the expected way. By necessity, her performance needs to be troublingly ungiving and opaque, yet roiling and loaded beneath the surface until the last scene she has with her foolish advocate Lord Longford (Jim Broadbent) where her hair is falling out and she is dying of emphysema but still smoking. Morton's Myra insists that "evil can be a spiritual experience, too." She is unpenitent, a woman with very little conscience, near-diabolical, near non-human, and Morton flinches from none of that.

As Mary Queen of Scots in *Elizabeth: The Golden Age* (2007), Morton stole the movie clear away from Cate Blanchett's Elizabeth with the size and daring of her playing, but it was in this period that Morton ran into health trouble. She had a stroke after being struck on the head with a piece of plaster on a set, and she had to spend a long period of time learning to walk and talk again.

When she returned, Morton had put on some weight, and her roles and movies were often not worthy of her. She made a brief appearance in David Cronenberg's *Cosmopolis* (2012), and she played the servant to Jessica Chastain's *Miss Julie* (2014), where she was not at her best. But *Code 46* and *Longford* showed just what she was capable of if given a chance.

Patricia Clarkson
On a Dare

A native of New Orleans, the smart, nervy, and naughty Patricia Clarkson had to wait until she was nearly 40 before she got her break-out part on film: Greta in *High Art* (1998). A very specific downtown Manhattan type of figure, Greta is skinny and droll and out-of-it, her eyes usually half-closed as she talks with her heavy German accent about her days as an actress in Rainer Werner Fassbinder movies. She is a stylish has-been or never-was and a drug addict, snorting heroin in the ladies' rooms of trendy bars, and her love affair with Lucy (Ally Sheedy), a noted photographer, is on the wane.

"I live for Lucy," Greta says, and then she corrects herself. "I mean, I live *with* Lucy." She is dissolute and depraved, a glazed sort of vampire attached to Lucy, but she is also glamorous and continually amusing. ("The smell of these eggs is *disgusting*," she says on one strung-out morning.) Seeming supine even when she is standing upright, Greta has armored herself in defenses and excuses, claiming a bad back as the reason why she needs her drugs, and muttering continually about how Fassbinder gave "Hanna" (Schygulla) the part she might have had.

Clarkson has fun with her German accent in *High Art*, calling interloper Syd (Radha Mitchell) a "psycho-phant" to Lucy, but it is clear that Greta herself is, or was, the sycophant and boot-licker to the passive and kindly Lucy in their social circle. When she realizes that she is losing Lucy, Greta breaks through her habitual haze to try to fight for their bad relationship with any means at her disposal. When Greta mentions how she gave up her career, Lucy is finally forced to cry, "Fassbinder's dead, you didn't have a career after that!" Greta's eyes widen like a scared kid when she hears this hard bit of truth, as if Lucy has pierced through all of her delusions and left her exposed.

Greta in *High Art* is a really juicy part, freshly and originally conceived and written by director Lisa Cholodenko, but Clarkson brings it that extra verve and oomph and multi-dimensionality to make her unforgettable, and essential. Her Greta is such a detailed and complete performance that she seems to exist outside of the film and even outside of Clarkson. I wouldn't be surprised to run into Greta downtown at some bar. That's how good and how convincing Clarkson is in *High Art*.

Clarkson had trouble getting cast in her early days because her looks said "ingénue" but her low and resonant voice always signaled authority and experience. She was the wife of Eliot Ness in *The Untouchables* (1987) and a leading lady to Clint Eastwood in *The Dead Pool* (1988), where she was menaced.

There were smaller roles and TV after that, and work on stage in the 1990s, but her work rate after *High Art* accelerated, so that she was sometimes making four to five films a year, usually in small parts in big films and lead roles in smaller films. She had made just four features in the 1980s and eight in the 1990s, but in the aughts she did 27, lavishing her talent on all kinds of pictures.

Clarkson is always inventive no matter what the task, and she shows her stage training in the expressive and original way she handles props. She played the neighbor in Todd Haynes's *Far from Heaven* (2002), fully understanding both the 1950s period and the style of that film, but some of her best work was often in obscure pictures.

In *Heartbreak Hospital* (2002), Clarkson gives a major comic performance as Lottie Ohrwasher, a dotty woman who lives for a soap opera she watches religiously. Clarkson unexpectedly emphasizes just how happy Lottie is in the world she has created in her apartment as she unleashes her hair sensually and stretches out near the shrine to her favorite male actor on the show.

Lottie in *Heartbreak Hospital* is a difficult role; it would be so easy to make her merely quirky or wistful, but Clarkson stretches her own imagination to create a radiantly unsettling, unpredictable oddball, getting a lot of mileage, as she did in *High Art*, out of how drastically different her face can look when she narrows her eyes or opens them wide. She makes Lottie a mousy sort of tigress, her eyes darting around the room with pleasure when she spots her favorite actor/character in the flesh. Clarkson's Lottie is very threatening, sweet and daffy but also deadly, and this is the kind of delightfully original work, daring but very grounded, that makes you wonder just how the actor did it.

Clarkson was a low-key Mrs. White in a TV movie of *Carrie* (2002), and then she got an Oscar nomination for supporting actress for playing Joy Burns, a mother with cancer, in *Pieces of April* (2003). Joy is funny and angry and basically detached from her family. "No wonder there's cancer, *she's* the cancer," she says of her daughter April (Katie Holmes), and Clarkson makes a harsh line like that rudely funny and intimidating because she says it so off-handedly, in that whiskey voice of hers.

A Clarkson performance always feels very lived-in, as if she has done extensive back-story work for the characters she plays, for nothing else could explain the richness of her women, the specificity, all the history that has led them to this moment and then that moment. And always Clarkson has her unmistakable yet flexible voice to rely on, one of the great movie voices, fully the equal in idiosyncratic expressiveness to the voices of Margaret Sullavan and Jean Arthur in their 1930s films.

In a role that won Mercedes McCambridge an Oscar in 1949, Clarkson could make no impact in *All the King's Men* (2006) because the poor editing actively destroys her performance, cutting on each of the moments she is trying to build at exactly the wrong time, but she was at her most sensual as the headmistress Ms. Traverse in *The Woods* (2006), being firm with her girls when she needs to be and playing her part with just the faintest whisper of camp to keep it fun. She was at her sexiest and most mysterious as the wife in Ira Sachs's *Married Life* (2007), showing her command of telling gestures, and then she gave three of her very best performances in 2008.

As Miss Dodger, the new high school drama teacher in *Phoebe in Wonderland*, Clarkson is close to magical, sly and hidden but with a tickled, pleasurable inner life that she teases the camera and her students with. Miss Dodger is an "eccentric" part as written, but Clarkson brings it her full attention and breathes so much appealing and unusual life into it, making this woman the kind of teacher everybody wants, the kind of teacher who serenely nods and gives permission rather than prohibiting and setting boundaries.

She did a memorable striptease as Ben Kingsley's cigarette-smoking mistress Carolyn in *Elegy*, eying him intensely as she drops each garment, but holding on to her detachment, too. What Carolyn offers Kingsley's David Kepesh, she says, is "pure fucking," and Clarkson limns a very no-strings sex kind of gal for us, easily bored when David complains about his son, but just as liable to jealousy—which she has to fight off—as the rest of the human race.

Clarkson shows here that she is so skilled that she can do two diametrically opposed things at once: at one point her eyes scan a room in a panicky way, and she does this panic full out while still keeping Carolyn's essential, even consummate cool and detachment. When David mentions an abortion she had, Carolyn speaks of it calmly with little regret, another choice on Clarkson's part that feels unerringly specific to the complex woman she is playing.

In Woody Allen's *Vicky Cristina Barcelona*, Clarkson brings the entire film to a halt with a short monologue, delivered just beyond the range of the camera, about her character's disappointment with her own life. She gives such weight to this monologue that it dominates the rest of the film, and so it came as no surprise when Allen offered her a full-scale lead part, seemingly tailored to her strengths, in *Whatever Works* (2009), where she does a real screwball comedy turn as a sheltered Southern lady who learns how to kick up her heels in Manhattan.

Finally, at 50, Clarkson was given a real starring vehicle of her own, *Cairo Time* (2009), which showed her liking for risk, and her integrity. In many ways most of that film is anti-dramatic. It is instead drifting and moody and exploratory in a way that finally comes to a head in a lovely scene where her tourist character Juliette is in a hotel room with a man she may have fallen in love with and they need to decide what to do, or if they should do anything.

Only a great actress could have sustained this film in such a low-key way up to and after this crucial scene, which is so difficult that Clarkson seems to be holding her breath through it just as we are for her. In her cloudy eyes here, which seem to feel the effect of hot weather, Clarkson signals that the only way to keep a desire pure, and powerful, is to never act on it.

She continues to work at an encouraging rate in all manner of films and TV shows, over-qualified for some of the things she does in commercial pictures, but starting to command independent vehicles in the manner of *Cairo Time*. Clarkson has already put together a body of work that rewards attention, viewings, and re-viewings. There are all sorts of stimulating and surprising nooks and crannies in this filmography, and there are sure to be far more.

Conclusion
Chaos Theory

What is acting talent? At its core, it is simply an expressive face and an expressive voice, and you cannot go too far without either of these things. Nicole Kidman has worked very hard at acting for over 30 years, and she has taken all kinds of worthy and challenging roles on film, but her hard, pretty face can only express about half an emotion at a time, and her voice is small and disembodied. And so her performances are a matter of her trying often desperately to express what her voice and face cannot express. On that basis, she can be somewhat touching.

Playing Virginia Woolf in *The Hours* (2002), for which she won an Oscar, Kidman is freed by the false nose she wears and seems like a different actress or a different person altogether, and on a modest level this is transformative Meryl Streep–like acting. But when the camera stays on her face for an extended scene at a concert in *Birth* (2004), Kidman's thoughts and feelings are not legible, whereas Streep's face is so freakishly expressive that it's possible to see specific words and even sentences and paragraphs of thoughts on it.

At the next level, there is having talent and knowing what to do with it. Cate Blanchett has been gifted with an extraordinarily expressive face and voice and access to any emotion that can be thought of, and so she is a prodigy in this way, but she uses her talent in a promiscuous manner to show off, and her roles and films are seldom worthy of her. An exception to this is *Carol* (2015), where she frames her over-dramatic tendencies much in the way Judy Davis might have. (Blanchett's Oscar-winning work in Woody Allen's *Blue Jasmine* {2013} is very much a Judy Davis–style performance, but without Davis's intellect and formidable sense of morality.)

Both Blanchett and Kidman are Australian, and both of them have said that they have been influenced by Davis, and so it seems at this point that Davis is just as important an influence on acting as Streep and Daniel Day-Lewis. Yet naturalism might be making a stealthy comeback. Look at the best work of Jennifer Jason Leigh or Samantha Morton, or Tim Roth or Gary Oldman, and you will see actors who don't mind muttering and getting off the track and disappearing.

In the work of Michael Fassbender and Ben Whishaw there is a new sort of openness to sex and femininity. These are two actors who are totally unconcerned with old-fashioned masculine worries about the value of pretending and display, which is what makes Sean Penn look like such a figure from another age. Maybe the ideal modern film from an acting standpoint would be something involving Fassbender, Whishaw, and Samantha Morton, or Jessica Chastain when she is at her most focused.

Chastain is a troubling yet emblematic figure of this new century. She was the focal point of perhaps the best modern American movie, Terrence Malick's *The Tree of Life* (2011), where she played a serene and charming but also dissatisfied and trapped maternal archetype. That film relies on her to a large extent, and she fills her every moment on screen with specific energy and intention. But she was amateurish on Broadway in the easy and surefire role of Catherine Sloper in *The Heiress* in 2012, a warning sign for what was to come from her.

Did Malick bring something out in Chastain, some organizing principle? It might have been noticed that directors are not particularly important in this book, at least in comparison to my first book on screen acting from 1912 to 1960. Of all the directors I have mentioned, Martin Scorsese is clearly the most dominant, with Woody Allen placing a distant second. Could it be said that director James Ivory played any decisive role in Anthony Hopkins's performance in *The Remains of the Day*? Or that Ronald Neame's direction was a crucial component of Maggie Smith's work in *The Prime of Miss Jean Brodie*? Only the most doctrinaire auteurist would think so.

The only major collaborations between director and actor covered here are the series of films that Scorsese made with De Niro and the films that John Cassavetes made with Gena Rowlands, both of which are somewhat creatively mysterious. Otherwise, from my point of view, the actor is often the auteur in this period, far more so than directors like Bob Rafelson or Alan J. Pakula or Sydney Pollack or Jim Sheridan or Lasse Hallström.

Certainly actors can be influenced, but it is often by other actors. Chastain spent a long time working with Al Pacino on various productions of Oscar Wilde's *Salome*, and so she brings a 1970s charge of Strasberg-like preoccupation to some of her work. This can lead to results of a very high caliber, as in her dangerously open playing of Strindberg's *Miss Julie* (2014) for Liv Ullmann, but it can also lead her to work where she feels hidden, vocally monotonous, or miscast. Chastain is a real 21st Century star in that she is very savvy about social media and promoting herself as righteous, and she has played the publicity game appealingly.

Modern-day actors like Chastain, Fassbender, and Whishaw have many options. They can choose the more narrow but emotionally gob-smacking way of working that Lee Strasberg pioneered, which led to the scene in the restaurant in *The Godfather* where Al Pacino's Michael Corleone has to decide whether or not to commit murder and also the scene where Ellen Burstyn's Sara Goldfarb admits to being lonely and old in *Requiem for a Dream*. These are towering heights of the acting art that came from wrestling with the most personal demons for Pacino and Burstyn.

Or younger performers can go the Olivier route that Anthony Hopkins, Maggie Smith, and Meryl Streep have followed, which allows an actor to achieve more and more consistently over a wider range of roles, with the warning example of Daniel Day-Lewis, who has excelled with the Stella Adler–style Method way of working but sometimes foundered when he moved more towards Olivier's externals and love of voices and disguises. Wherever these options lead actors in their prime today is an open question, for sometimes freedom can be inhibiting and some limits are needed, and sometimes limits need to be challenged, replaced, and upended.

Bibliography

Biskind, Peter. *Star: How Warren Beatty Seduced America*. Simon & Schuster, 2011.
Bosworth, Patricia. *Jane Fonda: The Private Life of a Public Woman*. Mariner Books, 2012.
Burstyn, Ellen. *Lessons in Becoming Myself*. Riverhead Books, 2007.
Coveney, Michael. *Maggie Smith: A Biography*. St. Martin's Griffin, 2017.
Dunaway, Faye. *Looking for Gatsby*. Simon & Schuster, 1995.
Edwards, Gavin. *Last Night at the Viper Room: River Phoenix and the Hollywood He Left Behind*. It Books, 2013.
Falk, Quentin. *Anthony Hopkins: The Authorized Biography*. Interlink Publishing Group, 1994
Fine, Marshall. *Harvey Keitel: The Art of Darkness*. Fromm International, 1998.
Fonda, Jane. *My Life So Far*. Random House, 2006.
Grobel, Lawrence. *Al Pacino*. Gallery Books, 2008.
Hershman, Gabriel. *Strolling Player: The Life and Career of Albert Finney*. The History Press, 2017.
Jackson, Laura. *Daniel Day-Lewis: The Biography*. John Blake, 2013.
Kael, Pauline. *5001 Nights at the Movies*. Henry Holt and Company, 1991.
Keaton, Diane. *Then Again*. Random House, 2011.
Kelly, Richard. *Sean Penn: His Life and Times*. Canongate, 2005.
Kenny, Glenn. *Anatomy of an Actor: Robert De Niro*. Phaidon Press, 2014.
Levy, Shawn. *De Niro: A Life*. Three Rivers Press, 2015.
McGilligan, Patrick. *Jack's Life: A Biography*. W.W. Norton, 1996.
Nolte, Nick. *Rebel: My Life Outside the Lines*. William Morrow, 2018.
Schulman, Michael. *Her Again: Becoming Meryl Streep*. Faber & Faber, 2016.
Spacek, Sissy. *My Extraordinary Ordinary Life*. Hachette Books, 2011.
Turner, Kathleen. *Send Yourself Roses: Thoughts on My Life, Love, and Leading Roles*. Springboard Press, 2008.
Walker, Beverly. *Jack Nicholson: Anatomy of an Actor*. Phaidon Press, 2014.
Wight, Douglas. *Leonardo DiCaprio: The Biography*. John Blake, 2014.
Winger, Debra. *Undiscovered*. Simon & Schuster, 2011.

Index

About Schmidt (2002) 10
Adjani, Isabelle 60
Adler, Stella 2, 3, 12, 35, 36, 68, 210
Admiral, Virginia 34, 37
Affliction (1997) 72, 73
Afterglow (1997) 72, 138
The Age of Innocence (1993) 62
Albee, Edward 135, 145, 169, 173
Albert Nobbs (2011) 169
Alfredo, Alfredo (1972) 30
Alice Doesn't Live Here Anymore (1974) 42, 119, 127
Alien (1979) 164
Alien: Resurrection (1997) 166
Alien 3 (1992) 166
Aliens (1986) 165
All Fall Down (1962) 14
All the King's Men (2006) 206
All the Little Animals (1998) 90
All the President's Men (1976) 30
Allen, Karen 20, 50, 66
Allen, Woody 46, 76, 129, 147–150, 152, 153, 185, 186, 187, 201, 206, 208, 209
Altman, Robert 14, 45, 84, 138, 145, 155, 175, 195, 197, 198, 199
American Buffalo (1996) 32
American Buffalo (play) 23
American Hustle (2013) 90
American Psycho (2000) 90, 97
Amistad (1997) 58
Anderson, Maxwell 27
Anderson, Paul Thomas 63, 64, 199
Anderson, Wes 45, 48
Andrews, Anthony 100
Angel (2007) 96
Angelopoulos, Theo 45
Angels in America (2003) 24, 193
Animal Crackers (1930) 148
Ann-Margret 56
Annie (1982) 51
Annie Hall (1977) 148
Anonymous Rex (2004) 116
Another Woman (1988) 46, 47, 48, 129
Antonioni, Michelangelo 9, 76
Anwar, Gabrielle 24
Any Given Sunday (1999) 24
Any Wednesday (1966) 104
Apocalypse Now (1979) 44, 69

Apted, Michael 156
Arizona Dream (1992) 111–112, 116–117
Armstrong, Gillian 152, 179, 182
Arnold, Andrea 95
Aronofsky, Darren 120, 121
Arquette, Rosanna 70
Artaud, Antonin 141
Arthur, Jean 149, 206
As Good as It Gets (1997) 10
Audrey Rose (1977) 56
Avatar (2009) 166
The Aviator (2004) 93
Awakenings (1990) 40
Away from Her (2006) 138–139

Baby (2000) 99
Baby Boom (1987) 152
Back Door to Hell (1964) 5
Backwards: The Riddle of Dyslexia (1984) 80
Bad Boys (1983) 75
Bad Lieutenant (1992) 44
Bad Timing (1980) 44
Badlands (1973) 154
Baker, Stanley 161
Baldwin, Alec 195
Baldwin, James 176
Bale, Christian 89–91
The Ballad of Jack and Rose (2005) 63
Bancroft, Anne 27, 131
Bang the Drum Slowly (1973) 34
Barbarella (1968) 105
Barefoot in the Park (1967) 105
Barfly (1987) 116–117
Barkin, Ellen 20
Barrymore, John 52, 59
Basinger, Kim 199
The Basketball Diaries (1995) 92
Bassett, Angela 84, 85
Bastard Out of Carolina (1996) 197
Bates, Kathy 196
Batman (1989) 10, 23
Bauer, Steven 22
Baumbach, Noah 33, 197
A Bear Named Winnie (2004) 96
Beat (2013) 102
Beat the Devil (1954) 71
Beatty, Ned 48
Beatty, Stephen Ira 12

213

Index

Beatty, Warren 9, 12–16, 19, 47, 112, 138, 150
Beckett, Samuel 49
Beckinsale, Kate 185, 191
Bed Among the Lentils (1988) 134
Bedford, Brian 133
Beharie, Nicole 97
Belafonte, Harry 84
Benigni, Roberto 72
Bening, Annette 12, 15, 16
Bennett, Alan 134–135
Benny, Jack 147
A Bequest to the Nation (1973) 143
Bergman, Ingmar 131
Bertolucci, Bernardo 37, 162
The Best Little Girl in the World (1981) 194
Bethune, Zina 42
Big Bad Love (2001) 159
The Big Chill (1983) 167
The Big Lebowski (1998) 67
The Big Short (2015) 91
The Big Wedding (2013) 41
Billy Liar (1963) 136, 137
Binoche, Juliette 61
The Birdcage (1996) 48
Birdman of Alcatraz (1962) 86
Birth (2004) 208
Biskind, Peter 12, 150
Bisset, Jacqueline 69
Black, Karen 7
Black Widow (1987) 161
Blanchett, Cate 141, 203, 208
Bloom, Claire 55
The Blue Boy (1994) 191
Blue Jasmine (2013) 208
Blunt (1987) 57
Bobbitt, Sean 97
Bobby Deerfield (1977) 20, 21, 22
Body Heat (1981) 170, 172
Bogarde, Dirk 136
Bogart, Humphrey 71, 125
Bogdanovich, Peter 65, 80, 82
Bonnie and Clyde (1967) 14, 47, 112, 117
Boogie Nights (1997) 199
The Border (1982) 10
The Bounty (1984) 57, 60
Bowles, Jane 162
Bowles, Paul 162
The Boxer (1997) 63
Boyer, Charles 20, 125
Bradford, Barbara Taylor 357
Bradshaw, Mark 99
Branagh, Kenneth 40, 190
Brando, Marlon 6, 13, 18, 19, 21, 34, 35, 36, 37, 49, 74, 107, 147, 189
Brecht, Bertolt 23
Brennan, Walter 27, 64
Brideshead Revisited (2008) 101, 193
Bridges, Beau 65
Bridges, James 160
Bridges, Jeff 65–67
Bridges, Lloyd 65

Brief Encounter (1945) 57
Bright Star (2009) 99, 101
Broadbent, Jim 203
Broken Blossoms (1919) 155
Brook, Peter 141, 142
The Browning Version (1994) 52
Bruce, Lenny 30
Bugsy (1991) 15, 44
Bukowski, Bobby 81
Bulworth (1998) 16
The Bunker (1981) 56
Burnett, Carol 51
Burstyn, Ellen 1, 2, 42, 80, 118–123, 127, 210
Burton, Iris 80
Burton, Richard 54
Bye Bye Man (2016) 117
Byrne, David 74

Caan, James 18, 24
Cagney, James 5, 6, 22, 63
Caine, Michael 47, 134
Cairo Time (2009) 207
California Suite (1978) 133
The Calling (2002) 116
Cameron, James 165, 166
Camille (1936) 19
Campion, Jane 45, 99
Cannery Row (1982) 70, 160
Cape Fear (1991) 40, 72
Captain Fantastic (2016) 88
Carbon Copy (1981) 85
Carlito's Way (1993) 75, 87
Carnal Knowledge (1971) 7
Carney, Art 120
Carol (2015) 208
Caron, Leslie 12, 15
Carradine, Keith 43
Carrey, Jim 173
Carrie (1952) 27, 28
Carrie (1976) 155
Carrie (2002) 205
Carrie (2013) 200
Carrington (1995) 192
Carter, Helena Bonham 60, 192
Carter, Lynda 163
Casino (1995) 40
Cassavetes, John 38, 76, 124–129, 209
Cassavetes, Nick 129
Casualties of War (1989) 75
Cat Ballou (1965) 105
Catch Me If You Can (2002) 93
The Catcher in the Rye 130
Cazale, John 19, 20, 75
Chalfant, Kathleen 192
Chamberlain, Richard 141
Chaney, Lon 155
A Change of Seasons (1980) 56
Charlie Bubbles (1967) 50
Chastain, Jessica 203, 209
Chayefsky, Paddy 115
Chekhov, Anton 3, 55

Chief Dan George 29
A Child Is Waiting (1963) 124
Children of the Revolution (1996) 187
China Doll 25
The China Syndrome (1979) 109
Chinatown (1974) 8, 114, 117
Chinese Coffee (2000) 24
Cholodenko, Lisa 204
Chow, Lesley 183
Christie, Julie 12, 14, 72, 136–139
Cimimo, Michael 38
Clarkson, Patricia 204–207
Clayburgh, Jill 20
Clift, Montgomery 39, 49, 61, 95
Close, Glenn 167–169
Coal Miner's Daughter (1980) 156
Coburn, James 72
Code 46 (2003) 202, 203
Cohn, Sam 190
Collins, Jackie 57
Collins, Joan 12
Comes a Horseman (1978) 109
Coming Home (1978) 109
Confidence (2003) 33
The Congress (2013) 45
Conrad, Joseph 42
The Contender (2000) 67
The Conversation (1974) 47
Cookie's Fortune (1999) 199
Coppola, Francis Ford 44, 47, 147, 172
Coppola, Sofia 23, 173
Corman, Roger 5
Cosmopolis (2012) 203
Cougar Club (2007) 116
The Counselor (2013) 98
Coveney, Michael 133
Coward, Noël 131
Cox, Brian 202
Craig, Daniel 102
Crawford, Joan 115
Crazy Heart (2009) 67
Crimes of Passion (1984) 171–172
Crimes of the Heart (1986) 152, 156
Criminal Justice (2008) 101
Cronenberg, David 88, 97, 200, 203
Cross Creek (1983) 176
The Crucible (1996) 63
Crudup, Billy 202
Cruise, Tom 32, 90, 94
Cruising (1980) 20, 22
Cry Baby Killer (1958) 5
Cry Freedom (1987) 85
Cutter's Way (1981) 65
Czarniak, Henry 148

Dale, James Badge 97
The Dance of Death (1969) 27
Dancy, Hugh 101
Danes, Claire 93
Dangerous Liaisons (1988) 168–169
A Dangerous Method (2011) 88, 97

A Dangerous Woman (1993) 162
The Danish Girl (2015) 103
Danner, Blythe 165
Danny Collins (2015) 25
Dano, Paul 63, 64
Dante, Joe 80
Dark Blood (2012) 82, 83, 187
Dark Victory (1976) 55
Darling (1965) 136, 138
Dash and Lilly (1999) 187
Davies, Terence 129
Davis, Bette 2, 3, 23, 24, 55, 115, 128, 151, 169, 180, 183, 186
Davis, Brad 95
Davis, Judy 3, 82, 179–189, 191, 208
Davis, Viola 86
Day, Doris 104
Day-Lewis, Daniel 2, 60–64, 93, 208, 210
Dead Again (1991) 190
Dead Man Walking (1995) 75
The Dead Pool (1988) 205
Dean, James 2, 13, 79, 126, 128
Death and the Maiden (1994) 166
Death of a Salesman (1985) 32
The Death of Ivan Ilych 161
Deconstructing Harry (1997) 187
The Deep (1977) 69
The Deer Hunter (1978) 38
DeGeneres, Ellen 153
de Havilland, Olivia 95
Dench, Judi 57, 140, 141
De Niro, Robert 2, 19, 34–42, 63, 73, 75, 87, 90, 92, 93, 162, 163, 189, 209
De Niro, Robert, Sr. 34
Dennis, Sandy 149
De Palma, Brian 22, 34, 75, 155
Depardieu, Gérard 37, 165
The Departed (2006) 10
Depp, Johnny 92, 111–112
Derek, Bo 56
Dern, Bruce 7, 8
DiCaprio, Leonardo 40, 63, 83, 92–94, 146–147
Dick Tracy (1990) 15, 23
Didion, Joan 20
Dirty Grandpa (2016) 41
The Disappearance of Aimee (1976) 115
Disney, Walt 193
Django Unchained (2012) 93
Doctor Zhivago (1965) 136–137
Dog Day Afternoon (1975) 17, 20, 21, 24, 25
Dogfight (1991) 81
$ (1971) 15
The Dollmaker (1984) 110
A Doll's House (1973) 55
A Doll's House (1973, Losey version) 109
Dolores Claiborne (1995) 196
Donat, Robert 99
Donen, Stanley 44, 50
Donnie Brasco (1997) 24
Don't Look Now (1973) 138

Doré, Gustave 155
Dostoyevsky, Fyodor 19
Douglas, Illeana 40
Douglas, Melvyn 47
Douglas, Michael 167, 171, 172
Down and Out in Beverly Hills (1986) 70
Down in the Delta (1998) 176
The Dresser (1983) 52
The Dresser (2015) 59
The Dressmaker (2015) 189
Drive, He Said (1971) 7
Dromgoole, Patrick 130
The Duellists (1977) 42
Duke, Patty 20
Dumb and Dumber To (2014) 173
Dunaway, Faye 8, 14, 105, 107, 111–117, 170
Dunne, John Gregory 20
Dunston Checks In (1996) 116
Durang, Christopher 152, 164, 165, 166
Durning, Charles 17
Duvall, Shelley 155

Eastern Promises (2007) 88
Eastman, Carole 8
Eastwood, Clint 65, 76, 128, 205
Easy Rider (1969) 5–6
The Edge (1997) 58
An Education (2009) 193
Edwards, Gavin 79
Eichner, Billy 200
84 Charing Cross Road (1987) 57
Ejiofor, Chiwetel 175
Elegy (2008) 206
The Elephant Man (1980) 56
Elizabeth R (1971) 143
Elizabeth: The Golden Age (2007) 203
Empire of the Sun (1987) 89, 90
The End of the Affair (1999) 199
The Entertainer (1960) 49
Erin Brockovich (2000) 52
Eureka (1983) 48
Eva (1962) 161
Evening (2007) 169
Eversmile, New Jersey (1989) 60
Everybody Wins (1990) 71, 161, 62
The Exorcist (1973) 119
Explorers (1985) 80
The Eye of the Storm (2011) 189
Eyes of Laura Mars (1978) 115

The Fabulous Baker Boys (1989) 66
Faces (1968) 124–125
The Falcon and the Snowman (1985) 75
Falk, Peter 125
Family Business (1989) 26
A Family Thanksgiving (2010) 117
Far from Heaven (2002) 199, 205
Far from the Madding Crowd (1967) 136
Farber, Manny 36, 37
Farewell to the King (1989) 70
Farrow, Mia 186

Fassbender, Michael 95–98, 209
Fassbinder, Rainer Werner 204
The Fast Lady (1962) 136
Fast Times at Ridgemont High (1982) 75, 194
Fat City (1972) 65, 66
Fatal Attraction (1987) 167–169
Fearless (1993) 66
Feiffer, Jules 8
Fences (2016) 86
Ferguson, Matthew 184
Ferrara, Abel 44, 45
A Few Good Men (1992) 10
The Fighter (2010) 90
The Final Option (1982) 180
Fincher, David 166
Fingers (1978) 43, 45
Finney, Albert 49–52, 59, 150, 151
The First Wives Club (1996) 152
Fish Tank (2009) 95, 96
Fishburne, Laurence 84
Fisk, Jack 154, 156
Fitzgerald, F. Scott 38, 164
Five Easy Pieces (1970) 6, 11, 24, 44
Flanagan, Fionnula 69
Flesh + Blood (1985) 195
Flight (2012) 86
Fonda, Bridget 40, 195
Fonda, Frances 104
Fonda, Henry 104, 109
Fonda, Jane 104–110
Fonda, Peter 6
For Colored Girls Who Have Considered Suicide When the Rainbow Is Enuf (1982) 176
For Queen and Country (1988) 85
For Those Who Think Young (1964) 118
The Fortune (1975) 15
Fortunes of War (1987) 190
48 Hrs. (1982) 70
Foster, Jodie 92
Fox, Michael J. 80
Franco, James 78
Frank (2014) 98
Frankie and Johnny (1991) 20
Franklin, Pamela 132
Frears, Stephen 103
The French Connection (1971) 46, 47
Freundlich, Bart 200
Friedkin, William 47
Friels, Colin 185
Fun with Dick and Jane (1977) 109

Galaxy Quest (1999) 166
Game Change (2012) 200
Gandhi (1982) 60
Gangs of New York (2002) 63, 93
Garai, Romola 96
Garbo, Greta 19, 136
Garland, Judy 124
Garr, Teri 47
Gazzo, Michael V. 43
Genet, Jean 144

George, Susan 30
Georgia (1995) 196
Gere, Richard 149, 159
Gerwig, Greta 163, 197
Ghostbusters (1984) 165
Ghosts Never Sleep (2005) 116
G.I. Jane (1997) 87
Gia (1998) 116
Gibson, Mel 152, 164, 169, 179
Gielgud, John 49, 57, 59, 99, 101
Gilbert, Melissa 120
Gilliatt, Penelope 145
Ginger in the Morning (1974) 155
Gish, Lillian 126, 150, 155
Glengarry Glen Ross (1992) 23
Gloria (1980) 128
Glory (1989) 85
The Go-Between (1971) 137
Go Tell It on the Mountain (1984) 176
Godard, Jean-Luc 109
The Godfather (1972) 1, 17, 18, 20, 25, 31, 147, 210
The Godfather: Part II (1974) 18, 35, 147
The Godfather: Part III (1990) 23, 152
Goin' South (1978) 9
The Gold Diggers (1983) 138
Goldblum, Jeff 190–191
Goldman, Bo 8
Gonet, Stella 85
The Good Father (1985) 57
The Good Mother (1988) 152
Goodbye Charlie (1964) 118
Goode, Matthew 101
Goodfellas (1990) 40
Goodman, John 67
Gorillas in the Mist (1988) 165
Grace Quigley (1984) 70
The Graduate (1967) 27, 28, 30
Graham, Heather 199
The Grand Budapest Hotel (2014) 45
Grant, Cary 5
Grant, Hugh 103, 183
Gray, James 83, 116, 123
Greene, Graham 200
Greer, Germaine 12
Greetings (1968) 34
Griffith, Melanie 165
Grobel, Lawrence 20, 22
Grotowski, Jerzy 100
Guare, John 164

Hackman, Gene 21, 46–48
Hagen, Uta 65
Half Moon Street (1986) 165
Hallström, Lasse 209
Hamlet (1969) 55
Hamlet (1990) 169
Hanks, Tom 86
The Happening (1967) 112
Hargreaves, John 180
Harris, Barbara 30

Harris, Julie 183
Harrison, Jenna 100
Harron, Mary 90, 97
Harry and Tonto (1974) 120
Hartley, L.P. 137
Harvey, James 40
Harvey, Laurence 136
The Hateful Eight (2015) 194
Hawke, Ethan 79, 80
Hayden, Sterling 18
Haynes, Todd 101, 198–199, 205
Head, Edith 147
Head, Murray 143
Health (1980) 175
Heart Beat (1980) 69, 156
Heart of Midnight (1988) 195
Heartbreak Hospital (2002) 205
Heartbreakers (2001) 166
Heat (1995) 24, 40
Heatherton, Joey 12
Heaven Can Wait (1978) 15, 138
Hedda (1975) 143
The Heiress (1949) 95
Hell or High Water (2016) 67
Hellman, Lillian 12
Hellman, Monte 5
The Help (2011) 157
Henry, Buck 12
Henry, Justin 31
Henry V (1989) 190
Hepburn, Audrey 50
Hepburn, Katharine 3, 16, 70, 167, 180
Hi, Mom! (1970) 34
High Art (1998) 204, 205
The High Cost of Loving (1958) 124
High Rolling in a Hot Corvette (1977) 179
High Tide (1987) 181–182, 187
Hill, Dana 50
Hill, Jonah 94
Hinckley, John 37
Hinson, Hal 81
A History of Violence (2005) 88
Hitchcock, Alfred 88
Hitchcock (2012) 59, 65
The Hitcher (1986) 195
Hoffman, Dustin 15, 19, 26–33, 36, 38, 46, 74, 75, 163
Holbrook, Hal 64
Holcroft, Edward 102
Holiday Heart (2000) 176
Hollywood Wives (1985) 57
Holmes, Katie 205
Holy Smoke! (1999) 45
Hoodwink (1981) 180
Hoosiers (1986) 47
Hopkins, Anthony 1, 21, 53–59, 189, 191, 193, 209, 210
Hopkins, Miriam 33
Hopper, Dennis 6
Hot Millions (1968) 131
The Hours (2002) 200, 208

Howard, Arliss 159
Howard, Trevor 144
Howards End (1992) 57, 190, 191
Hudson, Rock 68
The Humbling (2014) 24
The Hunchback of Notre Dame (1982) 57
Hunger (2008) 95
Hunter, Holly 45
Hunter, Tab 68
Hurlyburly (1998) 76
The Hurricane (1999) 86
Hurry Sundown (1967) 105, 112
Hurt, William 170, 172
Husbands and Wives (1992) 186
Huston, Anjelica 197
Huston, John 51, 52, 63, 65, 114

I Am Sam (2001) 76
I Heart Huckabees (2004) 33
I Love Trouble (1994) 72
I Never Sang for My Father (1970) 47
Ibsen, Henrik 55, 57, 131, 144
The Ice Storm (1997) 166
The Iceman Cometh (1973) 65
I'm Not There (2007) 101
Impromptu (1991) 182–184, 186, 191
In America (2002) 202
In the Bedroom (2001) 157
In the Name of the Father (1993) 62, 190
The Incredible Sarah (1976) 141
The Indian Runner (1991) 87
Inge, William 13, 14, 195
Inglourious Basterds (2009) 95
Innaurato, Albert 164
The Insider (1999) 24
Interiors (1978) 150
Intimate Affairs (2001) 73
The Irishman (2019) 41
The Iron Lady (2011) 169
Irons, Jeremy 169
Ironweed (1987) 2, 10
Irving, Amy 155
Ishtar (1987) 15
Ivory, James 209

J. Edgar (2011) 93
Jack and Jill (2011) 24
Jackie Brown (1996) 40
Jackson, Glenda 140–145
Jagged Edge (1985) 66
Jagger, Mick 17
James, Henry 135, 197
Jane Eyre (2011) 96
Jarvis, Katie 95
Jefferson in Paris (1995) 72
Jennifer's Shadow (2004) 116
Jennings, Alex 135
Jesus' Son (1999) 202
JFK (1991) 157
Johnson, Celia 132
Jolie, Angelina 116

The Jolson Story (1946) 130
Jones, Tommy Lee 156
The Journey of the Fifth Horse 27
Julia (1977) 109

Kael, Pauline 12, 158, 159, 179
Kaleidoscope (1966) 15
Kalin, Tom 200
Kansas City (1996) 84, 197
Karvan, Claudia 182
Katt, William 155
Kazan, Elia 13, 38
Keach, Stacy 65
Keaton, Diane 9, 10, 12, 15, 19, 50, 93, 146–153
Keitel, Harvey 37, 42–45
Keller, Marthe 20
Kelly, Grace 114
Kenny, Glenn 41
Keyloun, Mark 160
Kidman, Nicole 208
The Kids Are All Right (2010) 200
Kier, Udo 78
King, Larry 163
King Kong (1976) 96
King Lear (2018) 59, 193
The King of Comedy (1983) 39, 40
The King of Marvin Gardens (1972) 7, 119
Kingsley, Ben 206
Kline, Kevin 85
Klute (1971) 104–109
Knight, Shirley 137
Knight of Cups (2015) 91
Knightley, Keira 97
Kramer vs. Kramer (1979) 31
Krieps, Vicky 64
Kubrick, Stanley 9
Kushner, Tony 24
Kusturica, Emir 111

L.A. Confidential (1997) 199
The Lady in the Van (2015) 135
Lake, Veronica 125
Lancaster, Burt 86
Lane, Diane 87
Lange, Jessica 3, 9, 31, 58, 96, 189
Lapine, James 184
Larkin, Chris 133
The Last Detail (1973) 7, 8
Last Exit to Brooklyn (1989) 195
The Last of the Mohicans (1992) 62
The Last Picture Show (1971) 65, 66, 119
Last Tango in Paris (1973) 37, 107
The Last Temptation of Christ (1988) 44
The Last Tycoon (1976) 38
Laughton, Charles 62
Law, Phyllida 192
Lawrence, D.H. 6, 142
Lean, David 49, 136, 180
Lee, Joie 85
Lee, Spike 45, 85, 86
Legal Eagles (1986) 161

Leigh, Jennifer Jason 194–197, 208
Leigh, Vivien 14, 136
Lennon, John 154
Lenny (1974) 30
Leonard, Robert Sean 191
Leone, Sergio 40
Lester, Richard 137
Leto, Jared 90, 121
Letterman, David 90
Letts, Tracy 163
Levi, Primo 99
Lewis, Jerry 39, 94, 188
Life Is Beautiful (1997) 72
Life with Judy Garland: Me and My Shadows (2001) 188
Lilith (1964) 14, 47
Lincoln (2012) 60, 64
The Lindbergh Kidnapping Case (1976) 55
The Lion in Winter (1968) 55
The Lion in Winter (2003) 55, 169
Little Big Man (1970) 29, 113, 117
The Little Drummer Girl (1984) 152
Little Eyolf (1982) 57
Little Nikita (1988) 81
The Little Shop of Horrors (1960) 5
A Little Thing Called Murder (2006) 188
Little Women (1994) 89
Lloyd George (1973) 55
The Local Stigmatic 23, 24
Lola Versus (2012) 163
London Spy (2015) 102, 103
Lonely Are the Brave (1962) 124
The Lonely Passion of Judith Hearne (1987) 2, 134
Longford (2006) 202, 203
Look Back in Anger (1989) 190
Looking for Mr. Goodbar (1977) 149
Looking for Richard (1996) 20
Lorenzo's Oil (1992) 72
Losey, Joseph 109
Lost in Translation (2003) 76
Love Actually (2003) 192
Love Affair (1994) 16
Love and Death (1975) 148, 151
Love and Pain and the Whole Damn Thing (1973) 133
Love Story (1970) 140
Love Streams (1984) 128
The Lovers (2017) 163
Luck 33
Luhrmann, Baz 93, 180, 189
Lumet, Sidney 71, 81
Lutter, Alfred 119
Lynch, David 56, 154, 157

Macbeth (2015) 98
MacGraw, Ali 140
The Machinist (2004) 90
MacLaine, Shirley 158
The Madam's Family: The Truth About the Canal Street Brothel (2004) 123

Made in Heaven (1987) 161
Madonna 12, 75
Magic (1978) 56
Magnani, Anna 187
Magnolia (1999) 199, 200
Mahon, Kevin 39
The Maids (1975) 143
Main Street (2010) 123
Malcolm X (1992) 85
Malick, Terrence 76, 91, 98, 154, 209
Malkovich, John 89, 168, 181
Mamet, David 23, 25, 32
A Man of No Importance (1994) 52
The Man with Two Brains (1983) 170
Mancini, Henry 50
Manhattan (1979) 150
Manhattan Murder Mystery (1993) 152
Manhunter (1986) 202
Mann, Anthony 88
Mann, Michael 24
Mansfield, Katherine 142
Manville, Lesley 64
The Many Loves of Dobie Gillis 13
A Map of the World (1999) 166, 199
Map to the Stars (2014) 200
Marat/Sade (1967) 141
Marathon Man (1976) 26
Marley, John 124
Married Life (2007) 206
Martin, Steve 170
Marvin, Lee 154
Marvin's Room (1996) 93, 146, 152
Marx, Groucho 148
Mary, Queen of Scots (1971) 143
Mary Shelley's Frankenstein (1994) 40
Mathis, Samantha 82, 83
Matthau, Walter 141
Mazursky, Paul 70, 120
McCabe & Mrs. Miller (1971) 14, 138
McCambridge, Mercedes 206
McCrea, Joel 65
McCullers, Carson 177
McDowell, Malcolm 116
McGovern, George 14
McGregor, Ewan 90
McKellen, Ian 59
McNally, Terrence 117
McNeice, Ian 134
McQueen, Steve 30, 113
McQueen, Steve (director) 95, 97, 175
Me, Natalie (1969) 20
Mean Streets (1973) 35
Meet the Parents (2000) 40
Meisner, Sanford 68, 147
The Member of the Wedding (1997) 177
Mercer, David 120
The Merchant of Venice (2004) 24
The Messenger: The Story of Joan of Arc (1999) 32
Metroland (1997) 89
The Meyerowitz Stories (2017) 33

Miami Blues (1990) 195
Mickey One (1965) 14
Midnight Cowboy (1969) 28, 32
Midnight Express (1978) 95
A Midsummer Night's Dream (1935) 92
A Midsummer Night's Dream (1999) 90
Mike's Murder (1984) 160, 161
Milch, David 33
Milius, John 70
Milk (2008) 76
Miller, Arthur 63, 162
Miller, Henry 118
Miller's Crossing (1990) 52
Minnelli, Liza 38
Minnelli, Vincente 118
Minnie and Moskowitz (1971) 126
Mirren, Helen 140
The Mirror Has Two Faces (1996) 67
Miss Firecracker (1989) 176
Miss Julie (2014) 203, 209
Miss Mary (1986) 138
Missing (1982) 156
Mississippi Burning (1988) 47
Mr. Skeffington (1944) 23
Mitchell, Radha 204
Mo' Better Blues (1990) 85
Modine, Matthew 198
Mommie Dearest (1981) 112, 115, 116
Monroe, Marilyn 162
Montgomery, Elizabeth 55
Moore, Demi 87
Moore, Julianne 167, 198–200
Moore, Mary Tyler 12
Moranis, Rick 165
Moreau, Jeanne 49, 161
Moriarty, Cathy 39
Moriarty, Michael 35
The Morning After (1986) 66, 110
Morrow, Vic 194
Mortensen, Viggo 87–88, 97
Morton, Samantha 201–203, 208, 209
Morvern Callar (2002) 202
Mrs. Harris (2005) 123
Mrs. Parker and the Vicious Circle (1994) 195
Mrs. Soffel (1984) 152
Much Ado About Nothing (1993) 190–191
Mulligan, Carey 97
Mulroney, Dermut 80
Muni, Paul 63
Murder on the Orient Express (1974) 50
Murphy, Eddie 70
Murphy, Michael 150
Murray, Bill 76, 134, 165
The Music Lovers (1971) 141
Mussolini and I (1985) 57
My Beautiful Laundrette (1985) 60
My Brilliant Career (1979) 179–181
My Brother Jonathan (1985) 60
My Brother Tom (2001) 99, 100
My House in Umbria (2003) 135
My Left Foot (1989) 60, 61, 62

My Own Private Idaho (1991) 2, 78, 79, 80, 81
My Own Private River (2012) 78, 82
Mystic River (2003) 76

Nanny McPhee (2005) 193
Nanny McPhee Returns (2010) 193
The Natural (1984) 167
Neame, Ronald 209
Neeson, Liam 186
Neill, Sam 185
The Neon Bible (1995) 129
Network (1976) 112, 114, 117
New York, New York (1977) 38
New York Stories (1989) 70, 71
Newman, Paul 13, 136
Newsies (1992) 89
Nichols, Mike 27, 28, 192, 193
Nicholson, Jack 5–11, 15, 23, 24, 31, 36, 38, 150, 152, 158, 172
Nick Nolte: No Exit (2008) 73
A Night in the Life of Jimmy Reardon (1988) 81
Night Moves (1975) 48
Night Must Fall (1964) 50
Nimoy, Leonard 182
Nine (2009) 64
1900 (1976) 37, 38
Nixon (1995) 58
Nolte, Nick 68–73, 160, 162
North Dallas Forty (1979) 69, 72
Norton, Edward 41
Notes on a Scandal (2006) 141
Nunn, Trevor 100
Nyman, Michael 192
Nyong'o, Lupita 175
N.Y.P.D. 20

Oates, Joyce Carol 78
Oates, Warren 155
O'Connor, Kevin J. 63, 64
Odets, Clifford 181
An Officer and a Gentleman (1982) 159, 160
Oh! What a Lovely War (1969) 132
Oldman, Gary 208
Olivier, Laurence 1, 2, 26, 28, 49, 54, 55, 56, 57, 58, 59, 63, 103, 131, 210
On Golden Pond (1981) 109
On My Own (1991) 184–185
Onassis, Jacqueline Kennedy 12
Once Upon a Time in America (1984) 40
One Against the Wind (1991) 185
One Flew Over the Cuckoo's Nest (1975) 9, 24
One Woman or Two (1985) 165
O'Neal, Ryan 19
The Only Game in Town (1970) 15
Ono, Yoko 154
Opening Night (1978) 127–128
Orbach, Jerry 24
Othello (1965) 130
Othello (1981) 56
Our Souls at Night (2017) 110

Ovitz, Mike 161
Ozon, François 96

Pacino, Al 1, 2, 17–25, 31, 36, 38, 40, 47, 75, 87, 139, 150, 152, 163, 209, 210
Pack of Lies (1987) 120
Paddington (2014) 102
Page, Geraldine 154
Pakula, Alan J. 107, 109, 209
Palin, Michael 134
The Panic in Needle Park (1971) 20, 21
Papillon (1973) 30
The Parallax View (1974) 14
A Passage to India (1984) 180
The Passenger (1975) 9
Passion Fish (1992) 176
Patric, Jason 195
Peckinpah, Sam 30
Peggy Sue Got Married (1986) 172
Penn, Arthur 29, 112, 113
Penn, Sean 74–77, 87, 201, 209
People Vs. Jean Harris (1981) 120
A Perfect Murder (1998) 87
Perfume: The Story of a Murderer (2006) 33, 100
Perkins, Anthony 171
Perry, Frank 115
Pesci, Joe 39
Peter and Paul (1981) 56
Peter's Friends (1992) 190
Petulia (1968) 137
Pfeiffer, Michelle 20
The Phantom of the Opera (1925) 155
Philadelphia (1993) 86
Philipe, Gérard 99, 101
Phoebe in Wonderland (2008) 206
Phoenix, Joaquin 82, 83, 99
Phoenix, River 2, 78–83, 187
The Piano (1993) 45
The Piano Lesson (1995) 177
Pieces of April (2003) 205
Pinsent, Gordon 139
Pinter, Harold 145
Pit Stop (1969) 118
Play It Again, Sam (1972) 147
Plimpton, Martha 81
Poitier, Sidney 84
Polanski, Roman 8, 114, 166
Pollack, Sydney 186, 209
Polley, Sarah 138–139
The Portrait of a Lady (1996) 87, 89
The Poseidon Adventure (1972) 47
Postcards from the Edge (1990) 48
The Postman Always Rings Twice (1981) 9
Potter, Sally 138
Powers, Stefanie 57
Prayers for Bobby (2009) 166
Preminger, Otto 105, 112
Primary Colors (1998) 192
Prime Cut (1972) 154
The Prime of Miss Jean Brodie (1969) 131–133, 209

The Prince of Tides (1991) 71, 72
A Private Function (1984) 134
Prizzi's Honor (1985) 10, 172
Promise Her Anything (1966) 15
Providence (1977) 120
Pryce, Jonathan 82, 187, 191
Psycho (1998) 87
Pulp Fiction (1994) 45
The Pumpkin Eater (1964) 131
Puzzle of a Downfall Child (1970) 113, 116–117

Q & A (1990) 71
Quartet (2012) 33
The Queen (2006) 141
Queers (2017) 102
A Question of Love (1978) 128
The Quick and the Dead (1995) 92

Rabe, David 76, 165
Rachel Getting Married (2008) 163
Rafelson, Bob 209
Raggedy Man (1981) 156
Raging Bull (1980) 2, 39, 41, 90
Rain Man (1988) 32
Rampling, Charlotte 189
Ray, Nicholas 128
Rebel Without a Cause (1955) 126, 128
Redford, Robert 13, 19, 27, 30, 73, 110
Redgrave, Vanessa 21, 53, 74, 103, 130, 135, 143, 191
Redman, Joyce 50
Reds (1981) 9, 15, 150
Reed, Oliver 142
Reeves, Keanu 79, 81
Reitman, Ivan 161
The Remains of the Day (1993) 2, 57, 58, 190–191, 209
Remember My Name (1978) 175
Requiem for a Dream (2000) 1, 2, 120–122, 210
Reservoir Dogs (1992) 44
Resnais, Alain 120
Resurrection (1980) 119–120
The Return of the Soldier (1982) 145
The Revenant (2015) 94
Reversal of Fortune (1990) 169
Revolution (1985) 23
Revolutionary Road (2008) 93
Reynolds, Burt 199
Rhames, Ving 176
Rich Man, Poor Man (1976) 69
Richard II (2012) 101
Richardson, Ralph 49
Richardson, Tony 10
Richert, William 81
Rickman, Alan 192
Rigg, Diana 57
The River (1984) 156
Robards, Jason, Jr. 69
Robbie, Margot 94
Robbins, Tim 202
Roberts, Eric 116, 156

Roberts, Julia 52, 72
Rocket to the Moon (1986) 181
Roeg, Nicolas 44, 45, 48
Rollover (1981) 109
Roman J. Israel, Esq. (2017) 86
The Roman Spring of Mrs. Stone (1961) 13
Romancing the Stone (1984) 170
Romeo + Juliet (1996) 93
A Room with a View (1986) 60, 134
Rooney, Mickey 92, 94
Rose, Charlie 1
Ross, Herbert 133
Ross, Katharine 28
Rossetter, Kathryn 33
Rota, Nino 19
Roth, Philip 24
Roth, Tim 208
Rowlands, Gena 46, 124–129, 189
The Royal Tenenbaums (2001) 48
Rudolph, Alan 45, 73, 138, 161, 175
Rules Don't Apply (2016) 16
Running on Empty (1988) 81
Rush (1991) 195
Russell, David O. 90
Russell, Ken 140–142, 145, 171
Russell, Theresa 31, 161
Ryan, Robert 34, 38
Ryder, Winona 166

Sachs, Ira 206
Safe (1995) 198
St. Elsewhere 85
Salinger, J.D. 130
Salome's Last Dance (1988) 141
Same Time, Next Year (1978) 120
Sanda, Dominique 38
Sandler, Adam 24
Sarandon, Chris 17
Sarandon, Susan 75
Sarrazin, Michael 106
Saturday Night and Sunday Morning (1960) 49
Saturn 3 (1980) 44
Savage, Fred 120
Savage Grace (2007) 200
Saving Mr. Banks (2013) 193
Scarecrow (1973) 21, 47
Scarface (1983) 20, 22
Scent of a Woman (1992) 23, 24
Schatzberg, Jerry 20, 21, 113
Schepisi, Fred 189
Schlesinger, John 28, 136, 142
Schrader, Paul 35, 45, 72
Scorsese, Martin 10, 35, 38, 39, 40, 41, 42, 44, 45, 62, 63, 70, 93, 94, 119, 209
Scott, Campbell 196
Scott, George C. 137
Scott, Ridley 42
Scott, Tony 86
Sea of Love (1989) 20, 23
The Secret Agent (1996) 89

Segal, George 85, 141
Selby, Hubert 195
Sense and Sensibility (1995) 192
Serial Mom (1994) 173
Serkis, Andy 203
Serpico (1973) 20, 21
Seven Brides for Seven Brothers (1982) 80
Shadowlands (1993) 58
Shakespeare in Love (1998) 141
Shame (2011) 97, 98
Shampoo (1975) 14, 15, 138
Shange, Ntozake 176
Shanghai Surprise (1986) 75
Shattered Trust: The Shari Karney Story (1993) 120
Shaw, Fiona 61
Sheedy, Ally 204
Sheen, Martin 154
The Sheltering Sky (1990) 162
Shepard, Sam 73, 82, 187
Shepherd, Cybill 36
Sheridan, Jim 62, 63, 209
She's So Lovely (1997) 76
The Shining (1980) 9
Shire, Talia 19
Shoot the Moon (1982) 50, 51, 52, 150, 151
The Shooting (1966) 5
Short Cuts (1993) 195, 198
Shutter Island (2010) 93
The Silence of the Lambs (1991) 57
Silent Tongue (1993) 82
Simon, Neil 134
Simpson, Jim 165
A Single Man (2009) 200
Single White Female (1992) 195
Sirk, Douglas 199
Sister Mary Explains It All (2001) 152
Six Dance Lessons in Six Weeks (2014) 129
Six Degrees of Separation (1993) 86
Skyfall (2012) 102
Sleeper (1973) 147, 150, 151
Slipstream (2007) 59
Sluizer, George 82, 83, 187
Slumber Party '57 (1976) 159
Small, Michael 104
Smith, Maggie 1, 33, 130–135, 189, 191, 209, 210
Smith, Will 86
The Snowman (2017) 98
Something's Gotta Give (2003) 10, 152
Sondheim, Stephen 193
Song to Song (2017) 98
Sophie's Choice (1982) 2, 22
Sorkin, Aaron 98
Sorrentino, Paulo 110
Sorvino, Paul 22
South Pacific (2001) 169
Spacek, Sissy 154–157
Spencer, Charles 100
Spielberg, Steven 64, 89, 93
Splendor in the Grass (1961) 13
Stamp, Terence 48, 98

Stand by Me (1986) 81
Stanislavski, Konstantin 2, 68
Stanley, Kim 128
Stanwyck, Barbara 147, 202
The Star Wagon 27
Starman (1984) 66
State of Grace (1990) 75
Steiger, Rod 137
Steinbeck, John 160
Stephens, Robert 130–132
Steve Jobs (2015) 98
Stevie (1978) 144
Stewart, Patrick 143
Still Alice (2014) 200
Stone (2010) 41
Stone, Oliver 22, 58
Stoned (2005) 100
Stoppard, Tom 169
Storaro, Vittorio 37
Stowe, Madeleine 62
La Strada (1954) 76
The Straight Story (1999) 157
Straight Time (1978) 31, 33
Strange Interlude (1988) 141
Strangers: The Story of a Mother and Daughter (1979) 128
Strasberg, Lee 1, 2, 3, 17, 18, 19, 22, 35, 36, 39, 44, 105, 106, 115, 188, 119, 121, 123, 127, 149, 150, 154, 156, 192, 209
Straw Dogs (1971) 30
Streep, Meryl 2, 3, 22, 31, 48, 93, 135, 146, 147, 152, 164, 169, 188, 190, 208, 2010
A Streetcar Named Desire (1951) 6
Streisand, Barbra 67, 71, 72
Sturges, Preston 65
Suddenly, Last Summer (1993) 135
Suffragette (2015) 103
Sullavan, Margaret 99, 158, 206
Sunday Bloody Sunday (1971) 60, 142–143
Sunday in New York (1963) 104
Supergirl (1984) 116
Surviving (1985) 80
Sutherland, Donald 108, 138
Sweet and Lowdown (1999) 76, 201

The Tall Guy (1989) 191
Taps (1981) 75
Tarantino, Quentin 40, 44, 45, 93, 95, 194, 197
Tatum, Channing 194
Tavernier, Bertrand 45
Taxi Driver (1976) 35, 36, 37, 40, 42
Taylor, Elizabeth 15
Taylor, Lili 81
Taylor, Rod 131
Taymor, Julie 58, 101
The Tempest (2010) 101
Terminator Salvation (2009) 90
Terms of Endearment (1983) 10, 158, 160
Thalberg, Irving 38
Thank God It's Friday (1978) 160

Thelma and Louise (1991) 44
There Will Be Blood (2007) 60, 63, 64
Thewlis, David 93
They Shoot Horses, Don't They? (1969) 105–108
The Thing Called Love (1993) 80, 82
This Boy's Life (1993) 40, 92
This Must Be the Place (2011) 74
This So-Called Disaster (2003) 73
The Thomas Crown Affair (1968) 113
Thompson, Emma 58, 190–193
Three Days of the Condor (1975) 114
360 (2011) 59
The Three Musketeers (1973) 114
3 Women (1977) 155
Thunderbolt and Lightfoot (1974) 65
Tibaldi, Antonio 184
Titanic (1997) 92, 93, 94
Titus (1999) 58
To Be the Best (1992) 57
Toback, James 43, 45
Tolstoy, Leo 161
Tom Jones (1963) 50
Tomei, Marisa 157
Tootsie (1982) 31, 32
Torn, Rip 154
Total Eclipse (1995) 93
A Touch of Class (1973) 140
Tout va bien (1972) 109
The Towering Inferno (1974) 114
Town & Country (2001) 16
Towne, Robert 8, 15
Training Day (2001) 86
Trash (1970) 154
Travels with My Aunt (1972) 133
The Treasure of the Sierra Madre (1948) 63
The Tree of Life (2011) 76, 209
The Trench (1999) 99
The Triple Echo (1972) 143
Trixie (2000) 73
Tropic of Cancer (1970) 118
Tropic Thunder (2008) 73
True Grit (2010) 67
Tucker: The Man and His Dream (1988) 66
Turner, Barbara 194, 196
Turner, Kathleen 170–174
Turner, Ted 110
Turtle Diary (1985) 145
Tushingham, Rita 201
12 Years a Slave (2013) 98, 175, 178
The Twilight of the Golds (1996) 116
Two for the Road (1967) 50, 52
Two Lovers (2008) 83

Ullmann, Liv 12, 209
The Unbearable Lightness of Being (1988) 61
Under the Skin (1997) 201
Unforgiven (1992) 46, 48
Unhook the Stars (1996) 129
The Unloved (2009) 201
The Untouchables (1987) 205
Urban Cowboy (1980) 159, 160

Vadim, Roger 105
Van Sant, Gus 78, 81, 87
Velvet Goldmine (1998) 90
Verhoeven, Paul 195
A Very English Scandal (2018) 103
V.I. Warshawski (1991) 173
Vicky Cristina Barcelona (2008) 206
Vidor, King 65
The V.I.P.s (1963) 131
The Virgin Suicides (1999) 173
Voight, Jon 28
Voyage of the Damned (1976) 114

Wahlberg, Mark 199
A Walk on the Moon (1999) 87
Walken, Christopher 165
Wallis, Hal 143
Walsh, M. Emmet 31
War and Peace (BBC, 1972–73) 53, 54, 55
The War of the Roses (1989) 172
Warhol, Andy 29, 154
Warnecke, Gordon 60, 61
Warner, Deborah 145
Washbourne, Mona 144
Washington, Denzel 84–86
Washington Square (1997) 52, 135, 197
Wasikowska, Mia 96
Waters, Ethel 177
Waters, John 67, 173
Wayne, John 185
Weaver, Doodles 164
Weaver, Sigourney 164–166
Wedding Belles (2007) 96
Weigel, Helene 23
Weir, Peter 66
Weiss, Peter 141
Welch, Raquel 12
Weld, Tuesday 13, 69, 73, 149
Weller, Peter 51
West, Mae 22, 171
Wharton, Edith 63
Whatever Works (2009) 207
What's Eating Gilbert Grape (1993) 92
What's Love Got to Do with It (1993) 84
When a Man Loves a Woman (1994) 120
When You Remember Me (1990) 120
Where Angels Fear to Tread (1991) 187
Whishaw, Ben 33, 78, 99–103, 209
Who Framed Roger Rabbit (1988) 172
Who Is Harry Kellerman and Why Is He Saying Those Terrible Things About Me? (1971) 29

Who'll Stop the Rain (1978) 69
Who's That Knocking at My Door (1967) 42, 44
The Wild Ride (1960) 5
Wilde Salomé (2011) 20
Wilder, Gene 48
Williams, Cynda 85
Williams, Heathcote 23
Williams, Kenneth 130
Williams, Tennessee 13, 135
Williamson, Nicol 55
Willis, Gordon 104
Willson, Henry 68
Wilson, August 86, 177
Winger, Debra 70, 71, 158–163
Winn, Kitty 20
Winningham, Mare 196
The Winter Guest (1997) 192
Winter of Our Dreams (1981) 180
Winterbottom, Michael 202
Wit (2001) 192
The Witches of Eastwick (1987) 10
Witness (1985) 87
The Wolf of Wall Street (2013) 93, 94
Wolfit, Donald 52
A Woman Called Golda (1982) 182
A Woman Under the Influence (1974) 125, 127, 128
Women in Love (1970) 140, 142
Wong, Anna May 113
Wood, Natalie 12, 13
Woodard, Alfre 175–178
The Woods (2006) 206
Working Girl (1988) 165
The World According to Garp (1982) 167
Wright, Robin 45, 75
The Wrong Man (1957) 109
Wyler, William 27

The Yards (2000) 116–117, 123
The Year of Living Dangerously (1982) 164
You Only Live Once (1937) 109
Young, Gig 106
Young Cassidy (1965) 131, 136
Young Frankenstein (1974) 48
Youth (2015) 110

Zeffirelli, Franco 131
Zinnemann, Fred 177
Zuniga, Daphne 117